Settler Imperialism

Settler Imperialism

Alaska Natives and the Myth of the Last Frontier

Jess Arnett

MINNESOTA

University of Minnesota Press
Minneapolis
London

The University of Minnesota Press gratefully acknowledges the generous support provided for the publication of this book by Oberlin College.

Portions of chapter 4 are adapted from "Unsettled Rights in Territorial Alaska: Native Land, Sovereignty, and Citizenship from the Indian Reorganization Act to Termination," *Western Historical Quarterly* 48, no. 3 (2017): 233–54, https://doi.org/10.1093/whq/whx038.

Published by the University of Minnesota Press
111 Third Avenue South, Suite 290
Minneapolis, MN 55401–2520
http://www.upress.umn.edu

ISBN 978-1-5179-1693-0 (hc)
ISBN 978-1-5179-1694-7 (pb)

A Cataloging-in-Publication record for this book is available from the Library of Congress.

Printed in the United States of America on acid-free paper

UMP BmB 2026

Contents

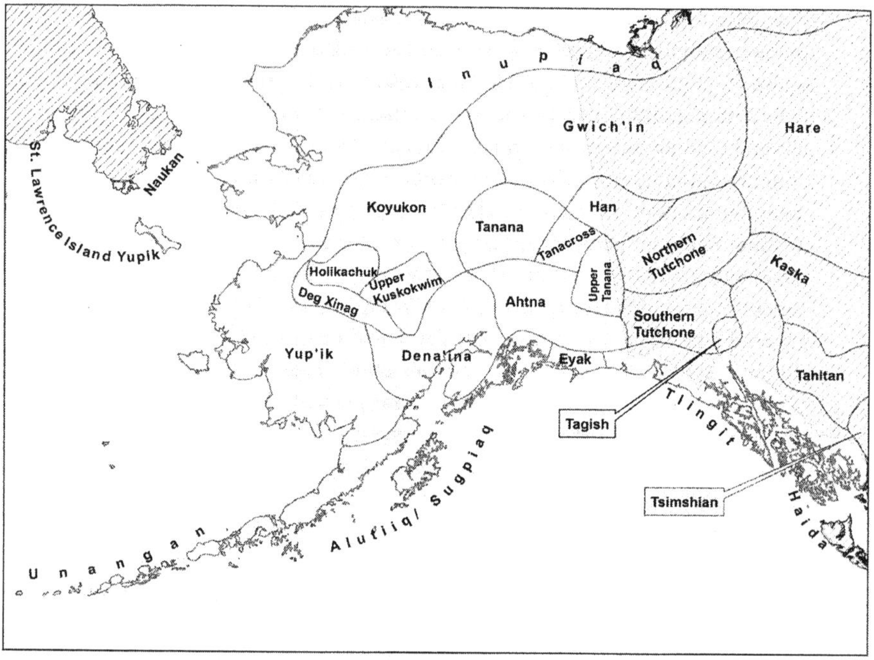

MAP 1. Alaska Native language map. Originally designed by Michael E. Krauss, digital map created by Gary Holton, Jim Kerr, and Colin West, *Indigenous Peoples and Languages of Alaska Map* (Alaska Native Language Center and University of Alaska Anchorage Institute of Social and Economic Research, 2011). This version is as adapted in Juliana Hu Pegues's *Space-Time Colonialism: Alaska's Indigenous and Asian Entanglements* (University of North Carolina Press, 2021).

Introduction

Between Empire and Frontier

Law and the Periphery of the Nation Proper

On April 12, 1902, Frederick Moore (Tlingit) sent a letter to the US Attorney General Philander Chase Knox from his home in Juneau. He introduced himself as a missionary "among my people in the District of Alaska" where "since said time I have devoted my entire attention to their welfare."[1] He continued that "their condition at the present time" was "very critical" due to the arrival of corporate fishing operations "who invariably attempt to locate [their operations] at the points and on the property hitherto occupied by the Indians." He described how "speculators" traveled up and down the coasts looking for suitable cannery sites "to be sold to corporations" to whom they "represent that they own and have a right to sell." He attested that once armed with this dubious title, the "purchaser invariably comes upon the ground and attempts by force and coercion to oust the natives and drive them away." The canneries then "send out their fishing boats . . . from one to one hundred miles on either side . . . stretching their nets . . . thus entirely cutting off the food supply of the Indians" who have "held and occupied" these lands "for a time whereof the memory of the Indian runneth not to the contrary."

Moore argued that it had been well known that the "Alaska Indians . . . have hitherto been self-supporting and it has never been necessary for the Government to make any provisions" for them. In a few short years, the corporate canneries had devastated the Indigenous salmon economies of Southeast Alaska, and he warned that if these conditions were not remedied through an affirmation of Native land rights, starvation would most certainly result. Moore requested that the attorney general provide him with a statement from the federal government that outlined the status of Alaska Natives and their rights in the land. He described how "in many cases" he had "advised the Indians to post their notice and claim . . . at the mouths of those streams and to forbid the white men from coming thereon," but "these notices" had been "disregarded and the District Attorney has hitherto failed to give us any relief whatever." He concluded with an appeal to the attorney general that surely "the Government . . . will protect these people in their homes and prevent the encroachment of the white people upon their rights."[2] Attorney General Knox forwarded Moore's request to the US attorney Robert Friedrich in Juneau, instructing him to "immediately investigate cases of alleged encroachments upon the lands of the natives." He contemplated that while "disposed to think that . . . it is the duty of this Department to endeavor to protect them in the courts to the same extent to which it protects the interests of Indians . . . the real status and rights of these natives have never been clearly defined and determined."[3] He forwarded Friedrich a copy of Moore's letter along with a memorandum detailing "certain laws and decisions bearing upon this subject," averring that "if the courts shall decide that these natives are not, like the Indians, wards of the nation, our responsibility will thereupon cease."[4]

I encountered this copy of Frederick Moore's letter to the US attorney general at the very bottom of a file at the National Archives and Records Administration in Washington, DC. It was the only document in that file to reference Indigenous land rights in Alaska, and it lay buried under dozens of petitions to the US House of Representatives from sportsmen's associations, chambers of commerce, civic associations, and trade boards. These petitions consisted of prewritten and circulated resolutions memorializing Congress to pass legislation organizing the District of Alaska into a territory of the United States. The petitioners lamented that "the District of Alaska possesses many . . . resources of natural wealth," including "untilled agricultural lands, undeveloped mineral belts, great fishing banks, and forests of valuable timber" that would remain unexploited and useless without "laws . . . by which title to land for the settler can be obtained."[5] They implored Congress to "open the land to settlement" by providing for a formal territorial government along with funding for "the construction of wagon roads, railroads, and telegraph lines." They also requested the federal government to preserve Alaska's status as "the greatest game country remaining on this continent" by extending hunting regulations.[6] While pursuing

FIGURE 1. Frederick L. Moore, 1888. Sheldon Jackson Papers, Presbyterian Historical Society, Philadelphia, PA. Photograph by Caleb Lysander Howe and Son.

different ends, both Moore and the petitioners sought a resolution to the uncertainties around the status of Alaska Natives and land that, by 1902, had become a persistent characteristic of the territory's position within the US settler colonial formation. Moore's letter sought to protect and preserve Indigenous land, subsistence economies, and ways of life, and the petitioners sought the mechanisms by which to transform land into property and transfer that property into individual, corporate, and state possession.

The tensions reflected in this archival folder are at the heart of this book. In the chapters that follow, I trace Alaska Native strategies in the preservation of their legal, political, and social orders, land, and sense of being and place from the initiation of US possessory claims in 1867 to the passage of the Alaska Native Claims Settlement Act (ANCSA) in 1971. I do so in the context of important developments in US settler colonial and imperial formations, situating Alaska as a critical and distinct break in previous patterns of US territorial expansion. I argue that this shift strained the legal frameworks that had heretofore defined the legal status of Indigenous Peoples in lands claimed and occupied by the United States. This occurred at the entanglement of two distinct but ultimately related developments: the targeting of Alaska by corporate and government interests who sought to establish imperial relations outside of the settler state and the cessation of treaty making with all Indigenous nations in territories claimed by the United States, a move accomplished by congressional fiat in 1871. Thus, the initiation of possessory claims in Alaska signaled the commencement of imperial ambitions distinct from contiguous western expansion in the context of a dramatic shift in continental Indian policy.

Without the old tools of dispossession at their disposal, Alaska became a critical location where government, corporate, and settler interests simultaneously sought out new methods of land appropriation while assembling the emergent structure of US empire in what most government officials understood as a noncontiguous, overseas colonial possession. Thus narrated as first empire rather than the last frontier, Alaska lay outside of what they considered to be properly national territory and was not intended for full integration into the settler state.[7] These government officials incorporated this assumption into their engagements with Alaska Natives, and in addition to refraining from treaty making, they proffered a theory of Asian origins for Alaska Natives, refused to designate Alaska as Indian Country, and excluded Alaska Natives from the jurisdiction of the Bureau of Indian Affairs (BIA). While treaties, Indian reservations, and subjection to BIA oversight unequivocally represented "instruments of overt conquest," they nevertheless established the legal basis for Native sovereignty and land rights within the US legal system.[8] Their absence would become the basis by which government officials and lawmakers would deny a nation-to-nation relationship between the US federal government and Alaska Native nations from that moment forward, setting in motion what legal scholars characterize as over a century of "theoretical uncertainty about the legal status of the Indigenous Peoples of what is now the state of Alaska."[9]

These uncertainties were solely in the minds of these government officials, and their assumptions regarding Alaska Native political organization, sovereignty, and land regulations did not reflect realities on the ground. In the early years of possessory claims, the US military and initial corporate and settler interlopers were situated mostly in Tlingit and Haida homelands and therefore beholden to Tlingit and Haida legal orders.[10] Nevertheless, as the military, settlers, corporate fisheries, and timber operations increased encroachment on Tlingit and Haida lands and lives, many Alaska Natives responded by adapting and incorporating notions of US law into their strategies to preserve their ways of life, their political autonomy, and their social, economic, and cultural institutions. These strategies and the institutions they aimed to sustain were grounded in place, which ordered all other elements of material and spiritual life, including the social and legal orders that structured their relationships to each other and to the land.[11] Moore's letter to the US attorney general in 1902 is an example of this syncretism. Having worked with various Tlingit communities in voicing opposition to violations of their land laws and disruptions to their subsistence economies, Moore had ample experience mobilizing Tlingit legal orders against and through US legal frameworks. He drew on settler conceptions of property while indicting the underhanded maneuvers of the "speculators" and the legality of the title they fraudulently claimed the right to sell, while situating his objections in the context of Tlingit clan ownership and regulation of fishing streams and Tlingit protocols of permission.[12] He also demonstrated that he knew, as did his respondent Knox, that the precise nature of Indigenous land rights in Alaska had yet to be clearly defined in US law. He pressed the attorney general for a definitive statement that would render Tlingit land regulations legible to, and thereby enforced against, settlers and corporations seeking to establish themselves in Tlingit homelands.

Historians typically interpret this reluctance of the federal government to establish a uniformity of territorial expansion and Indigenous–US relations in Alaska as neglect. I argue instead that it is symptomatic of a new legal formation that I call "settler imperialism." I define *settler imperialism* as the constellation of statutory and case law that lawmakers, judges, federal and territorial officials, and corporate interests constructed to subvert Alaska Native sovereignties and land relations. This constellation arose out of and subsequently facilitated the persistence of legal uncertainty concerning the status of Indigenous Peoples in Alaska and their lands.[13] Beginning with the purchase of Russian interests in Alaska and continuing throughout the twentieth century, Congress, along with the federal executive agencies, resisted extending the established frameworks of continental expansion that had been characterized by constitutionally prescribed methods for the acquisition of Indian lands and the statutory regulations that facilitated the incorporation of territory through provisions established in the Northwest Ordinance and the Trade and Intercourse Acts.[14] In their place, these interests debated, drafted, proposed, and enacted legislation that allowed access to Native lands for settlement, infrastructural and extractive projects, and military operations. While often acknowledging and debating the implications of these uncertainties, lawmakers and government officials failed to resolve them. Instead, they crafted legal language that deliberately bypassed nation-to-nation negotiations for land through the disavowal of Alaska Native sovereignty.

I argue further that the construction and maintenance of the settler imperial formation in Alaska was contingent on two dual ambiguities: the first around Alaska Native legal status and the second around Alaska's relationship to properly national territory. These ambiguities had a specific and discrete dispossessive function in the context of the first US claim to a territory conceptualized as a noncontiguous imperial space. As described by political theorist Robert Nichols, dispossession in the contiguous states and territories operated through a recursive logic by which land is transformed into property and transferred to non-Indigenous "owners" and Indigenous land rights are only recognized recursively through retroactive attribution.[15] In this formulation,

Nichols argues that the making of property out of land and the taking of that property were temporally "fused," demonstrating that in the very moment that settlers transferred control over the land from Indigenous people to themselves, they simultaneously "recoded its meaning" such that the transference of land is what transformed it into a "discreet entity" to which one could have proprietary rights.[16] The temporal and spatial nature of this process is particularly relevant to the Alaska context, especially with regard to the end of treaty making writ large and Alaska's persistent reputation as the last frontier. Alaska lacked the customary legal mechanisms (treaties) to convert land into property and for the first decades of US possessory claims remained illegible as an extension of the western frontier that had represented regions as always already becoming part of the settler state.[17] Scholars of settler colonial studies have long argued that, contrary to the popular national myth of calculated and orderly negotiation for Indigenous lands to which the US settler population could expand, the primary mode of territorial acquisition was achieved through the illegal intrusions of settlers into Indigenous lands. Referred to as the "frontier rabble" by anthropologist Patrick Wolfe, these intruders seized and claimed lands in contravention of treaty rights, which provoked a variety of responses, up to and including war, from the Indigenous people whose land regulations the trespassers had violated.[18] This in turn often prompted additional land cessions by which the federal government would retrospectively redeem the illegality of preemptive land seizures through "purchase," and the rabble was poised to receive title to the property that had been generated out of their theft.[19]

In Alaska, the dual ambiguities that government officials created around the racial and legal status of Alaska Natives and Alaska's relationship to the nation proper disrupted this dispossessive process in both spatial and temporal terms and at two critical junctures. Historians have often attributed the federal government's slow development and incorporation of Alaska into the settler state to the persistently low numbers of white people in the territory. In this presumption, they are partially correct.[20] What they fail to perceive was how their fixation on the last frontier narrative presumed that Alaska had always been conceived of as a settler space and was destined to culminate in statehood. While conceding that Alaska's noncontiguity and geographical distance presented significant logistic barriers to the frontier rabble, I suggest that it also facilitated delay by both Congress and federal agencies in defining the relationship of Alaska to the nation proper and, by default, the legal status of Alaska Natives in relation to tribal nations in the contiguous states. This paused the simultaneous making and taking of land as property; with no rabble to initiate extralegal seizure, the federal government was not compelled to extend land laws to a territory that it did not intend—at least initially—to become part of the nation proper.[21] This elongated the temporal window between the initiation of possessory claims by treaty between the United States and another supposedly discovering nation (Russia) and the necessity to incorporate land as property into the national territory of the United States, constituting the first juncture by which ambiguity was inserted into the dispossessive process. Government officials had fancied Alaska as a new venture in overseas colonialism with an uncertain relationship to the United States, which allowed them to frame Alaska Natives as distinct from Indigenous people in the contiguous United States. Because of the uncertainty around Alaska's ambiguous relationship to states and statehood, government officials hesitated in defining the legal status of Alaska Natives. This ambiguity is reflected in the attorney general's response to Moore's letter, penned thirty-five years after the Treaty of Cession, that "the real status and rights of these natives have never been clearly defined and determined."[22]

These ambiguities operated to pause the dispossessive process at this juncture until the turn of the century, when political and public discourses were focused on the social and economic implications of the closing of the frontier and the imperial debates following the Spanish-American War. These national crises necessitated a reframing of Alaska within the US imperial formation, and Frederick Moore's protest of increasing encroachment on Tlingit fishing economies and the petitions from would-be settlers clamoring for land laws and infrastructure in Alaska are symptomatic of this impending shift. In recent decades, scholars have been examining the legal and political discourses that arose in response to the seizure of additional noncontiguous territories in 1898 and the doctrines of incorporated and unincorporated territories in which they culminated. While rightly focusing their analysis on the strategic and political justifications for US annexation of additional territories, along with the implications for the inhabitants thereof, these scholars likewise allow the frontier narrative of Alaska to cloak its central role in this transformative imperial process.[23] At the turn of the century, legal scholars and Supreme Court justices debated various theories of territorial status and their constitutionality, ultimately rebranding Alaska as an extension of frontier expansion. Framing Alaska this way allowed government officials and the Supreme Court to distinguish between Alaska and other noncontiguous territories as they had previously distinguished Alaska from the contiguous states. In this sense, invoking a frontier narrative of Alaska provided a foil against which the Supreme Court could define and situate unincorporated territories within the US legal system and the geopolitical structure of empire.

Congress responded to this narrative shift by passing a series of organic acts and amendments for Alaska and officially designated the longtime customs, military, or civil district as an incorporated territory in 1912. I argue that this transition from district to organized/incorporated territory relocated ambiguity in the dispossessive process from the moment of making and taking to the moment of retroactive attribution. As a newly minted incorporated territory, twentieth-century Alaska bore witness to an accelerated rate of military, corporate, and settler expansion and the rapid appropriation of Native land. Critically, incorporated status did not change the ambiguity of Alaska Native land rights in US law. Armed with nearly fifty years of federal refusal to define the legal status of Alaska Natives, government officials, corporate interests, and lawmakers continued to categorize them as "native but not Indian," as "associations but not tribes." In the US legal system, tribal nations are the recognized entities to which the federal government attributed collective land rights and the authority to dispose of them. The denial of tribal status allowed these settler actors to imagine that Alaska Natives had never been formally removed from their homelands, casting doubt on the fact of a legal and compensable taking and inserting ambiguity into the eligibility of Alaska Natives for retroactive recognition as former owners of the land.

Within these temporal windows, from 1867 to 1912 and from 1912 to 1971, Congress and the courts constructed the legal constellation of settler imperialism through piecemeal and contradictory statutory and case law that refrained from conclusively defining the legal status of Alaska Natives and their land. Drawing on the ambiguity embedded in the process of dispossession, they constructed this legal framework to maintain a status quo in which they refrained from confirming or denying the existence of Aboriginal title and, by default, the nationhood status of Alaska Native polities. To this end, they managed first to extract from, and then subsequently fully appropriate, Native land without the use of treaties or other constitutionally prescribed means.[24] While the operational function of ambiguity shifted in the twentieth century, the settler imperial formation has been informed throughout the duration of US possessory claims by the racialization of Alaska Natives as Asian in origin.[25] These imagined Asian origins, perpetuated by tourists and missionaries along with government officials, underpinned the administrative exclusion of Alaska Natives from the BIA on account that they were considered "races of a questionable, ethnical type," which effectively "located the rights, and therefore political strategies, of Alaska Natives as distinct from those of other Indigenous people in the United States."[26] This is not lost on Alaska Native activists and Alaska Native studies scholars, who have long argued that the "lack of clarity for Indigenous rights" following the Treaty of Cession had tremendous impacts on Alaska Natives as the "United States continued to neglect any aspect of Indigenous sovereign ownership of land."[27] They consistently point to the ways the US government "chose not to make treaties with Alaska Native tribes in an attempt to avoid the sovereign recognition of our [Alaska Native] nations," and the federal government leveraged the ambiguity this historical refusal engendered to facilitate continuous and ongoing dispossession.[28]

In spite of US refusal to recognize their nationhood status, Alaska Natives mobilized Indigenous legal and political orders and engaged US law to establish and maintain diplomatic relations. These strategies included pursuing citizenship as a means by which they could access US legal and political institutions, adapting a variety of political and economic organizational structures and expressions, and identifying and leveraging components of federal Indian law that they found useful in the preservation of their societies and their land relations. As Moore's letter demonstrates, they knew early on that the federal government was treating them differently than tribal nations in the contiguous states. Moore's appeal to the attorney general for clarification of Alaska Native land rights does not, however, suggest that he and other Native leaders sought to achieve an identical formulation of the recognition of their Indigenous land and sovereignty rights. Rather, they sought to define their relationship to the federal, territorial, and state governments, settlers, businesses, and corporations on their own terms.[29] To this end, they articulated their own legal and political orders in the courts, Congress, and territorial and state legislatures while adopting terms such as *citizen, Indian, tribe,* and *property* to convey their legal rights while also recoding them to resonate with the ways they related to each other and to the land.

In particular, many Alaska Natives paid close attention to the ways government officials and lawmakers coupled the recognition of Indigenous nationhood and land rights to the concept of wardship, and they oriented their strategies in opposition to that linkage.[30] In the absence of treaties, this significantly increased the valence of citizenship in their efforts to stymie military, settler, and corporate encroachment. Beginning in Southeast Alaska, Tlingit, Haida, and Tsimshian peoples embraced citizenship as an important category that would distinguish them from wards, though not in ways that equated to assimilation and abandonment of their Indigenous identities and legal and political rights. Many argued vehemently that they had never been wards, nor had they ever been tribes, as federal Indian law had defined these categories, and they resisted these designations. They advocated for an Indigenized expression of citizenship that they could mobilize in defense of their land. This strategy was not entirely unique as Native people across the United States likewise employed citizenship in their resistance efforts against dispossession, disenfranchisement, and marginalization; however, the context and function of Alaska's racialized and territorial ambiguities made this approach especially important.[31]

Conversely, government officials, corporate interests, and lawmakers employed the rhetoric of citizenship to discredit Alaska Native nationhood and claims to collective land rights, and they leveraged the ambiguities of Alaska Native legal status to these ends. These settler actors attributed Alaska Native advocacy for citizenship and equal rights to what they perceived as the absence of tribal nations and collective land rights recognized through treaties or the existence of Aboriginal title in Alaska. They concluded that this had resulted in a less contested and more efficient process of assimilation by which the former methods of land acquisition were not necessary. While they repeatedly leveraged these conclusions against Alaska Native land rights and sovereignty, they also came to argue that the lack of reservations, treaties, and recognized tribes in Alaska ought to serve as a model for federal Indian policy in the contiguous states. These arguments became particularly potent in the backlash to the Indian Reorganization Act at mid-century when the federal government developed policy ultimately leading to the unilateral termination of over one hundred tribal nations. In this context, this book demonstrates how lawmakers and government officials brought imperial techniques and logics back to inform domestic policy, thus reifying settler colonial governance and dispossession.[32] Despite Alaska's distinctiveness in the US imperial formation, the vacillations of federal Indian law between recognizing tribal nations as sovereign entities and seeking to terminate, dissolve, and assimilate Indigenous nations nevertheless reverberate through Alaska and back again.

The imperial ambitions that shaped the legal landscape in Alaska were also central to the trajectory of US empire and the management of the relationship between domestic and imperial spaces that is critical to hegemonic and settler colonial dominion. Alaska lies at the critical juncture where frontier logics became entangled with extractive, hegemonic, extranational objectives, and this entanglement necessitated the formulation and mobilization of new categories of peoples and territories within the purview of US empire. Taking into consideration Chickasaw scholar Jodi Byrd's concept of Indianness as a "site through which U.S. empire orients and replicates itself," I explore the ways the category of "Indian" functioned in Alaska, where it was often "oppositionally juxtaposed" against the Indigeneity of Alaska Natives.[33] This particular deployment of Indianness informed the ways government officials came to measure the rights of Indigenous Peoples in noncontiguous territories, and through it new methods of territorial governance emerged. In this way, this book casts an eye to the moments when Alaska, as a geopolitical asset, anchored a framework for ordering other noncontiguous territories within this imperial matrix while also serving as the material and geographical place from which the United States launched and managed hegemonic operations. In both roles, Alaska functions as a critical location in what legal historian Christina D. Ponsa-Kraus describes as the "elaborate process of combined inclusion and exclusion, expansion and retraction, projection and limitation, intended for territories at the margins of the nation."[34] The tentative and often ambiguous nature of this process further reflects how Alaska's exceptionally long duration as a customs district, unorganized territory, then incorporated territory allowed for corporate-nation-state interests to work out the mechanics of empire.

I trace the emergence and development of settler imperialism in six chapters, each focusing on key moments in which Alaska Natives confronted and challenged the intrusion of government officials, corporate interests, lawmakers, and settlers in their homelands. In doing so, I locate and track the ways these interests animated and mobilized ambiguity to facilitate access to land in the absence of customary instruments of dispossession and as a conduit for empire building. Chapter 1 begins with an analysis of the entanglements of Tlingit sovereignty and US possessory claims in the immediate aftermath of the 1867 Treaty of Cession. I argue that Tlingit resistance to encroachment on their territories and disavowal of their legal, political, and territorial orders drew US military personnel, government officials, Congress, and judges into debates about Alaska and its Indigenous inhabitants. Three critical cases, *United States v. Seveloff* (1872), *United States v. Kie* (1885), and *In re Sah Quah* (1886), mark significant locations in which the courts codified racial and legal distinctions between Alaska Natives and Indigenous peoples and tribes in the contiguous states. In articulating these distinctions, the courts determined that Alaska was not Indian Country and that Alaska Natives were neither US citizens nor members of tribal nations. Labeled by one judge as "dependent subjects," the courts made no further determinations as to Alaska Native political status or land rights within the US legal system.[35] The exclusion from citizenship notwithstanding, the refusal to acknowledge sovereignty and Aboriginal title in Alaska inadvertently interrupted the conditions of possibility required to convert land into property. While frustrating Alaska Natives along with subsequent settler and corporate interests alike, these court cases situated ambiguity as a cornerstone of future legislation and policy.

Chapter 2 takes up Tlingit, Haida, and Tsimshian land rights and citizenship activism as they responded to the influx of corporate fisheries, mining activity, and a growing interest in timber harvesting in their homelands. Likewise responding to the growth of corporate and settler activity, Congress passed two organic acts and two land statutes between 1884 and 1926 that I argue embedded the legal uncertainties of Alaska Native land rights into the legal and administrative structures of the territory even as they redefined Alaska's relationship to the nation proper. Importantly, these processes unfolded amid the imperial debates following the Spanish-American War and the US Supreme Court's ruling in the Insular Cases. Alaska figured prominently here, as government officials, Supreme Court justices, and legal theorists contemplated the nature of its relationship to national territory in their deliberations about the constitutional status of the additional noncontiguous territories seized in the 1898 Treaty of Paris. In these debates, they renarrated Alaska as the last frontier in their efforts to carve out the doctrine of incorporation by which the federal government would structure the territorial governance in areas determined to reside permanently outside of the settler state and the political status of their inhabitants. While culminating in the designation of Alaska as an incorporated territory, the ambiguity around the legal status of Alaska Natives and their land carried over as settler, military, and corporate interests utilized the new territorial land laws to claim Indigenous homelands as property. This relocated ambiguity into the process of retroactive attribution as Alaska Natives shifted their legal strategies for preserving their land relations from citizenship—conveyed unilaterally in 1924—to obtaining recognition of their land rights within the US legal system.

Chapter 3 follows the development of Alaska Native land claims strategies as Tlingit attorneys along with members of the Alaska Native Brotherhood and Alaska Native Sisterhood sought to define the relationship of US citizenship, land, and federal Indian law through Indigenous political and legal orders. I argue that they mobilized the ambiguities and uncertainties in their legal status to shape their relationship to the federal and territorial governments during critical shifts in national policy reflected in the Indian Reorganization Act (IRA). Many Tlingit activists recognized that the ambiguity in their legal status frustrated their efforts to assert their land rights and subsistence-based political economies. They also recognized that this same ambiguity had the potential to cloud the legality of the titles sought by settler and corporate interests. They employed this potential in compelling Congress to include them in specific provisions of the IRA and to pass the 1935 Tlingit and Haida Jurisdictional Act authorizing them to pursue land claims suits against the US government. Together, the IRA amendments and jurisdictional act represented strategies for dislodging the ambiguity that government officials and lawmakers had relied on to disavow Alaska Native nationhood and to justify their exclusion from legal frameworks that would recognize their land rights. I examine these policies in the context of imperial reorganizing, as the federal government simultaneously consolidated all incorporated and unincorporated territories into the new Division of Territories and Island Possessions.

Chapter 4 charts Alaska Native efforts to mobilize their vision of Indigenous land rights and citizenship as government officials, lawmakers, and corporate timber and fishing interests sought to rescind the IRA in Alaska. These contests were framed by intensifying corporate resource extraction efforts and the militarization of the territory leading up to, during, and in the aftermath of WWII. I argue that government officials sharpened the racial and legal distinctions they had created between Alaska Natives and tribes in the contiguous states to facilitate Alaska's increasing role in establishing US global hegemony. Federal officials and lawmakers understood this project to be contingent on federal access to land for military infrastructure and corporate access to land for resource extraction. These two interrelated projects hinged on the ambiguity around the status of Alaska Natives and their land, which government officials and Congress employed in the unilateral expansion of military bases in Southcentral Alaska, and the opening up of land in Southeast Alaska to timber corporations through the Tongass Timber Act. Both processes were made possible by the ways federal officials and lawmakers cast doubt on the existence of Aboriginal title in Alaska. Significantly, the Tongass Timber Act explicitly established the legislative means by which settlers and corporations could appropriate Native land while bypassing Tlingit land rights indefinitely. As such, it demonstrates the ways settler imperialism, as a constellation of law premised and contingent on ambiguity, facilitated the material and physical act of dispossession while suspending, indefinitely, the retroactive recognition of Alaska Natives as the original owners of the land.

Chapter 5 tracks ambiguity as a function of the settler imperial formation by examining Tlingit and Haida responses to the passage of the Tongass Timber Act and increasing territorial bids for Alaska statehood. I argue that in this context, their strategies increasingly reflected the ways ambiguity prompted them to explore resolutions to their land rights and the preservation of their legal and political orders outside of existing legal frameworks that confined possible settlements to the realm of retroactive attribution and compensation as the original owners of the land. Especially poignant in the Termination Era in which lawmakers sought both the justification for and the means to extinguish tribal status in the contiguous states, Alaska Natives doubled down on their argument that their Indigenous land rights were integral to their US citizenship and a necessary means by which they would contribute to the development of Alaska in the event of statehood. To this end, they positioned the unresolved status of their land rights as a barrier, warning that the lack of clarification could frighten off investors, leaving the future state struggling to achieve economic stability. By coupling their land rights to statehood, they advanced their vision of citizenship, sovereignty, and the potential for government-to-government relations through mutual interest in the future of Alaska. Importantly, the post-WWII Alaska Native land claims activism and debates about Alaska statehood occurred alongside and as part of the reclassifying of other noncontiguous territorial possessions within the United States' imperial formation. Statehood for Alaska ran headlong into federal and military ambitions for the function of the territory in maintaining and reproducing empire. Complicating the conclusions of some historians that various interests impeded statehood solely for economic concerns and party politics, this chapter concludes by demonstrating that full incorporation into the Union did not bring Alaska's role in empire to an end but instead reified it.

Chapter 6 examines land claims litigation leading up to the passage of ANCSA. I argue that two important lawsuits—*Tlingit and Haida Indians of Alaska v. United States,* filed in the US Court of Claims, and *Natives of Palmer, Alaska v. United States* filed in the Indian Claims Commission—demonstrate the ways the federal government reformed settler imperial ambiguity from a legal discourse of unresolved uncertainties in racial and legal status into a systematic and circular logic of dispossession in the poststatehood era. This logic relied on the division of Alaska Natives into three racial categories (Indian, Aleut, and Eskimo) immediately following statehood, to which lawmakers and government officials ascribed divergent land rights and tribal status.[36] This, along with the contradictory and controversial outcomes of *Tlingit and Haida* and *Natives of Palmer,* further persuaded Alaska Natives to seek a land claims settlement that included both the restoration of Native lands to Native possession and a monetary settlement for lands appropriated by the state and federal governments. As before, they positioned their land rights as a barrier to corporate access to and transportation of petroleum resources located in the northernmost region of the United States. This settlement came to fruition in the 1971 Alaska Native Claims Settlement Act, and I track the ways members of the Alaska Federation of Natives, among numerous individuals and organizations, sought to infuse the critical elements of their legal, political, and social orders into its provisions. Lawmakers and corporate interests nevertheless foreclosed many of these possibilities, and ANCSA is often characterized as having complicated legacies and contradictory outcomes. These challenges aside, ANCSA does represent the cumulative and cooperative efforts of Alaska Natives to navigate a new imperial formation that was predicated on racial and legal distinctions intended to facilitate the disavowal of their nationhood, sovereignty, and land by perpetuating and reproducing ambiguity and uncertainty as a legal strategy of empire.

This book traces the development of the settler imperial formation in Alaska, identifies its objectives, and maps out some of the ways it functions on the ground in specific legal spaces. It is not a comprehensive overview of all statutory and case law in Alaska's history, nor does it claim absolute consistency of these policies and imperial strategies throughout Alaska. Likewise, it also does not suggest that all Alaska Native communities responded similarly or with the same objectives in mind. With "twenty different language groups and seven or eight broad cultural groups, depending on interpretation," Alaska Natives are as diverse as the homelands to which they have adapted themselves perfectly since time immemorial.[37] Most of this book focuses on events and peoples in Southeast Alaska, given that this region was the location of colonial governance and denser settler populations, with some case studies drawing on events in central or Interior communities. It disrupts the frontier mythologizing that characterizes Alaska, past and present, but demonstrates why it is imperative to understand what that narrative eclipsed and how it informs Indigenous–US relations and US global hegemonic projects. To achieve this, the book at times focuses a great deal of attention on the development and discourses of empire among government officials, corporations, judges, lawyers, and lawmakers as they sought ways to nullify Alaska Native political and legal orders that structured their relationships to land and their exercise of their inherent sovereignty. It is imperative, though, to recognize that the legal and political landscape in Alaska looks the way it does because of what Alaska Natives did. The settler imperial formation becomes visible when analyzing the ways Alaska Natives developed strategies in navigating it, and this book aims to trace their historical and ongoing interventions in US empire.

Methods and Positionality

I am a non-Native historian who grew up on Dena'ina homelands in Southcentral Alaska, and this book is one of the many outgrowths of my experiences there. Cognizant of the historical and ongoing colonialisms developed in tandem with Western academic research paradigms and the power relations they engendered, it is crucial to situate myself in relation to the communities that I write about in this book. My family relocated to Eagle River (just north of Anchorage) from southwest Ohio in January of 1994 when I was twelve years old, and the transition from the humid subtropical climate of Cincinnati to the subarctic coastal mountains was an abrupt but welcome change. People ask me what it was like to grow up there, often with a tinge of skepticism as if to say they appreciate the "adventure" of it but they themselves couldn't imagine being so peripheral to the trappings of "mainstream" society or dealing with the cold.[38] I always respond that our move there was the best thing that ever happened to me, and I prefer the cold anyhow. Far more important than the weather, though, was how different the cultural, political, and social landscape of Alaska was in contrast to suburban Ohio with regard to the complex histories and relationships between Alaska Natives and the settler, corporate, and military communities and the colonial projects they represent. Coming to understand these dynamics and myself brought me, over the course of several decades, to this book.

Our arrival in Alaska coincided with two important developments in Alaska Native politics: escalating legal contests over subsistence rights in the years following the 1980 passage of the Alaska National Interest Lands Conservation Act and the 1993 naming of nearly 230 Alaska Native Villages as federally recognized Indian tribes. State officials balked at these developments, leading to years of conflict over subsistence rights and federal funding programs, while tensions flared among many white settlers who perceived them as race-based privileges that unfairly disadvantaged them. This rhetoric is not new, though it carries a particular valence given Alaska's distinct history even as it is persistently wielded against tribal sovereignty across the United States.

Nevertheless, Native sovereignty in Alaska remains an intensely contested subject today (as elsewhere) as evidenced in the proliferation of litigation challenging Alaska Native sovereignty and subsistence rights stemming from these statutes and policies. I became more interested in the discourses framing Native subsistence, the Alaska Native Corporations, Alaska's oil economy, citizenship, and colonialism, among other related issues, into my young adulthood through conversations with Native community members, friends, and classmates. It wasn't until I was a master's student at New York University that I thought about Alaska Native land and sovereignty activism as an area of potential research. Most of my coursework there was situated in postcolonial studies, and I suppose I sought to contextualize what I knew about Alaska in these frameworks.

To this end, I put together a reading list after my mom sent me a copy of Iñupiaq scholar and activist William L. Iġġiaġruk Hensley's memoir *Fifty Miles from Tomorrow: A Memoir of Alaska and the Real People,* which was published in 2008. Maria Shaa Tláa Williams (Tlingit) edited an anthology entitled *The Alaska Native Reader: History, Culture, Politics* the following year, and after reading these books I wanted to know more about ANCSA and the legislation and policy that Williams and Hensley describe. After spending a few years in California, I knew that the legal history in Alaska was different from that in the contiguous states, and I wanted to understand why and what that meant for the ongoing contests over subsistence and sovereignty and the discourses of race and modernity that constituted the undercurrent of life in Alaska. My master's thesis more or less attempted to trace the settler legal history of ANCSA, and in doing so it became clear that the more important story was the ways Alaska Native interventions in US colonialism shaped the Alaska that I grew up in.

By the time I sought admittance to a PhD program, I'd lived outside Alaska for several years and I knew that much of the research and writing would be conducted out of state, presenting challenges to the relationships with community members that are imperative for this kind of project. I made a commitment to return to Alaska as frequently as possible and have conversations with friends and community members about my research ideas and what I found in the archives. Given the diversity of Alaska and the statewide focus of this book, my research questions did not originate in the context of any one Alaska Native community.

Rather, Alaska Native community members and representatives, archivists, and Alaska Native, Indigenous, and non-Indigenous academic colleagues in Indigenous studies fields with whom I talked through my thinking and consulted on drafts and archival materials encouraged me to pursue this project and have been central to its development. For example, in the early stages of research and writing I worked in the Sealaska Heritage Center's William L. Paul Sr. Archives and Special Collections, an Indigenous archival institution that houses an extensive collection of material relating to Tlingit, Haida, and Tsimshian activism. In using these collections, I consulted with the archivists on the materials I was using and how I would write about them, and I shared some early drafts to this end. Recognizing and taking seriously that many stories are not mine to tell, I rely only on published works from members of the relevant community to describe, interpret, or explain the intellectual and theoretical frameworks that underpin the actions or strategies of the Alaska Natives who made this history and whose stories I trace through the archives. Whenever I conduct research in Anchorage (or just return home for a visit), I've been fortunate enough to have multiple conversations with a friend, community member, and elder in Eklutna, who is the descendant of some of the prominent activists in this book. While outside of Alaska, it has been crucial for me to build relationships with other scholars working in Alaska Native studies, and I am grateful to them for inviting me to participate in several Alaska Native studies panels and roundtables to discuss my research with them and for their feedback, insight, and guiding of this project for the last decade. I am grateful for the continuous support and encouragement from multiple institutions and people as I worked to untangle settler imperialism.

1

Creating an Imperial Jurisdiction

Tlingit Law and Homelands at the Margins of Indian Country

The United States initiated possessory claims to what is now the state of Alaska by signing the Treaty of Cession with Russia on March 30, 1867.[1] When the US Army officials raised the US flag at Sitka, most Russian presence was confined to a smattering of trading posts that clung precariously to the Alaska coast. Per the treaty, Russian inhabitants of the territory could request to be returned to Russia within a period of three years, and most opted to do so, leaving the small US military contingent to negotiate their presence in Tlingit homelands and their relationship with Tlingit society. Tlingit accounts of these early years of US possessory claims reveal that the small army contingent that arrived in Southeast Alaska realized quickly that Tlingit operated under a complex legal system that the Russians had been unable to subvert.[2] In fact, Russians often remained barricaded in their forts, relying on Tlingit for food and survival. When Tlingit tired of Russian presence, they burned their forts to the ground.[3] For the first three decades of US presence in Alaska, military officers, prospectors, and missionaries likewise found themselves obliged to recognize Tlingit tribal law, in which Tlingit continued to handle their own legal affairs internally and compelled the US military to fulfill sanctions imposed by Tlingit on white people in the event of a transgressions.[4] Legal disputes and violent conflicts were often the result of a refusal to adhere to Tlingit law.[5]

Tlingit legal order is structured through the clan system, which demarcates belonging, kinship, and the ownership of tangible and intangible property, including land.[6] Clans are held responsible and liable for the wrongdoings of their members, and clans are obliged to compensate the injured party for damages. Tlingit scholars demonstrate that well into the second decade of US possessory claims, the US military was frequently obliged to compensate clans for violations of their laws even as they attempted to assert an increasing amount of legal authority over Tlingit affairs.[7] As Tlingit legal orders and assertions of sovereignty over their homelands impeded US presumptions of authority, Tlingit people increasingly found themselves in US courts where attorneys and judges began carving out a distinct variety of American jurisprudence that reflected the turn toward extranational empire that the "purchase" of Alaska had signaled. Their rulings relied on the statutory and racial distinctions that government officials and Congress had articulated in the first five years of possessory claims. In conjunction with Alaska's remote location and its illegibility as a potential settler space, these rulings were vague and often iterated in the negative in that they defined what Alaska and Alaska Natives were not, rather than delineating their legal relationship to the United States. Specifically, these early rulings declared that land in Alaska was not Indian Country and that Alaska Natives were not to be recognized as nations. Without proffering a definitive alternative, early case law introduced ambiguity into the legal relationship of Alaska Natives to the federal government.

This chapter charts the settler imperial structure as constructed by government officials in response to Tlingit challenges to US authority and the ways the ambiguities on which this structure was contingent became codified and perpetuated through the territorial courts. It begins with an analysis of the founding assumptions of US possessory claims reflected in the Treaty of Cession, the Alaska Act of 1868, and the administrative exclusion from the Bureau of Indian Affairs (BIA). Uncertain of what Alaska's future would be in relation to contiguous states and territories, Congress withheld fundamental elements of federal law and policy that had characterized previous decades of westward expansion. This hesitancy to incorporate Alaska into legal uniformity was likely informed by the Treaty of Cession, which contained vague clauses regarding the legal and political status of Alaska's inhabitants. In this vein, the Johnson administration did not dispatch treaty commissioners, nor did lawmakers extend the Northwest Ordinance and the Trade and Intercourse Acts to Alaska, thereby suspending the prescribed legal mechanisms by which the federal government had historically appropriated Indigenous land and incorporated that land into the nation-state. Instead, they designated Alaska as a customs district in 1868 with no indication that further instruments of territorial governance or land negotiations with Alaska Natives would be forthcoming. The commissioner of Indian Affairs followed suit, infusing racial ambiguity into the emergent administrative framework by declaring that

Alaska Natives occupied an undefined racial category and ought to be excluded from BIA oversight.

In these early years, Congress only supplemented these statutory withholdings in response to Tlingit challenges to the meddling of military officers in their affairs. As Tlingit people enforced their own laws and legal orders in contradiction to the assumptions and expectations of US military officers, they increasingly found themselves under arrest and tried in US territorial courts. Between 1872 and 1886, three critical cases came before the Oregon and Alaska courts concerning the legal status of Alaska Natives and the nature of Alaska as a territorial possession. *United States v. Seveloff* (1872), *United States v. Kie* (1885), and *In re Sah Quah* (1886) each mark a crucial moment in the development of settler imperialism as judges interpreted the Treaty of Cession, Alaska's designation as a customs district, and the racial distinctions that government officials had used to differentiate between Alaska Natives and tribal nations and peoples in the contiguous states. Occurring in the immediate aftermath of the cessation of treaty making, these rulings meant that any further characterization of Alaska and its Indigenous inhabitants would require additional legislation. But instead of passing clarifying legislation, subsequent Congresses continued the practice of refraining from concrete definitions or procedural approaches to Alaska Native land, political relations, and territorial governance until the turn of the century when the frontier rabble and commercial fishing interests arrived in critical mass.

The Treaty of Cession and Early Settler Imperial Relations

When the United States signed the 1867 Treaty of Cession with Russia, many lawmakers understood the transaction as formalizing possession of the nation's first noncontiguous territory. Secretary of State William H. Seward had negotiated the $7.2 million deal by which the United States secured Russian interests in 375 million acres of the northwesternmost region of North America. He and Charles Sumner had convinced Congress to ratify the treaty with descriptions of Alaska's vast natural resources and as a strategic bridge to eastern markets, the former referring to the Aleutian Islands as the "stepping-stones between the two continents."[8] The language of the treaty itself may not have appeared remarkable to lawmakers or government officials at the time, and yet it included subtle but fundamental differences from prior treaties involving land cessions between the United States and other European "discovering" nations.[9] While in some ways adhering to the standard language and format of other nineteenth-century expansion treaties, it contained clauses regarding the political status of the inhabitants and the nature of the lands ceded that Congress and the courts would later interpret to distinguish Alaska Natives and their land rights from tribal nations in the contiguous states and territories. As such, it marked the ways that government officials conceived of Alaska and their intentions for it as constituting a break from previous patterns of continental expansion characterized by subsequent incorporation into the nation-state.

Articles III and VI signaled this shift and became important cornerstones on which lawmakers and the courts would configure Indigenous–US relations in Alaska. Article III extended US citizenship to "the inhabitants of the ceded territory . . . with the exception of the uncivilized tribes," whom it declared would be "subject to such laws and regulations as the United States may, from time to time, adopt in regard to aboriginal tribes of that country."[10] This seemingly innocuous clause did two things: It excluded Indigenous Alaskans from citizenship while denying nationhood status for Alaska Native Nations. Exclusion from US citizenship was not unusual and reflected nineteenth-century naturalization law in the contiguous states regarding Indigenous people who were likewise excluded from citizenship prior to the 1924 Indian Citizenship Act. However, while legal precedent in the contiguous states had excluded Indigenous people from citizenship, it had nevertheless typically recognized the nationhood status of tribes—a designation omitted from the Treaty of Cession with Russia. In doing so, this treaty set Alaska Natives on a trajectory characterized by "an ambiguous legal status marked by a racialized discourse of civilization" whereby "legal and political rights, therefore, hinged not on nation-to-nation negotiations but on individualized citizenship, and qualifications for citizenship . . . depended on demonstration and performance of being 'civilized.'"[11]

Perhaps anticipating the end of treaty making generally, I argue further that the language of Article III established the basis by which this "ambiguous" political and legal status of Alaska Natives could remain undefined indefinitely. Instead of defining the precise negotiating status of Alaska Natives, the treaty subjected them to "laws and regulations" that Congress may impose from "time to time." This was a subtle but significant departure from prior treaty language that had more clearly designated the responsibilities of the federal government to Indigenous inhabitants of territory ceded from one "discovering" nation to another. For example, Article VI of the Treaty Between the United States of America and the French Republic for the Louisiana Purchase in 1803 commits the United States to "execute such treaties and articles as may have been agreed between Spain and the tribes and nations of Indians," thereby recognizing the sovereignty of the Indigenous nations within what became the Louisiana Territory.[12] Furthermore, the 1848 Treaty of Guadalupe Hidalgo, while distinguishing between Mexican citizens and Indigenous tribes, committed the United States to arbitrate the relationship between the two while extending citizenship to the former.[13] To this effect, the United States ultimately honored treaties signed between Indigenous nations and Mexico and citizens of the Republic of Texas before entering into treaties with the Comanche, Apache, and Kiowa, among others in the region—a path not taken in Alaska.[14] Leaving the legal status of Alaska Natives undefined in a context in which the mechanics of expansion were changing and uncertain in a region virtually inaccessible by the "frontier rabble" animated the temporal function of ambiguity in Alaska Native–US relations.

In concert with Article III, Article VI of the Treaty of Cession also came to play a role in sustaining and mobilizing ambiguity in Alaska throughout the nineteenth and twentieth centuries. Whereas Article III had addressed the political status of Alaska's Russian and Indigenous inhabitants, Article VI concerned the status of land. It declared that the territory ceded was "free and unencumbered by any reservations, privileges, franchises, grants, or possessions, by any associated companies, whether corporate or incorporate, Russian or any other, or by any parties, except merely private property holders."[15] At the end of negotiations, the United States agreed to pay Russia a total of $7.2 million for their interests in Alaska, though the $.2 million was added to the original sum of $7 million after Secretary Seward insisted on the language in Article VI. He had written to the Russian Minister in March of 1867, offering "with the approval of the President" to "add two hundred thousand dollars . . . on that account," and he forewarned the minister that he "much regard[ed] it as an ultimatum."[16] By rendering land in Alaska free and clear of any property rights save that of individual property holders, the treaty authors established the legal means by which future lawmakers, federal and territorial officials, corporations, and settlers would deny the existence of Aboriginal title in Alaska. This in turn allowed them to perpetuate doubt and uncertainty regarding the eligibility of Alaska Natives to be compensated (retroactively) as the prior owners of lands from which they had been dispossessed.

Together, Articles III and VI created the conditions by which ambiguity became the underlying principle in all future negotiations of Alaska Native political status and land rights. Future lawmakers and corporate interests would come to argue that Aboriginal title had never existed in Alaska because, according to Article III, Alaska Natives would be subject to congressional legislation rather than negotiated with via treaty. Furthermore, they would argue that, in the event that Aboriginal title had existed at any point prior to US possessory claims, the Treaty of Cession had extinguished it.[17] The changes adopted in the treaty between the United States and Russia marked an important shift in the ways the United States sought to define the legal status of Indigenous inhabitants of territories ceded by one "discovering" nation to another. This had implications beyond Alaska, demonstrating the ways Alaska functioned as a distinct space in which lawmakers and government officials worked out techniques and practices of imperial possession.[18] Not long after the conclusion of treaty negotiations, Congress passed its first legal code for Alaska, designating it as a customs district. The act did not establish a territorial legislature, office of the governor, or a territorial court system in accordance with expansion procedure established in the Northwest Ordinance, and it made no mention of Alaska Natives.[19]

The significance of these ambiguities became clear as Tlingit enforced their own legal orders in response to violations of the US military. Oral histories attest that after the arrival of Americans in 1867, clan leaders decided to pursue diplomatic relations rather than war. They cautioned government and military officials that they "owned Alaska, that Russians had lived in Alaska only with their permission."[20] US military officials arrived with different assumptions in mind, and in many ways they were aware of the unique conditions under which the United States had claimed possession of Alaska. Correspondence between Colonel Jefferson C. Davis and his superiors reveals their understanding that the ambiguity engendered by the lack of treaty obligations and a territorial civil government diminished their accountability. When Colonel Davis arrived in Alaska, his official orders communicated by Major General Henry W. Halleck reflect these new conditions and their implications for Indigenous people in noncontiguous territories. Halleck instructed him that "in the absence of any organized civil Territorial Government," Davis would "act as their general superintendent, protecting them from abuse and regulating their trade and intercourse with our own people." He warned, however, that "military officers have no authority to make Indian Treaties. You will therefore enter into no negotiations of that kind, or attempt to bind our government to any contracts of agreements without special authority and under special instructions."[21]

Presumptions of US authority in Tlingit homelands lead to frequent altercations, and just two years after US arrival in Tlingit territory, these tensions had erupted in military violence. The 1869 bombardments of Kake and Wrangell both arose from instances in which Tlingit clans had first sought restitution for injury or death of a clan member in accordance with Tlingit law. The bombardment of Kake and its aftermath especially demonstrates the ways the lack of treaties and a civil government informed Davis's military initiatives in Alaska. The Kake War began with an affront to three clan leaders by a white soldier, which led to one clan leader seizing the soldier's rifle in response to the offense. When Davis sent troops to arrest the leaders, the resulting conflict resulted in wounded soldiers, Tlingit fatalities, and the arrest of a Tlingit leader. Davis attempted to put Sitka on lockdown, surrounding the village with gunship artillery, with which soldiers shot and killed Tlingit as they attempted to leave Sitka by canoe. When pressed by clan leaders for restitution for the deaths, Davis refused, after which the clan leaders killed two trappers out of a party of four that they encountered on Admiralty Island. To Tlingit, this satisfied the requirements under Tlingit jurisprudence, but to Davis it likely represented an entirely separate and unprovoked incident, and he responded by shelling three villages and two forts. While the Kake Tlingit had evacuated these sites prior to the shelling, the US military burned the villages to the ground; unable to return to their homes, exposure, starvation, and illness resulted in additional Tlingit fatalities.[22]

Perhaps anticipating an investigation and subsequent reprimand for these actions, the army appeared to have concealed the incident by omitting any mention of it in Fort Sitka's US Army Post Report for January.[23] Despite these efforts, the army's handling of the events that transpired at Kake did reach Jefferson's superiors and the public; however, it is evident that Davis and his counterparts anticipated that the lack of civil authority and enforceable treaty obligations would impair any potential consequences. In the midst of escalating conflicts between Tlingit and the army, Lt. Col. Robert Scott wrote Davis musing that he was quite fortunate to not be "hampered by a civil government, Indian Bureau, etc. in Alaska, and had therefore a good square chance to pitch in and punish such tribes as many become ugly."[24] Davis obviously concurred, remarking just a year later in his annual report that "the Indians throughout the Territory have generally shown a desire to observe peaceful relations with the whites. Having no farcical treaty obligations to observe, none, of course, have been violated, and one of the principle causes of war between the races has thereby been avoided."[25] Davis, Scott, and the military generally understood that the absence of federal regulations and treaty obligations to mitigate their actions in Alaska facilitated the abrogation of tribal sovereignty and any accountability for violently doing so. The military engaged in countless acts of violence in contravention of treaty rights and federal regulations in the contiguous states, and though the explicit absence of any structure to regulate Indigenous–US relations in Alaska through citizenship or nation-to-nation negotiation resulted in violence, it also contributed to the ambiguity that came to inform debates over Alaska Native legal status and their land rights for the next hundred years.

Tlingit Sovereignty in US Territorial Courts

As the military resisted Tlingit legal authority and sought to consolidate control in Southeast Alaska, they increasingly arrested Tlingit people and charged them in US territorial courts. The events surrounding the 1869 bombardments, however, were only the beginning of Tlingit efforts to prevail upon US military and government officials to respect their legal orders and their authority over matters in their homelands. In the decades following the end to treaty making in the contiguous United States, the US District Court of Oregon and the District Court of Alaska (established by the 1884 First Organic Act for Alaska) were compelled to consider the legal status of Alaska Natives amid broader reconfigurations of Indigenous–US relations. On the West Coast, the preceding two decades bore witness to an initial fraying of nation-to-nation relations between tribal nations and the federal government with Congress's refusal to ratify eighteen treaties with California tribal nations and challenges to the nature and applicability of Indian Country in land west of the Rocky Mountains.[26] These processes were contested and piecemeal on the West Coast, but Alaska's noncontiguity and the Asian racialization of Alaska Natives allowed government officials to apply this emerging technique of nonrecognition unilaterally and across Alaska. In 1872 when the Board of Indian Commissioners recommended that the "the inhabitants of Alaska be placed under the care of the Department of the Interior" and proposed that funds be set aside from the Indian Department for that purpose, Interior Secretary Columbus Delano balked.[27] Rejecting the proposal, he argued that "Congress has not yet provided any territorial government for Alaska" and that "the Indian Service, embracing all the Indians of the United States is applicable to such persons only"; he concluded that such an appropriation would be inappropriate because "it is exceedingly doubtful whether the inhabitants of Alaska . . . belong to the same race or family of men as the Indians of the North America."[28] His decision was based on the opinion of Commissioner of Indian Affairs Francis Amasa Walker, who sought to distinguish between "tribes nearer at hand, and with which the Government has long sustained relations," and those in regions outside of the United States proper. Regarding Alaska, Walker had "never believed that the natives of Alaska were Indians within the meaning of the Constitution," and he argued that Indian status should not be "extended unnecessarily to races of a questionable ethnical type, and occupying a position practically distinct and apart from the range of undoubted Indian tribes of the continent."[29]

The courts ratified this administrative exclusion along with the legal distinctions introduced by the Treaty of Cession, Alaska's status as a customs district, and the refusal of the federal government to sign treaties with Alaska Natives in the following decade. Between 1872 and 1886, three cases were pivotal to this process, and each arose out of Tlingit resistance to increasing US intrusion into their lands and disregard for Tlingit legal systems. To this end, the main legal question in these cases was whether US courts had jurisdiction to adjudicate the alleged offenses, which hinged on whether the courts determined that Alaska was

Indian Country. If they found that Alaska was Indian Country, such a ruling would establish the existence of Aboriginal title in Alaska and invoke the constitutional protections of Indian lands as mandated in the Trade and Intercourse Acts. This would presumably require negotiations on a nation-to-nation basis for the transference of Alaska Native land into US possession, situating these cases at the critical juncture of the making of land into property and the transferring of that property from Indigenous people to non-Native possession. The final decisions in each ultimately concluded that Alaska was not Indian Country, nullifying the legal concept that had, in the settler legal system, defined land that was not yet property. Collectively, these three cases represent the point at which the abstract racial and legal ambiguities articulated by government officials from the signing of the Treaty of Cession reconfigured the dispossessive process by disrupting the material making and taking of property. This severely undermined the methods by which Alaska Natives could establish their land rights in US law, while simultaneously facilitating and hindering settler, federal, and corporate objectives for the next hundred years.

The first case to consider Indian Country in Alaska—*United States v. Seveloff*—came before the District Court of Oregon in 1872.[30] That year, the US military arrested a distillery operator of Tlingit and Russian descent by the name of Ferueta Seveloff. Seveloff was charged with violating Articles 20 and 21 of the Trade and Intercourse Acts, which prohibited the introduction of "spirituous liquors" into lands considered—at least by the US military—to be Indian Country. His arrest marked an important dispute in Tlingit–US relations, as many Tlingit and Creole people had developed small liquor operations during the Russian era. The Russians had not regulated alcohol among Alaska Natives, and it was considered a legitimate and important trade commodity.[31] The case, therefore, reflected the military's efforts to exert authority in Tlingit country and the ways that the United States was reconfiguring the legal mechanisms by which they might do so.[32]

Because Alaska had no court system of its own, the case came before Oregon District Court Judge Matthew Paul Deady. Amid the fracturing application of federal Indian law along the coast, Deady espoused what legal scholars refer to as an ambitious "racist, expansionist, pioneer ideology" that "held that white settlement of most of the western territory of the United States was both economically and politically desirable and an act of personal heroism on the part of settlers."[33] To this end, he and other jurists felt that Indian Country as a legal concept and the treaty negotiations that they mandated were outdated and a hindrance to settlers, for whom possession of the North American continent was their birthright. As a judge, he championed an 1853 Oregon Supreme Court case ruling that had concluded that Oregon Territory only became Indian Country upon the enactment of an 1850 federal statute creating the Willamette Valley Treaty Commission, which extended the 1834 Trade and Intercourse Acts to that territory. Widely regarded as flawed legal thinking at the time of its issuance, *United States v. Tom* concluded that prior to the 1850 statute, only specific sections of the Trade and Intercourse Acts concerning liquor restrictions were applicable in the territory insomuch as they "enhanced the safety of white settlers."[34] To Deady, then, the legal concept of Indian Country restricted settler appropriation of land as property by inserting a waiting period between preemptive seizure and redemptive purchase.

Seveloff's attorneys adopted the conclusions, if not the same logic, from *Tom* and likewise argued that Alaska was not Indian Country because Congress had not specifically designated it as such. They did this not so much to dislodge Indian Country restrictions regarding land rights but to achieve an acquittal on the basis that the restrictions on liquor included in the Trade and Intercourse Acts were not in force in Alaska. Conversely, attorneys for the United States argued that the Trade and Intercourse Acts applied to Alaska proprio vigore from the time of purchase in 1867 as they had elsewhere across the continent. In fact, Secretary of State Seward had argued as much in an 1869 letter to the secretary of war when he stated that designation of new territory as Indian Country "by a happy elasticity of expression, widening as our dominion widens, includes the territory ceded by Russia."[35] Given Deady's aversion to the restrictions of Indian Country, he accepted Seveloff's defense, ruling that Alaska was not subject to the Trade and Intercourse Acts. Importantly, his reasoning relied on the 1868 statute that had designated Alaska as a customs district rather than a territory. Section 4 of that act had explicitly reserved the regulation of spirituous liquors to the president of the United States in Alaska. This power was typically exercised by Congress per Articles 20 and 21 of the Trade and

Intercourse Acts, and thus by designating these powers to the president, Deady concluded that Congress had intended the 1868 act to supersede prior legislation.[36]

Deady ruled that Alaska was not Indian Country and found Seveloff not guilty. What happened next is telling; rather than respond by establishing a legal uniformity, Congress passed an act extending only Sections 20 and 21 of the Trade and Intercourse Acts to Alaska.[37] While this may seem like an expedient solution to the issue of regulating liquor in the territory, the selective application of only two sections speaks to the ways the rulings in *Tom* and *Seveloff* resonated with shifting congressional attitudes toward US relations with Indigenous people, their political status, and the nature of their land rights. Alaska's noncontiguity, uncertain relationship to the nation proper, and the ambiguity that government officials had already established around Alaska Native racial and legal status made this divergent statutory response much easier to justify. For Alaska Natives, this buttressed the emerging settler imperial formation by unilaterally eliminating the statutory recognition of their land and sovereignty in the US legal system.

The Trade and Intercourse Acts—first enacted in 1790, subsequently renewed, and then made permanent in 1834—established federal jurisdiction in the regulation of Native and non-Native relationships, which constituted one of the cornerstones of the nation-to-nation relationship. Most importantly, the federal government defined and recognized tribal, collective ownership of Indian land in the Trade and Intercourse Acts. The final 1834 version contained a preemptive land clause, declaring that purchases of land from Indians would be invalid "unless the same shall be made by treaty or convention entered into pursuant to the Constitution."[38] Legal designation as "Indian Country," then, brought with it the recognition of Indigenous land rights and nation-to-nation negotiating status.

By 1882, Judge Deady would go on to decide five more Indian Country cases that had implications for the legal status of Alaska Natives and their homelands, each relying on *Seveloff* and *Tom*. Following the passage of the 1884 First Organic Act for Alaska, the new Alaska territorial courts continued to take up the question in *United States v. Kie* and *In re Sah Quah,* decided in 1885 and 1886, respectively.[39] More specifically, these cases involved questions of jurisdiction over Tlingit internal tribal affairs and reflected the persistence of Tlingit legal and political orders and the ways Tlingit people had begun to draw on aspects of US law in navigating increasing US encroachment in their homelands. The first of the two cases arose when a Tlingit man identified as Charles Kie allegedly murdered his wife, a Tlingit woman known as Nancy. It is likely that Charles Kie's clan handled the matter internally, adhering to Tlingit legal expectations to compensate Nancy Kie's clan for her death. In complete derogation of Tlingit sovereignty, the military arrested Charles Kie and charged him in the new District Court of Alaska despite the fact that the United States had never before attempted to interfere in intra-Tlingit matters. Kie's attorneys challenged the presumption of US jurisdiction by arguing that Alaska was Indian Country and that the US courts had no authority to try him for manslaughter. Because Kie had committed his offense after the US Supreme Court ruling in *Ex Parte Crow Dog* in 1883 but before the Major Crimes Act went into effect after its passage in 1885, his attorneys held that the court lacked jurisdiction regarding crimes committed by one Indian against another Indian in lands designated as Indian Country. Alaska District Court Judge Ward McAllister Jr. rejected this argument, and citing the ruling in *Seveloff*, held that Alaska was not Indian Country. Kie was convicted of manslaughter and sentenced to ten years imprisonment and a fine of one hundred dollars.

Kie's attorneys appealed the case, which came before Judge Deady in the District Court of Oregon. Unsurprisingly, he upheld *Seveloff* and his additional Indian Country decisions by identifying the 1868 act that had designated Alaska as a customs district as the definitive basis by which Alaska had been excluded from the Trade and Intercourse Acts.[40] He elaborated that post *Seveloff*, Congress's explicit extension of only Sections 20 and 21 of the Trade and Intercourse Acts had further demonstrated the federal government's intent that Alaska was not on the same legal footing as contiguous states and territories with regard to Indian lands and the territory's Indigenous inhabitants. Like McAllister, who concluded that save for the "purposes of section 20 and 21 of the act of 1834, [Alaska] is not 'Indian Country' in any other sense," Deady ruled that Alaska had been deliberately excluded from the designation.[41] Despite having established support for his ruling in the context of the 1868 act, he went further in arguing for legal distinctions between Alaska Natives and Indians of the continent, asserting absolute US jurisdiction over Alaska Native affairs and denying Alaska Native nation-to-nation negotiating status and the existence of Aboriginal title in the territory. Citing Articles III and VI of the Treaty of Cession, which, respectively, had excluded Alaska Natives from US citizenship and guaranteed that land in Alaska was free and clear of any and all reservations save private individual property, he concluded that it had not been "at all probable that the aborigines of Alaska can or will be considered as dependent or domestic nations, or people having any title to the soil of the country, to be extinguished by the United States, as were the Indian tribes north and west of the Ohio River."[42]

Perhaps the most definitive formulation of these arguments appeared in *In re Sah Quah,* which arose in 1886 when Sah Quah, identified in court records as Haida, walked into a courtroom in Sitka, requesting "a paper from the Big Chief so I could walk around like any other man." In response, the District Court of Alaska Judge Lafayette Dawson issued a notice of petition of a writ of habeas corpus. The notice charged a Tlingit man by the name of Nah-Ki-Klan with holding Sah Quah as a "slave and chattel," thereby "restrain[ing] him of his liberty . . . illegally and wrongfully."[43] Per the notice, Nah-Ki-Klan was commanded to bring Sah Quah and appear in the new Alaska District Court "to be called or charged" the following week. Both Sah Quah and Nah-Ki-Klan appeared as ordered on April 26, 1886, and following a brief hearing, the court issued the writ granting Sah Quah his freedom. Local newspapers hailed the court's decision as righteously eliminating one of the last vestiges of slavery in the United States, and local assimilationist-minded missionaries undoubtedly considered the opinion a boon for their efforts. Legal scholars have long suspected that *Sah Quah* had been a collusive case, brought about by missionaries seeking a condemnation of Tlingit culture through a rebuke of slavery and slave trading.[44] While the court's decision to issue the writ likely did not have much immediate effect on Tlingit governance or day-to-day life, it synthesized the rulings in *Seveloff* and *Kie,* cohering the constellation of legislative and administrative exclusions and designations that government officials and lawmakers had proffered in the preceding years regarding Alaska.

Court documents show that Nah-Ki-Klan rejected the court's demand that he release Sah Quah, arguing that both he and the petitioner were "Indians of the Thlinket or Koloshian race . . . in communities independent of any other law, authority, or jurisdiction, in all their civil and domestic relations."[45] Written in English by an interpreter whose intentions and motivations are unclear, Nah-Ki-Klan's response articulates a thorough rebuke of US authority in Tlingit matters and on Tlingit lands. It continues by arguing:

> That the United States has never acquired, by treaty, by conquest, or by consent of the said uncivilized tribes or of the uncivilized inhabitants of Alaska any authority to impair the recognized rights of said Indians, under their said immemorial usages, in the property and services of their slaves, or in any other respect. The said United States has never attempted to assert any such authority, by any enactment of their law, under which the jurisdiction of this court can be asserted for the severance of any of the relations or customs established by said immemorial usage, or the abrogation of any of the rights of persons or property among said uncivilized natives, or by which said rights may be impaired or regulated by any of its courts.[46]

In concluding his statement, Nah-Ki-Klan denied that his relationship to Sah Quah constituted slavery, stating that "the defendant denies that he is as such a slave-holder, under said established customs, amenable to the order or authority of this court."[47] Nah-Ki-Klan signed the prepared response with an x-mark.

The case went to a brief trial in which questioning focused more on the nature of slavery among Tlingit, though the legal question at hand was the extent to which Tlingit were subject to US law, specifically the Thirteenth Amendment. Elaborating beyond the question of Indian Country, this case would hinge on whether Judge Dawson concluded that Nah-Ki-Klan and Sah Quah were members of sovereign nations in which US law has no jurisdictional authority. As to the issue of slavery, Tlingit witnesses, including Sah Quah, seemed determined to thwart this intrusion into their affairs. According to court records, Sah Quah testified that he had been captured by Flathead Indians in British Columbia, sold to the Chilkat, and remained with them until Nah-Ki-Klan "took pity" on him "and brought me down here [to Sitka]."[48] When asked by attorneys representing Sah Quah or by Judge Dawson if he was enslaved by Nah-Ki-Klan, he refused to answer in the affirmative, stating only that "he is my father."[49] Studies of Pacific Northwest Coast slavery have identified slave holding and trading as integral to Indigenous

Northwest Coast societies in terms of political, social, and economic stratification and have documented the role of enslaved people within intertribal relations.[50] Tlingit, along with other Northwest Coast communities, enslaved people through war and trade, and enslaved persons were valuable for their labor and also played important roles in potlatches and other ritual activities. Most enslaved people were owned by kin groups and were "of considerable importance to the economy of many Northwest Coast communities in two ways: they were a significant commodity in intergroup transactions . . . and their labor power was important in many subsistence activities and other mundane tasks."[51] While significant to Indigenous political economies in the Northwest Coast and elsewhere in North America, it is important to note that scholars distinguish between Indigenous slavery and captive taking and the plantation-based racial chattel slavery that developed in the US South as "a form of property and system of compulsory labor entailing permanent and hereditary status."[52]

Nevertheless, Sah Quah continued to define his relationship to Nah-Ki-Klan on his own terms. When pressed by his own appointed attorney whether "you consider yourself a slave of this man ever since you left Yakutat," he responded, "No, sir," and when asked whether "you consider yourself a son," he affirmed, "Yes, sir." Sah Quah conceded that he had sought out a "paper . . . so I could walk around like any other man" but argued that his obligation to Nah-Ki-Klan only included assistance in the construction on the latter's house, to be completed "in the fall of the year."[53] Additional Tlingit witnesses refused to conclusively answer questions regarding slavery or to provide any specificity regarding the practice within Tlingit culture. For example, a woman referred to in court documents as Marchia was called to testify but responded only vaguely, insisting that she knew very little of "Indian ways" when it came to slavery.[54] She admitted to having once been enslaved but would not disclose any details of her experiences, leading one newspaper article to describe her as a reluctant witness who "at once became a know-nothing, as to all else concerning it, stating that she was young and had forgotten all she knew about slaves and did not know how she became free."[55] Nah-Ki-Klan did not testify.

The resistance of Tlingit witnesses to questions about slavery lends credence to the suspicion of scholars that this was a case orchestrated by white settlers to justify colonization and assimilation objectives.[56] And importantly, it provides an example of the ways Tlingit people, in conjunction with their own legal and social orders, sought to incorporate some of the tools and concepts from US law in navigating their daily lives. Sah Quah does not specify in his testimony that the "paper" he sought was for the purpose of freeing him from Nah-Ki-Klan. In the context of an increasing missionary presence and the exclusion of Tlingit from white areas of town, it could be just as plausible that what Sah Quah sought was a document from a white court of law that might allow him to navigate the changing legal and racial landscape in which Tlingit and US sovereignties and political orders were becoming more entangled.

The record does not tell us what happened to Sah Quah or Nah-Ki-Klan after they left the courtroom that day, though it is likely that they carried on just as they had before. Judge Dawson's opinion, though, carried far-reaching implications. The question before the court was not so much whether Nah-Ki-Klan truly enslaved Sah Quah but whether the court had the authority to issue the writ and force Sah Quah's release. This meant that Dawson needed to determine the extent to which and under what legal authority Tlingit people were subject to US law. In this sense, he understood that his opinion should define "what, then, was the legal status of Alaska Indians."[57] Like those before him, Dawson answered this question not by delineating the legal status and the nature of Alaska Native rights in US law but instead by describing what Alaska Natives and Alaska as a US possession were not. He concluded that Article III of the Treaty of Cession had reserved the authority to "make laws and regulations" for "the aboriginal tribes of that country" to Congress alone, "indicating very clearly that they were . . . regarded as subject to some power superior to their own untamed inclinations." He affirmed the findings in *Seveloff* and *Kie* that Alaska was not Indian Country because Congress had only extended Sections 20 and 21 of the Trade and Intercourse Acts to the district, thereby "the intention was to withhold or exclude from the territory all the other sections of the act." He continued that even though some Alaska Natives had "connected themselves with the mission churches and . . . adopted civilized habits of life . . . they are not citizens within the full meaning of that term." Finally, he concluded that Alaska Natives were not privy to the policy inherent in the Northwest Ordinance of 1787 by which the "various Indian tribes . . . have been treated as free and independent" as reflected in the practice of treaty making.[58]

In assessing the absence or inapplicability of these familiar legal categories and frameworks of US–Indigenous relations, Judge Dawson concluded that Alaska Natives "are now regarded as dependent subjects, amenable to the penal laws of the United States, and subject to the jurisdiction of its courts."[59] The category of "dependent subjects" and the ambiguity it embodies are at the heart of settler imperialism. In classifying Alaska Natives this way, Dawson joined his fellow judges, along with government officials and lawmakers, in creating a "third category under federal law that had never existed, where you had Indians with no recognized land rights or sovereignty."[60] In doing so, Dawson's ruling demonstrates how the mid-nineteenth-century confluence of possessory claims to noncontiguous territory and the end of treaty making in the contiguous states created the conditions of possibility for a radical reframing of the dispossessive process and the material form of US empire. Government and corporate interests sought to establish overseas dominions as a means to assert imperial relations and thereby increase wealth through resource extraction without the burdens of nation-to-nation negotiations. To this end, they pursued methods by which they could unilaterally disavow Indigenous nationhood and rights "to the soil of the country." Because their primary objective was to consummate possession of territory in the absence of treaties or similar agreements, government officials and Congress abandoned the legal theory and attendant practices of Indian Country in the founding possessory documents relating to Alaska. As both theory and practice, Indian Country had represented, legally, the anticipation of "property" in that the designation of lands as Indian Country animated the legal mechanisms by which it could be appropriated. Indian Country likewise designated those residing within it as having a predetermined legal status as sovereign. To successfully abandon Indian Country, government officials needed to abandon the category of "Indian," which they accomplished by ascribing an Asian racial identity to Indigenous people in Alaska. Thus, Commissioner Walker's 1872 determination that Alaska Natives were not Indian and therefore should be excluded from BIA jurisdiction relegated Alaska Natives to an emergent and yet indeterminate logic of US empire. This ambiguity notwithstanding, for Walker, his contemporaries in Congress and other agencies, and their successors, it followed that only Indians could inhabit Indian Country.

From this moment on, refusing Indian Country in Alaska succeeded in complicating Alaska Native legal and political strategies against dispossession, though the ambiguity these refusals engendered cut multiple ways. What these officials and lawmakers did not anticipate was that in abandoning Indian Country and clouding the legal status of Alaska Natives, they had deprived themselves of the primary means by which they could establish clear title to the lands they were appropriating. In the twentieth century, Alaska Natives threatened that this ambiguity could derail settlement and development in the territory, granting them significant influence over determining the status of land in the absence of Indian Country. In the spaces these officials left undefined and therefore ambiguous, Alaska Natives mobilized their own systems of landownership and political theory. To them, designation of land in Alaska as Indian Country mattered little as they conceived of and articulated their own relationships with the US federal government. This became evident at the turn of the century when an influx of settlers and corporate fishing operations to Southeast Alaska prompted Tlingit, Haida, and Tsimshian across the region to organize in protest of the derogation of their land rights. Informed by the ways the federal government treated them differently than their counterparts in the contiguous states, they sought out ways to incorporate elements of settler institutions and rhetoric into their own legal and political systems. They then recoded and redeployed them in ways that situated the ambiguity that had been intended to facilitate their dispossession as a barrier to the settler imperial appropriation of their land.

2

Conceiving a New Frontier

Tlingit Diplomacy, US Imperial Expansion, and the Doctrine of Territorial Incorporation

On December 14, 1898, Frederick Moore served as a translator at a meeting between nearly a dozen Tlingit leaders and Alaska Governor John Brady in a schoolhouse in Juneau, Alaska. They had assembled for the purposes of levying their concerns emanating from the rapid influx of white people into their territory with the arrival of corporate fishing and mining operations. They had come from Wrangell, Hoonah, Taku, and Juneau, and one after another, they explained how white miners and fisherman, employed by the mining and fishing companies, had taken their streams and hunting and trapping grounds and intruded on their village sites without any notice, negotiation, or recourse. Many of them bore witness to place-names and oral histories, establishing the genealogy by which they knew and owned their lands and related the consensus that "all our people believe that Alaska is our Country."[1] Importantly, they expressed their offense and surprise that white settlers would not negotiate with them for compensation for the use of their land and that this refusal was a deviation from their understanding of US law. They knew that the United States had negotiated for land with Native tribes in the contiguous states, and they situated themselves as landowners deserving of similar treatment, warning that they knew "that down below (the States) that [if] a man possessed a certain property and another man comes along and wants that property he pays for it."[2]

Importantly, many of those who testified emphasized Tlingit land and legal orders and proposed methods by which they could persist in their customs while issuing permission for specific activities such as mining. So long as settlers were mindful not to disturb their subsistence and the social and cultural orders it sustained, they were willing to facilitate settler presence. These diplomatic gestures were largely ignored, as government officials and lawmakers became more resolute in their assumptions that Alaska Natives had no recognizable land rights or the political authority to assert them. Believing the fiction that the Treaty of Cession had extinguished any Aboriginal right in the land, they descended on Tlingit villages, fishing streams, and hunting grounds. Thus, by the turn of the century, the withholding of Indian Country status in Alaska had created a pathway for settlers and corporate interests to obtain title to land in Alaska without negotiation or compensation, and they eagerly took advantage of the absence of treaty rights or Aboriginal title.

This meeting at the schoolhouse in Juneau took place just four days after the signing of the Treaty of Paris that concluded the Spanish-American War and was thus situated within a critical restructuring of US empire and Alaska's function within this emerging imperial formation. This restructuring necessitated a reframing of Alaska in relation to the nation proper, which catalyzed a more rapid migration of settlers and corporate interests into Southeast and Interior Alaska. In response to the global geopolitical remapping and increasing anxiety over the "closing of the frontier," Congress passed two organic acts and adopted two land statutes for Alaska between 1884 and 1926. The First Organic Act for Alaska established a minimal civil government and changed Alaska's designation from a customs district to a "civil and judicial district" equipped to implement US mining laws.[3] This adjustment in land law by which prospectors could acquire title to mining claims prompted lawmakers to include a provision regarding Alaska Native land rights. Unable to determine what land rights they sought to ostensibly protect, Congress simply inserted a clause stating that Alaska Natives should not be "disturbed in the possession of lands actually in their use and occupation or now claimed by them." They further mandated that the specific nature of lands possessed through "use and occupation" would be defined in "future legislation by Congress," thereby reincorporating the temporal ambiguity initiated by Article III of the Treaty of Cession and projecting it, once again, indefinitely. By the time of the schoolhouse meeting in Juneau, Congress had also extended US townsite laws and the Homestead Act to Alaska, resulting in the exponential invasion of corporate operations and white settlers that the Tlingit Chiefs gathered to protest in 1898.

In the aftermath of the Spanish-American War and the imperial debates that followed, these struggles over land in Alaska took on added significance as the US Supreme Court took up the question of the political status of territories seized in the 1898 Treaty of Paris and their inhabitants in the Insular Cases.[4] From 1901 to 1922, the court heard over two dozen cases regarding territorial status in which it conceived of, defined, and reified the new legal doctrine of incorporation by which the federal government could distinguish between territories it considered part of the nation proper and thus availed of the Constitution and those it considered external possessions and therefore excluded from constitutional purview. To authenticate the new category of unincorporated territory, the Supreme Court justices, other jurists, and lawmakers conjured a new frontier narrative for Alaska, proffering it as a settler space and a potential state, which allowed them to define territories that were not intended for incorporation. This new frontier narrative, arising amid these two decades of imperial reconfiguration, led Congress to enact the Second Organic Act for Alaska in 1912, designating Alaska as an organized incorporated territory of the United States.

This chapter tracks the ways Alaska Natives intervened in these legal configurations by situating Indigenous legal orders and political theories of land, settler-state citizenship, and Indigenous nationhood at the crux of US empire. In response to increasing land rights activism, lawmakers attempted to substitute the collective land rights previously recognized in Indian Country status by passing the Alaska Native Allotment Act of 1906 and the Alaska Native Townsite Act in 1926. Echoing assimilation policy in the contiguous states and territories, each act provided for individual Alaska Natives to obtain either a "homestead" or title to the land on which they resided within a townsite. Neither statute resolved the larger question of the legal status of Alaska Natives and their land more broadly, resulting in what legal scholars refer to as a "confusion of cases" that proliferated in the twentieth century.[5] This ultimately facilitated extractive and settlement objectives without definitively resolving the ambiguity in Alaska Native legal status, thereby adding to the settler imperial framework. Despite this, the ambiguity underlying these contradictory rulings and settler imperial legislation became an important wedge that Alaska Natives used to prevent the unilateral foreclosing of their land rights. In the meantime, Alaska Natives mobilized around the pursuit of settler-state citizenship as a method to compel legal recognition of the rights in the land amid the turbulence and uncertainty of the transition from customs district to incorporated territory in Alaska.

Use and Occupation

In 1884, Congress passed the first of two Organic Acts for Alaska. The First Organic Act converted Alaska from a customs district to a civil, judicial, and land district and provided for a district court, a judge, a clerk, a handful of commissioners, and a marshal with four deputies. While extending the provisions by which individuals could secure titles to mining claims, Section 8 instructed that "nothing contained in this act shall be construed to put in force in said district the general land laws of the United States."[6] In addition to this departure from territorial legislation in the contiguous states regarding land, Congress also opted not to establish a territorial legislature or provide the district with a congressional delegate. In opening up the land to mining claims, lawmakers were confronted with the question of Native land rights, and in the absence of treaties and the legal frameworks of Indian Country they debated at length as to what rights they might be legislating for and by what means. In the end, they included a clause in Section 8 that "Indians or other persons in said district shall not be disturbed in the possession of any lands actually in their use or occupation or now claimed by them but the terms under which such persons may acquire title to such lands is reserved for future legislation by Congress."[7] Alaska Native activists and scholars have long pointed to the wording of this clause and its various interpretations as engendering controversy and confusion, which allowed the issue of Alaska Native land rights to be "skirted by Congress" in the following decades. They likewise contend that, even in its vagueness, the "Organic Act of 1884 is the foundation upon which Alaskan Native claims to land are based. It is the basic law which promises a final settlement."[8]

The 1884 act also provided the basis by which Congress, lawmakers, and government officials could sustain the uncertainty around Native land rights even after conversion of Alaska into an incorporated territory. As a settler imperial piece of legislation, its ambiguities functioned to elongate the temporal window of the dispossessive process by interrupting the transition from preemptive seizure to redemptive purchase, and its ambiguities are inserted in three phrases. Its opening phrase "Indians or other persons" suggests that Indigenous inhabitants of Alaska had the same legal designation in terms of rights in the land as settlers and corporate interests; the second phrase "lands actually in their use or occupation or now claimed by them" establishes a need-based contingency with no prescriptive method by which to determine the existence and extent of such need; and the third phrase reserving the method by which to initiate claims to "future legislation by Congress" further extends the path by which lawmakers could avoid Native land rights in Alaska indefinitely. These three phrases protected the preemptive claims by non-Natives and implied that future "other persons" would have the same rights as Alaska Natives in access to land, while clouding Native land rights in the uncertainty and subjectivity of need-based rights, allowing "use or occupation" to stand in for Indian Country and its attending implications of sovereignty until Congress decided what kind of use or occupation warranted negotiation for purchase or retroactive attribution.

Legal scholars argue that the "unspoken implication" of the use and occupation clause was that Indigenous people in Alaska did not have the same land rights as Indigenous people in the contiguous states.[9] Congressional debates over the 1884 act reveal that in the absence of treaties and Indian Country, lawmakers were unsure "by what tenure the Indians are there" and "what ordinarily characterizes their claim of title."[10] They fretted that failure to include some protection of "the rights of the Indian residents of Alaska" from "possible invasion" in the bill could potentially result in the government "ultimately expending large sums of money in investigation and finally in reimbursing them for their losses." In order to avoid the costs of redemptive purchase at some future date, they sought the means to facilitate non-Native access to land without violating the rights of Alaska Natives, which they refused to define. Preston B. Plumb, a senator from Kansas, captured the logical loop in which the committee members found themselves. He proposed that "the Indian shall at least have as many rights after the passage of this bill as he had before," and while he did "not know that they have any rights at all," he "only want[ed] to avoid the certain consequences which will result from the adoption of this bill" should it fail to prevent future circumstances that required compensation. His counterparts argued that for the time being, the bill avoided large-scale liability for land claims by refraining from extending US land laws in their entirety. The committee had chosen instead to designate Alaska a land district and apply only the US mining laws, which other committee members argued could not "possibly absorb any great extent of territory," therefore avoiding future costly settlements.[11] Without the need to immediately resolve the ambiguity around the legal status of Alaska Natives, Congress adopted the bill with the "use or occupation" clause, establishing the methods for preemptive seizure and delaying assessment of any need for redemptive purchase and retroactive attribution for the foreseeable future.

As the congressional debates in 1884 reveal, the implication that Alaska Natives did not have the same land rights as other Indigenous people was tightly bound to the implication that Alaska was not considered to be the same as other, contiguous, territories. At the time, Alaska's white population numbered only about four hundred, and the absence of the frontier rabble and the uncertainty that Alaska would become a settler state in the nation proper allowed lawmakers to justify their withholding of customary territorial governance in addition to their refusal to clarify Indigenous legal status and land rights. While contemplating the latter, some senators voiced concern over "what opinion the Committee on Territories holds in regard to the question of the operative force of the Constitution and laws of the United States within a territory . . . without an act of Congress to apply [them]?" Despite assurances from committee members that in crafting "this simple frame of government . . . for the extension of such laws as we thought the few inhabitants . . . needed," they had not violated any constitutional requirements, many continued to remark on the deviations the 1884 Organic Act contained from those typically enacted in the contiguous territories.[12] For example, Florida Senator Charles W. Jones suggested the proposed legislation was "a most remarkable bill, because I do not think there is anything like it in our annals." He continued that it was strange to set up a government for a territory without provision "for a legislative establishment," and to do so suggested that "the laws of the United States are not in force in this Territory, nor the Constitution of the United States."[13] Others concurred that as a judicial land district, they did "not think it is plain that this is to be an organized territory." They concluded that as such, Alaska was not privy to the mandate of the Revised Statutes of 1878 that "the Constitution and all laws of the United States which are not locally inapplicable shall have the same force and effect within all the organized Territories, and in every territory hereafter organized as elsewhere within the United States."[14]

The final two sections of the bill sustained these distinctions. Section 14 maintained presidential authority over the regulation of liquor, and Section 13 allocated funding for the "education of children of school age . . . without regard to race." Often cited as a testament to progressive policy toward Alaska Natives, the congressional record reveals that the motivation for racially integrated education in Alaska arose from the racial distinctions lawmakers and government officials had established between Alaska Natives and Indigenous people in the contiguous states and territories. Senator Henry L. Dawes, whose assimilationist ideology would coalesce in the devastating policy of allotment in the contiguous states and territories just three years later, proffered that Alaska Natives should not be classed "among the Indians in our own land. . . . They must be treated in a different manner." His counterparts agreed, then-Senator Benjamin Harrison reasoned that "these Indians in Alaska have never yet become public charges" and thus had not required "the system of annuities, treaty annuities, or annuities by special grants of Congress."[15] This rhetoric and reasoning was not new but rather endemic of the ways "government officials proffered racial categorization . . . of Alaska Native peoples as Asian" and therefore more civilized "in arguing the case for Alaska's purchase" nearly twenty years prior.[16] They elaborated on these distinctions in preserving the prohibitions and regulations of alcohol, warning against "the grave error in classifying the Indians of Alaska with our Indians" when "the condition of the two classes is very different."[17]

In the spirit of these debates, the final bill reflects the careful wording that lawmakers employed in delineating policy and law in Alaska. The senate substituted the word *district* for *territory* in several critical places—namely, in Section 9, which named and described the structure of government that they were crafting. They were explicit that Alaska would have no territorial legislature or a delegate to Congress. Perhaps most telling is the removal of the word *Constitution* from the provision that originally read "and the Constitution and laws of the United States not locally inapplicable to said district . . . are hereby extended thereto."[18] In this sense, the final bill, enacted into law on May 17, 1884, remained ambiguous on Indigenous land rights, the legal status of Alaska Natives, and foreshadowed debates about the frameworks of US expansion. This ambiguity would provide important precedent at the turn of the century when lawmakers were faced yet again with the task of regulating what constituted properly national territory.

The Alaska Frontier as a Function of Empire

Just over three weeks into the Spanish-American War, President William McKinley signed legislation extending United States homesteading laws to the District of Alaska. This decision reflected the ways that lawmakers and government officials were changing both the legal and the conceptual narrative framework of Alaska as part of a broader reconfiguration of territorial ordering at the edges of empire. At the conclusion of hostilities with Spain, the resulting possessory claims to additional noncontiguous territories in 1898 generated intense disputes regarding the political status of large populations of nonwhite inhabitants. These imperial debates coincided with anxieties around settler access to land and the future of American democracy as the frontier had been declared closed.[19] In this moment, Alaska became an important means by which lawmakers, government officials, judges and would-be settlers rationalized the exclusion of inhabitants of newly seized territory from the nation proper while creating a new frontier for settlement by US citizens. Prior to 1898, lawmakers and government officials had not generally conceived of Alaska as a settler space, and its status as a district provided the legal rationale for the constitutionality of holding territorial possessions indefinitely without extending citizenship, a territorial government, or statehood status. As lawmakers negotiated territorial jurisprudence with regard to Puerto Rico and the Philippines, they altered their thinking about Alaska. Lawmakers had previously reasoned that the district's low population and rugged terrain made it an unlikely candidate for territorial organization and eventual statehood. However, in this moment of imperial crisis, these characteristics became a convenient stage on which to craft a frontier narrative that naturalized the remote and noncontiguous land district as the logical terminus of Manifest Destiny. This allowed them to distinguish between territories slated for inclusion in the nation proper and those that were not, regardless of the population size or the citizenship status of their inhabitants.

This conceptual shift can be traced from the 1898 decision in *Endleman et al. v. United States*. Just two months before hostilities erupted between Spain and the United States, the US Ninth Circuit considered an appeal from two petitioners who had been convicted of "selling intoxicating liquors" in the District of Alaska. The defendants "moved to quash this indictment" on the grounds that, as US citizens, they had the constitutional right to hold property in the form of liquor on an equal basis with other citizens of US territories. They concluded that if Congress had the "power to regulate the sale of intoxicating liquors within the territories as a police regulation, it can only enact laws applicable to all the territories alike." The court rejected this defense, stating that "territories of the United States are entirely subject to the legislative authority of congress. They are not organized under the constitution," and therefore Congress was not required to establish a uniformity of law between states and territories. The ruling argued that the United States exercised complete "dominion and sovereignty" over its territories and could "legislate in accordance with the special needs of each locality," foreshadowing the ways jurists and lawmakers would conceptualize and debate various territorial statuses in delineating between what constituted future properly national territory and localities they might exclude indefinitely.[20] Furthering the legal basis for these distinctions took on new urgency during the war with Spain, and lawmakers, justices, and legal scholars began debating territorial legal theories in the context of three possibilities: the plenary theory, by which "Congress has absolute discretion in setting the constitutional status of each territory"; the theory of incorporation, by which there exists "differentiation between an incorporated and unincorporated territory" in which Congress exercises "absolute discretion to bring territories under the Constitution when it deems it convenient"; and the theory of immediate incorporation, by which the "Constitution governs a territory as soon as it is under the sovereignty of the United States."[21]

At the conclusion of the war with Spain, Alaska was central to defining and rationalizing each of these scenarios. Advocates of plenary authority argued that Alaska's tenure as a district supported the constitutionality of holding territories indefinitely. One jurist argued in the *Harvard Law Review* that Congress may establish "whatever form of administration it may think proper, not inconsistent with the principles and provisions of the Constitution of the United States. . . . No fixed limit of time can be assigned for the duration of such a regime. We have held Alaska under such conditions already for thirty years, and she is hardly more deserving of autonomy now than when she was a Russian province."[22] Proponents of incorporation theory and the theory of immediate incorporation disagreed, and while they recognized that *Endleman* might be the "popular authority" in support of the plenary theory for Alaska, they posited that it ought to be limited. They contended that Congress may, theoretically, "exert its power over territory within its jurisdiction and outside the limits of States without regard to the Constitution." However, they challenged the ability to arbitrarily withhold constitutional guarantees from territories generally.[23]

Others argued that *Endleman* should be understood as specific to Alaska, where the "meagre population" had justified the "deliberate departure from a sound rule" of customary territorial organization and presumed trajectory toward statehood. Conceived of as an extractive colony rather than internal to the settler state, one jurist suggested that Alaska would likely "become a veritable waste when the fur-bearing animals are exterminated and the gold is carried away."[24] At the beginning of 1898, many understood the absence of the frontier rabble and the reluctance of lawmakers to legislate for Alaska in a way that facilitated white settlement as evidence that Alaska might remain a temporary possession. As such, Congress was under no obligation to make changes in its status unless an increase in population necessitated additional delineation. By 1901, the legal challenges that would come to be collectively referred to as the Insular Cases required the federal government and the courts to confront these questions in the context of territories with much larger populations of nonwhite inhabitants. To justify the exclusion of Puerto Rico and the Philippines, they reframed Alaska's meager white population and vast tracts of supposedly inhospitable wilderness as exemplary of the ideal conditions for inevitable inclusion in the nation proper.

From *Downes v. Bidwell* in 1901 to *Balzac v. Porto Rico* in 1922, the Insular Cases chart this process and demonstrate the ways the legal concept of unincorporated territory relied on the ambiguities of Alaska Native legal status that had been initiated in the 1867 Treaty of Cession. The provision in Article III by which Russian citizens who remained in Alaska "shall be admitted to the enjoyment of all the rights, advantages, and immunities of citizens of the United States" became central to the development of the doctrine of incorporation that the Supreme Court ultimately adopted. Lawmakers and jurists argued that by extending citizenship to inhabitants of Alaska, "with the exception of uncivilized native tribes," the 1867 treaty reflected a uniformity with "all the treaties for the acquisition of territory on the continent of North America." This argument reflected a reimagining of Alaska that facilitated an important contrast with the treaty with Spain, which made "no such provision" for citizenship but "merely cede[d] Porto Rico and the Philippines" to the United States and left political status of "the native inhabitants" entirely up to Congress. The court affirmed that such language made it "clear" that "the government can acquire possessions without making them a part of the United States."[25]

Reimagining the 1867 treaty as an extension of expansion precedent marked the beginning of a shift in territorial discourse that allowed lawmakers and the courts to define Alaska as having been incorporated despite lacking both a territorial government and a substantial white population. This became a critical point when the US Supreme Court took up the Insular Cases. Beginning with the ruling in *Downes*, the court focused on the fact that the 1867 treaty had conveyed US citizenship on Russian inhabitants automatically after a period of three years whereby no further action was required by Congress for their naturalization. By comparison, the Treaty of Paris had not conveyed US citizenship to any inhabitants of the territories ceded by Spain. Instead, the authors specified that any "Spanish subjects, natives of the [Iberian] Peninsula," who remained in the territories after one year must make a formal "declaration of their decision to preserve" their allegiance to Spain. If they did not do so, they would not be awarded US citizenship but be assigned "the nationality of the territory in which they may reside."[26] The court concluded that by omitting the self-executing path to US citizenship for Spanish residents of the ceded territories, the treaty authors had designated citizenship as the operative factor in distinguishing between properly national territory and mere possessions.

This difference had significant implications for the ways lawmakers and government officials would come to question the legal status of Alaska Natives. Both treaties reserved the political status of specific categories of inhabitants to Congress indefinitely. Importantly, the Treaty of Paris defined non-Spanish inhabitants as "native inhabitants," whereas in the 1867 treaty, non-Russian inhabitants were referred to as "uncivilized native tribes."[27] This wording, however intentional, implied the existence or future existence of "civilized" or "settled" Native tribes in Alaska that could potentially claim the rights and privileges of US citizenship upon enactment of the treaty or assimilate to eligibility for citizenship in the future. This subtle but critical difference in verbiage determined that the political rights of members of "civilized" tribes would be recognized through citizenship while "uncivilized tribes" would inhabit a political status parallel to the nonwhite populations of the other US territories. The implied extension of US citizenship to categories of "civilized" nonwhite inhabitants paralleled the assimilatory logic of Indian policy in the contiguous states. Relegating "uncivilized native tribes" to a similar undefined status as their counterparts in other noncontiguous territories maintained their exclusion from the trappings of federal Indian policy—namely, the recognition of Aboriginal title and Indigenous nationhood. This parsing of Alaska Native legal status between those who could assimilate to citizenship similarly to Indigenous people in the contiguous states and those who had none of the constitutionally recognized rights as tribal nations and were also excluded from citizenship buttressed the theory of differentiated incorporation that the court sought to codify. It also reflected the tension between the alternating roles of Alaska as a settler and an imperial space that came to sustain the ambiguities in the dispossessive process while bridging the transition from westward expansion to extraconstitutional imperial administration.

The extension of US townsite laws in 1900 and the US Homestead Act in 1898 to Alaska reflected this shifting narrative and necessitated the relocation of ambiguity in the dispossessive process from the point of commodification and alienation of property to the point of redemptive purchase. Up until this point, the absence of a critical mass of settlers in Alaska to execute preemptive seizure allowed lawmakers to refrain from establishing legal frameworks for formal land appropriation as they wavered on Alaska's relation to properly national territory. As they resolved this question in the wake of the legal debates arising out of the Spanish-American War by incorporating Alaska into the conceptual frontier, they did so in a way that avoided the subsequent redemptive purchase that had typically characterized dispossession in the contiguous states. In the era of treaty making, lands not yet negotiated for were considered as "not yet recognized as within the bounds of the state," thus settler intrusion represented an illegality that was customarily resolved through retroactive compensation to those recognized recursively as the Indigenous prior owners.[28] Despite recognizing Alaska as "within the bounds of the state" and opening up land to appropriation and settlement, lawmakers carried over the ambiguity of Alaska Native legal status and that of their lands.

As Congress elaborated on the administrative structure of Alaska with the 1900 amendments to the 1884, or First, Organic Act for Alaska and the 1912 official designation as a fully organized territory in the Second Organic Act for Alaska, they refrained from defining Alaska Native land rights beyond the "use and occupation" clause of the 1884 act. This exacerbated the effectiveness with which the wave of frontier rabble and the corporations that employed them took advantage of the uncertain status of Alaska Natives and their land. Congressional extension of homesteading, mining, and townsite laws to Alaska initiated a rapid influx of white laborers who came to work for fishing and mining corporations and sought to establish varying degrees of permanent settlement. Armed with claims by lawmakers and administrators that Alaska Natives did not have similar land rights to tribes in the contiguous states, the commercial fisheries, mining companies, and potential settlers descended on Tlingit and Haida lands. When they encountered protest from clan leaders, the intruders produced legal records of titles that they had obtained with no consultation, notification, or negotiation.

In this new context, the 1898 meeting of the Tlingit Chiefs with Governor Brady in Juneau thus signified an important moment as they articulated their political, cultural, and historical relationships to the land and sought resolutions to increasing transgressions against their legal orders by white settlers and corporate extractive activities. Importantly, each Tlingit representative demonstrated that they perceived the distinctions that lawmakers and government officials had made between them and Indigenous Peoples and tribes in the contiguous states and the ways settlers and corporations used those distinctions to invalidate their land rights and legal and political legitimacy as nations. As such, they constitute a powerful example of Tlingit oratory and the mobilization of Indigenous political theory and diplomacy at the nexus of US empire. The procession of the speeches lays out, succinctly and directly, their concern for cultural and economic survival and the ways that Tlingit and their white neighbors might coexist. Scholars point out that the speeches were "well argued, well-balanced, and well-paced" and that the speakers were "eloquent and moving in their unanimous concern with land," though they did not include the typical level of poetic language customary of Tlingit oratory.[29] Perhaps signaling their command of Euro-American legal rhetoric and its transactional

FIGURE 2. Juneau Indian Village, 1898. Courtesy of Alaska State Library, Alaska State Library Place File Collection, ASL-P01-4853.

worldview to further emphasize the gravity with which they addressed the governor and his representatives, the speeches are direct and concise indictments of American behavior in Tlingit lands.

Furthermore, while they never say so directly, they all mobilize "land as at.óow" as "the cultural concept underlying the entire set of speeches." Meaning "an owned or purchased thing," *at.óow* is the fundamental concept that "underlies all dimensions of Tlingit social structure, oral literature, iconography, and ceremonial life." In addition to stories, names, artistic compositions or designs, songs, or events, at.óow can also be land or geographical features, thus these speeches constitute a collective counternarrative to Euro-American property regimes.[30] Because of this, the meeting transcript is worth unpacking at length.

The first speaker, Kah-du-shan, from Wrangell, began by asserting Tlingit sovereignty, political authority, and Tlingit legal orders relating to land. He reminded his listeners that "before the white people came to this country, Tlingit had laws and at every village there was a chief." He continued with a brief genealogy of Tlingit place-names, describing the ways his clan had historically used specific places as testimony that "this country belongs to us" and that they exercised a high degree of control over their territories. Kah-du-shan challenged the US purchase of Alaska, contending that the Russians were merely trading partners and had no means of surviving in Tlingit lands without maintaining appropriate trade relations. This was a subtle reminder that the Russians had been in Tlingit territory with permission, and Tlingit had historically met perceived threats to their property and other transgressions by destroying Russian forts and settlements, evicting their occupants. While acknowledging they were no longer as powerful militarily, Kah-du-shan censured the contrasting behavior of Americans, who had arrived unannounced and immediately began seizing Tlingit salmon creeks and disturbing their villages and hunting grounds. He criticized the ways that Americans "take our property, take away ground, and when we complain to them about it, they employ a lawyer and go to court and win the case."[31] This constituted an egregious violation of Tlingit legal systems regulating permission of access and posed an unacceptable threat to Tlingit life.[32]

The second and third speakers, Chief Johnson of Juneau and Koogh-see from Hoonah, affirmed Kah-du-shan's words before elaborating on the ways Americans had violated Tlingit law and how they might reconcile the errors. They asserted that "we know this is our country" and requested the return of fishing creeks and hunting grounds that had been taken without permission.[33] In Tlingit legal orders, access to "key production sites, even to non-matrikin, was typically extended if permission was sought," thereby validating the host's rights to the location and agreeing to respect their rights to the land.[34] To this end, Chief Johnson emphasized friendship, love, and cooperation, invoking Tlingit notions of kinship that informed the procedures of permission, stating, "We love you as children love their parents. . . . We love you as our friends," impressing upon his audience that they had not treated their Tlingit hosts with the appropriate and expected level of reciprocation. He stressed that they knew the United States government had encountered resistance from "Indians in the states about the land" and proposed finding a diplomatic solution by which Americans and Tlingit could coexist. Americans might remain in Tlingit land; however, he beseeched the governor for the return of "the places that brought us food," without which they would starve. The third speaker, Koogh-see, reiterated the diplomatic sentiments of Chief Johnson, acknowledging that "there are lots of things here which white men can make money out of. There is lots of gold in this country." He and his counterparts were prepared to permit mining, so long as it did not interfere with their hunting, trapping, and fishing, and he described the ways the fishing and canning operations had scared off their game and depleted the fish.[35]

Other speakers addressed the material impacts American intrusion had been having on Tlingit society more directly, and they employed Euro-American concepts of property and commodity economies to render their complaints legible to an audience ignorant of Tlingit society. Chief Kah-ea-tchiss from Hoonah described his ancestors' roles in the lucrative otter trade and how the arrival of "white people makes lots of smoke" which "drives the sea otter away." Because the Americans had entered Tlingit lands and waters without permission and had chased off the primary source of their livelihoods, he urged that they were owed compensation for the degradation of this economic staple. Juneau Chief Shoo-we-Kah reiterated this sentiment, recalling how a "white man by the name of Tom" entered his clan's creek and "took possession of it; [he] cut trees down and does not pay me anything." He described how he knew that if a man in the states wanted property that was in another's possession, "he pays for it," and he urged similar respect for Tlingit land and the livelihoods it supported using rhetoric that appealed to his listeners' economic and legal frameworks. He stated "we built this house and paid money for it. We paid for everything in this house, and take good care of this house. . . . In different villages here our people have property just like this house, and I would ask you to take good care of it and see that no one interferes with it."[36] He argued that Tlingit property regimes deserved equal respect and validation and gestured to the ways they could coexist with Euro-American objectives.

After Shoo-we-Kah's argument for the mutuality of both Tlingit and US legal systems, the speakers shifted their focus back to Kah-du-shan's opening complaint that their own legal orders had been ignored and that they had been denied recourse in the legal system that Americans had brought to their homelands. Chief Charley of Juneau captured their indignation at the wholesale abrogation of both Tlingit land rights and US property law. He balked at the presumption that "when [whites] want the ground they [could] simply move us from one place to another" without providing any legal remedy to protest such theft. He continued that "now all the creeks are claimed by the company [Treadwell Gold Mining Company] . . . and if you make a complaint and go into court, we are notified that it is too late now, that the paper is recorded and nothing can be done."[37] Importantly, the speakers accused Governor Brady and his counterparts of the theft of Tlingit lands in ways that they knew ran contrary to US–Indigenous relations in the States. The final speaker, Jack Williams of Juneau, spoke in Tlingit translated by Frederick Moore. He began by stating that "we have the same flesh as those Indians living down below in the States and we know the Government of the United States has provided food, clothing, houses for them." He informed Brady that he knew the United States negotiated with tribes in the States for the use and rights-of-way through Indian lands and that the government had set aside reservations where they would not be bothered by white people. He requested that the government set aside similar "places where we could make our homes as the people do at Fort Chester near Metlakahtla . . . where we could live by ourselves and have our property and homes where the white people could not bother us."[38]

As a whole, the procession of speeches reflect the ways Tlingit would customarily deal with interlopers who violated their legal orders and land regulations while situating themselves in the matrix of Indigenous–US relations. They followed Tlingit protocol of censuring those who "abused their privileges by staying too long, or taking too much, or violating some local ordinance" by inviting Governor Brady to the meeting, describing the offenses, emphasizing friendship, and informing him of how their ancestors had always used the land.[39] In this context, they also leveraged their knowledge of the ways the US government had treated with and negotiated with tribes in the contiguous states. Brady's response was pithy and condescending, though he alluded to the ambiguity of the 1884 Organic Act to deny Tlingit assertions of landownership. He posited that while "the laws remain yet to be made," the "Thlingit are entertaining wrong notions of how much land they own," revealing how ambiguity defended settler and corporate interests.[40] Nevertheless, by affirming their genealogies of landownership and claiming a kinship between themselves and "Indians down below," the Tlingit representatives in Juneau that day sought to render their land and sovereignty legible in the legal frameworks that the US government had heretofore used to mitigate its relationship to tribes. It also reveals that they perceived and found utility in their exclusion from these frameworks, and throughout the twentieth century they would alternately draw on these similarities and distinctions in advocating for their own legal, political, and cultural paradigms. This strategy proved useful as the implications of the Insular Cases came to bear on Alaska Native land rights in the courts and Congress.

In the first decades of the twentieth century, lawmakers and government officials struggled to reconcile the lack of legal uniformity of incorporated territorial status for Alaska with the distinctions they had created between Alaska Natives and tribes of the contiguous states. The result was a confusion of cases with contradictory rulings beginning in 1901 in the Alaska District Court and culminating in 1922 in the US Supreme Court. These cases reflect the challenges lawmakers faced with regard to the ambiguous legal status of Alaska Native land rights while shifting the basis by which a territory might achieve incorporated status from the citizenship eligibility of the inhabitants to its capacity to serve as a frontier for white settlement. While reimagining Alaska as a frontier, and therefore spatially and temporally conceived of as future public lands suited for white homesteading, Congress passed legislation that refrained from addressing the existence of Aboriginal title in the territory. As legal challenges to land titles arising from the alleged purchase of Alaska Native lands, lawmakers configured a process by which Alaska Natives could essentially "homestead" their own homelands in the form of allotments and townsites alongside potential white settlers rather than address land rights via nation-to-nation negotiations. The first of these cases considered whether Alaska Natives held their lands under Aboriginal title and therefore were prohibited from selling them to any entity but the federal government. *Sutter v. Heckman* arose from a dispute over tidelands by two corporate fisheries; Carl Sutter and his coplaintiffs claimed ownership based on their original purchase from Charles Dickson, who Sutter identified as an Indian. The district court found in favor of Sutter's claim, arguing that the First Organic Act did not bar Alaska Natives from conveying their lands, thus validating Sutter's title.[41] This decision upheld on appeal to the Ninth Circuit, where the court determined that the specific language in the 1884 act had intended to protect the region's "few inhabitants in the possession of lands, whatever character, by which they eked out their hard and precarious existence."[42] To this end, both courts agreed that Alaska Natives could convey title to their lands, which was constitutionally prohibited in lands designated as Indian Country and under the purview of Aboriginal title.

This case worked its way through the Alaska District and the US Ninth Circuit Courts in close proximity to when the US Supreme Court took up the first of the Insular Cases. The 1901 ruling in *Downes* unfurled the logic informing what became known as the doctrine of territorial incorporation. For this reason, the doctrine of incorporation and its probable implications for Alaska and the legal status of its inhabitants may not have been under consideration in *Sutter*. This changed by 1904 when the Alaska District Court began interpreting *Downes* to mean the extension of all US laws to Alaska, including federal Indian law. That year, two matters came before Alaska District Court Judge James Wickersham: the naturalization petition of a Creole man of Russian and Yup'ik parentage and a lawsuit brought by the federal government that sought to invalidate the individual sale of land by two Athabascan men to white prospectors.[43] In both, Wickersham articulated a theory of incorporation for Alaska, drawing on the citizenship clause of the 1867 Treaty of Cession whereby he delineated between two legal categories of Alaska Natives. Because the treaty had explicitly identified "uncivilized native tribes" as ineligible for citizenship, he concluded that there must be a class of "settled tribes" that were made citizens upon enactment of the treaty terms. He reasoned that members of settled tribes, who he argued had become US citizens by dint of the treaty stipulations, had been absolved of their tribal affiliations, including Aboriginal land rights, in lieu of the rights and privileges of citizenship. "Uncivilized native tribes," however, fell under the purview of federal Indian law upon incorporation of Alaska as an organized territory. Thus, when John Minook filed his intent to become a US citizen, Wickersham dismissed the petition on the basis that Minook was already a US citizen as a Creole member of a "settled tribe."[44] Conversely, he elaborated that because the Supreme Court had implied the incorporated status of Alaska in *Downes,* it should naturally follow that "the Indian tribes of Alaska [have] the same status before the law as those of the United States."[45]

The Supreme Court officially codified Alaska's incorporated status the following year in *Rassmussen v. United States.* Importantly, this decision affirmed citizenship as the marker of incorporated status despite the fact that Alaska still lacked a territorial government and remained sparsely populated. The case came before the court when Fred Rassmussen challenged his conviction for operating a brothel on the grounds that he had been denied a jury trial, thereby denying him his constitutional rights under the Sixth Amendment. Attorneys for the federal government denied that Rassmussen was entitled to a twelve-person jury, claiming that "Alaska was not incorporated into the United States, and therefore the Sixth Amendment did not control Congress in legislating for Alaska." They elaborated that "even if Alaska was incorporated into the United States . . . it was not an organized territory" because it did not have a full territorial government.[46] The court disagreed, ruling that the citizenship clause of the Treaty of Cession with Russia had expressed Congress's intent to "incorporate [the] acquired territory into the United States," establishing the precedent that citizenship rather than population size or the presence of an organized government constituted the criteria for incorporation.[47] Scholars have long analyzed the racial motivations of lawmakers and the Supreme Court justices in withholding citizenship and incorporated status from Puerto Rico, the Philippines, and Guam, though *Rassmussen* further naturalized the narrative of Alaska as part of the continental frontier, which functioned to sharpen distinctions between Alaska and the territories seized in 1898.

The Alaska courts interpreted *Rassmussen* to indicate Congress's intention that all aspects of the Constitution applied to the territory, including federal law regulating Indian lands. Wickersham issued a decision to this effect just months later in which the federal government sought to evict white prospectors from land they claimed to have acquired through purchase from two Salchaket Athabascans. In late March of 1905, the Salchaket men, identified in court documents as Chief Jarvis and Henry, had requested some neighboring white people to assist them in staking and filing notices of particular lands they owned "about one mile below the mouth of the Little Delta River and along the left branch of the Tanana River" in Alaska's Interior.[48] Roughly two weeks later, two other prospectors filed bills of sale in the Fairbanks Mining District at Delta City for the same lands, which they claimed to have purchased lawfully from Jarvis and Henry. This prompted the federal government to intervene, and Wickersham decided the case in favor of the United States. Elaborating on his opinion in *Minook,* he determined that Jarvis and Henry were members of "uncivilized tribes" and as such "they are entitled to the equal protection of the laws which the United States affords to similar aboriginal tribes within its borders."[49] Departing from the Asian racialization of Alaska Natives made by policymakers a quarter century earlier, Wickersham instead rationalized his conclusions on his perceived racial kinship between the Athabascans of Interior Alaska with the "Umpquas in Oregon, and the Navajos and . . . Apaches." More importantly, he averred that Congress's extension of "the mining, homestead, town site, coal land, and other general laws" of the United States to Alaska implied the extension of laws regulating Indian lands to the territory as well. Such would have designated Alaska Natives, including Chief Jarvis and Henry, "ward[s] of the government," whereby their "lands are not subject to disposal or sale or abandonment by him."[50] This ruling was the first time a court recognized Aboriginal title in Alaska.[51]

Despite this interpretation that incorporation implied the extension of federal Indian law to US territories, Congress and government officials hesitated to recognize collective landownership and nation-to-nation negotiating status for Alaska Natives. Instead, lawmakers and government officials largely maintained the racial distinctions and legal ambiguity around Alaska Natives and deliberated on legislative solutions they hoped would prevent large swaths of land in Alaska from falling subject to Native claims. The same year as *Rassmussen*, President Theodore Roosevelt requested a report on Alaska from Navy Lieutenant George T. Emmons, who advised Congress against seeking a large collective settlement or tribal reservation. He acknowledged the uncertain status of Alaska Natives, musing that "under the present code of laws the status of the native [of Alaska] has never been decided" and "whether or not the natives of Alaska are citizens of the United States . . . has never been judicially determined. Their position is anomalous. They have never come under the reservation act." Because of this, he argued that "tribal ties are very light" in Alaska and cautioned that "anything looking toward land indemnity or money payment or tribal reservation would be the greatest mistake here." Undoubtedly informed by assimilation rhetoric and policy, he imagined that the development of labor markets and an increasing amount of white settlers would enable Alaska Natives to "exercise their civic rights as any settlers in Alaska" and as such they "should be protected in their living, and the same rights of citizenship that are given to all."[52]

While waxing eloquent about citizenship, Emmons inadvertently mapped out the codified legal system of landownership and clan structure that he was attempting to argue did not exist in Alaska. In the same breath in which he evidenced the disintegration of tribal ties among Alaska Natives, he stated that they nevertheless organized in "geographic grouping[s] of families for mutual protection and social obligation" and that "the totem or family was the unit of life among these people." He continued that "the whole country was portioned off among the families as hunting reserves, berry grounds, or fishing sites and their laws of property and rights were very clearly defined and strictly observed."[53] What Emmons and others had clearly observed but sought to subvert was the intricate system of Tlingit jurisprudence represented in totemic law. Oral tradition along with the textual histories that were "carved onto the totem poles that lined the rivers of Southeast Alaska, on screens that filled the longhouses of each village, and . . . woven into the fabric of ceremonial blankets and clothes" told of "how each clan came to possess their land" and defined clan boundaries.[54] What Emmons reported was that even after forty years of US occupation, these legal orders were unmistakably intact and legible to government officials and lawmakers seeking to rationalize their denial of Alaska Native landownership and autonomous governance.

In response to Emmons's report and its emphasis on recognizing Alaska Native rights through the assimilatory pursuit of citizenship, Congress passed the Alaska Native Allotment Act in 1906. The language in the 1884 Organic Act did not distinguish between Native and non-Native inhabitants of Alaska in the protection of "Indians and other persons" from being disturbed in the possession of lands. Lawmakers thus concluded that Native and non-Native property rights were the same and that Alaska Natives were only entitled to the same land rights as settlers. To this end, the Alaska Native Allotment Act should not be interpreted as an extension of the General Allotment Act applicable in the contiguous states. It did not identify and associate lands with specific tribes but rather sought to establish a pathway by which Alaska Natives could obtain title to homesteads similarly to non-Natives settling in the district. The Alaska act also differed in that it was not self-executing, nor did it guarantee an allotment location that would be culturally, socially, or economically relevant to the person seeking title to it. Instead, individual Alaska Natives were required to file an application with the Department of the Interior to obtain a "*preference right* to secure by allotment the nonmineral land occupied by him"[55] Like the Homestead Act, the applicant was then required to provide proof of actual occupancy for a period of five years before an application would be approved, rather than qualifying for and potentially receiving an allotment by dint of membership in a tribal nation affiliated with reservation lands. Additionally, Alaska Native allotments were "deemed the homestead of the allottee and his heirs in perpetuity." For this reason, Alaska Native allotments were not considered trust lands, reflecting the ways lawmakers aimed to refrain from language that might imply the existence of Aboriginal title for which future redemptive purchase might be necessary.[56]

Between 1906 and 1960, the Interior Department issued only eighty Native allotments. The incompatibility of allotments with Alaska Native land regimes and subsistence lifeways, in addition to the tedious bureaucratic process, clearly made Native allotments unpopular, and it is not surprising that so few utilized its provisions to assert rights in the land. While generally resisting allotments, Tlingit, Haida, and Tsimshian in Southeast Alaska nevertheless continued their diplomatic organizing, founding the Alaska Native Brotherhood (ANB) in 1912 followed by the Alaska Native Sisterhood (ANS) in 1915. Through these new intertribal organizations, they began mobilizing their efforts toward establishing a naturalization process for Alaska Natives through the new territorial legislature, which they achieved in 1915. Members of the ANB and ANS knew from their interactions with administrators and the courts that there was significant debate about their legal status and that of their lands. Denied a pathway to assert Aboriginal land rights through treaty or negotiation, they saw citizenship as an important tool for influencing policy that affected their land. As US citizens, they would have access to the ballot box, the territorial legislature, the courts, and educational institutions where they could train to navigate the US legal system.[57] This approach would prove crucial, as the Alaska District Court and the US Ninth Circuit issued contradictory rulings on the nature of Alaska Native land rights in the coming decades while fishing and mining operations continued encroaching on Native lands and waters.[58]

The Homestead Act was perhaps less popular than Native allotments, with fewer than 1,000 homestead patents issued before 1940 and fewer than 3,500 issued in total by the time the act was repealed. This dismal number of homesteaders seeking to take advantage of inexpensive land at a time characterized by the social, political, and economic anxieties around the closing of the American frontier belies the logic by which Alaska came to be considered an incorporated territory. The frontier rabble of citizen settlers did not arrive as lawmakers had anticipated, demonstrating that the narration of Alaska as the natural terminus of westward expansion—and therefore that which could be considered properly national territory—was more fiction than fact. Lawmakers and judges nevertheless honed this frontier fiction when Congress passed the Jones–Shafroth Act in 1917, which restructured the Puerto Rican government and granted US citizenship to anyone born in Puerto Rico on or after April 11, 1899.[59]

The extension of citizenship to Puerto Ricans fundamentally undermined the contingency of incorporated territorial status on the citizenship status of a territory's inhabitants. The Federal District Court of Puerto Rico seized this opportunity to challenge classification of the territory as unincorporated, forcing the US Supreme Court to further emphasize Alaska as a frontier as opposed to a possession. In a ruling the following year *In re Tapia,* the court held that the Jones–Shafroth Act entitled US citizens residing in Puerto Rico to the provisions of the Constitution and Bill of Rights in their entirety. The Supreme Court of Puerto Rico followed suit in *Muratti v. Foote,* elaborating that "the history of incorporating the territories of the United States has been traced in the Insular Decisions and the *Rassmussen* case." The judges drew a deliberate parallel to Alaska, arguing that "to say that the acquisition of territory plus organized government plus citizenship" for Puerto Rico is not equal to "the case of Alaska" is "equivalent of denying the algebraic truth that a+b+c=a+c+b."[60] The US Supreme Court took up the obvious contradictions between Alaska's incorporated status until 1922 when it issued the ruling in *Balzac v. Porto Rico.* In *Balzac,* the justices stated that it was Alaska's frontier character rather than citizenship that provided for incorporated status, thus rationalizing the exclusion of territories with much larger populations.

Like *Rassmussen* nearly two decades earlier, *Balzac* arose from the denial of the Sixth Amendment right to a jury trial, and the US Supreme Court acknowledged the parallels. The opinion acknowledged that "a law of Congress or a provision in a treaty acquiring territory, declaring an intention to confer political and civil rights on the inhabitants of the new lands as American citizens may be properly interpreted to mean incorporation of it into the Union as in the case of Louisiana and Alaska." Unfortunately, such was not the case with Puerto Rico, whereas "Alaska was a very different case." Unlike the unincorporated territories, Chief Justice William Howard Taft wrote in the majority opinion that Alaska "was an enormous territory, very sparsely settled, and offering opportunity for immigration and settlement by American citizens. It was on the American continent, and within easy reach of the then United States."[61] Until the Spanish-American War, Alaska's minute population and distance from the contiguous states provided the rationale for withholding the legal frameworks of westward expansion and inclusion in the nation proper. Just two decades later, the court backed away from this logic in order to exclude Puerto Rico from incorporated status and instead reframed Alaska's deficits that had previously impaired the territory's likelihood of inclusion in the nation proper. The court renarrated noncontiguity and geographic distance as contiguity and proximity and Alaska's minute population as an opportunity for Euro-American immigration rather than a reflection of the territory's undesirable climate and locale, thus designating Alaska's frontier character as the undisputed criteria for incorporated status rather than citizenship. *Balzac* reveals the ways incorporated territories were fashioned in the same moment as unincorporated territories, and the reframing of Alaska was essential to make the necessary distinctions between a frontier and a possession. The imperial crisis following the Spanish-American War initiated a process by which the lawmakers and government officials sought legal methods to exclude additional territories and peoples at their discretion. To do this, they needed to redefine Alaska within the legal framework of westward expansion to more closely align with contiguous territorial possessory claims. They were careful, however, not to compromise the access to Native land and resources they had achieved by distinguishing Alaska Natives and Alaska Native lands from recognized tribal nations and lands designated as Indian Country in the contiguous states and territories.

In this way, they used Alaska as the backdrop against which they worked out the details of empire while carrying the ambiguity around Alaska Native legal status and that of their land rights through incorporation. Alaska's transition to "the last frontier" resolved the ambiguity in Alaska's relation to properly national territory, unpausing the transference and transformation of land into property. As a frontier open to homesteading rather than a distant territory with little promise for settlement, formal territorial incorporation rendered land in Alaska legible as fully actualized public lands. Going forward, lawmakers and government officials would come to argue that the necessity for redemptive purchase for those lands was unclear. They continued to draw on the racial and legal distinctions their forebearers had established in the nineteenth century to question whether Alaska Natives ought to be negotiated with or compensated for their land. This maneuver effectively relocated the temporal pause in the dispossessive process to the action of retroactive attribution by which Alaska Natives would, theoretically, be recognized as the "prior owners" of the land. In the decades following *Balzac,* lawmakers, government officials, and corporate interests continued debating whether or not Alaska Natives had any prior rights in the land while crafting legislation that enabled white settlement and Native dispossession until Congress might determine the nature of those rights at some future, undetermined date.

The uncertainties around Alaska Native land rights no doubt facilitated dispossession; however, Alaska Native land rights activists came to wield this ambiguity in ways that forced lawmakers and government officials to consider ways to resolve it. To this end, they hung the threat of Aboriginal title over potential or anticipated corporate development projects and settler ambitions while simultaneously pursuing an agreement that would be more conducive to their ways of life. To achieve this, they mobilized their ambiguous legal status, at times situating themselves as similar enough to tribes of the contiguous states to prompt federal officials and lawmakers to include them in aspects of continental Indian policy that they found useful. Conversely, they would often emphasize distinctions between themselves and other tribal nations to avoid the trappings of federal Indian law that undermined their objectives. Like the Tlingit leaders at the 1898 meeting with the governor, Alaska Natives continued the tradition of negotiating and navigating American presence in ways that would sustain their relationship to their land, thereby guaranteeing the collective continuance of their legal, political, social, and economic orders.[62]

3

Asserting Native Land Relations

Native Land Rights and Equal Citizenship in the IRA Era

Andrew Hope (Tlingit, Eagle, Kaagwaantaan) opened the 1920 annual convention of the Alaska Native Brotherhood (ANB) reporting that "all Natives of Sitka voted in the last election of November 2."[1] Four years before Congress passed the 1924 Indian Citizenship Act, Hope and his cohort serving on the ANB Citizenship Committee devised a plan by which Alaska Natives could claim their right to vote by signing an affidavit attesting to their status as US citizens per the General Allotment Act (Dawes Act) of February 8, 1887, and carrying it to the polling stations.[2] At the turn of the century, many Alaska Natives began exploring citizenship and voting as strategies to mitigate US occupation of their homelands. In 1920, they seized the rhetoric of assimilation reflected in the Dawes Act of 1887 to assert their voices in US colonial policy.

The ANB and Alaska Native Sisterhood (ANS) had successfully advocated for a path to citizenship through the Alaska Territorial Legislature in 1915, but the stringent nature of the process and its contingency on white approval of citizenship applications discouraged many from pursuing it. In order to secure a certificate of US citizenship under the territorial statute, a Native petitioner had to obtain the signatures of at least five white residents willing to testify that the petitioner had abandoned tribal ties and had lived a "civilized life" for at least one year. Most potential applicants likely resented the requirement that they submit to white approval of their eligibility for citizenship, and the process could be time consuming and disruptive to subsistence rounds and participation in wage labor. Thus, the ANB approached a local precinct judge with a theory that they might claim their rights to citizenship under provisions of the Dawes Act, which Congress had passed in the late nineteenth century, forming the legislative mechanism of assimilation policy that aimed to dissolve tribal nations and lands. Key to the ANB's theory was the clause proclaiming "every Indian born within the territorial limits of the United States who has voluntarily taken up . . . residence separate and apart from any tribe of Indians therein, and has adopted the habits of a civilized life, is hereby declared to be a citizen of the United States and is entitled to all the rights, privileges, and immunities of such citizens."[3]

By utilizing the Dawes Act this way, Alaska Natives made a case for their inclusion in federal Indian policy, thereby claiming US citizenship by way of their status as Indians. According to Hope, on election day all Alaska Natives of eligible voting age in Sitka printed out and signed an affidavit declaring that the signatory was "an Indian born within the territorial limits of the United States of America" who had set up residence apart from "any tribe of Indian" and "adopted the habits of a civilized life." The affidavit affirmed that as such, each individual could "claim [their] citizenship rights under the provisions of the Act of Congress of the United States, approved February 8th, 1887."[4] The decision to claim citizenship status through federal Indian law reflects the ways many ANB and ANS members understood their relationship to tribes in the contiguous states and the US legal and political institutions that framed their struggles for land rights. By declaring themselves Indians, they asserted a legal kinship as Indigenous people with inherent rights in the land in ways that might resonate with lawmakers and government officials. Furthermore, the renunciation of tribal ties in favor of a "civilized life" not only implied that tribal relations persisted in Alaska but also allowed those claiming to have taken up "residence separate and apart" from a tribe to define what that entailed. Most importantly, this strategy explicitly based Alaska Native claims to US citizenship on their status as Native people; rather than abandoning their Indigenous identities and lives in order to become citizens, they argued that their Indigeneity is what qualified them for citizenship, and citizenship became one of the many tools they employed in seeking recognition of their land rights.

The 1920 election strategy is just one example of how settler imperial ambiguities allowed Alaska Native activists to manipulate federal Indian policy and US legal institutions to ensure the continuance of their cultures, livelihoods, and social and political orders. By the turn of the century, many Alaska Natives were attending boarding schools and colleges or universities in the contiguous states where they encountered Indigenous people from tribal nations and communities across North America. Upon returning to their homelands, most were keenly aware that their legal status and their historical relationship to the federal government was markedly different from that of other tribes. Many of them took note of the reservation system and the Bureau of Indian Affairs (BIA) and the concept of wardship status that lawmakers and government officials attached to the federal recognition of tribal land rights. Wary of this context, they understood citizenship as one possible means to define their land relations and affirm the legitimacy of their social, economic, and legal structures within the rights rhetoric of the US legal system. To this end, many Alaska Native land rights activists understood the legal and racial distinctions lawmakers had established in the previous century along with the ambiguity these distinctions animated as potentially allowing them to influence how they might communicate their land rights in Congress and the courts. To do this, they alternately argued for inclusion or exclusion from various trappings of federal Indian policy or advocated for modifications to a given policy to reflect their needs and objectives more adequately.

This strategy became increasingly important as lawmakers and government officials debated the uncertainties inherent in the 1884 First Organic Act for Alaska in their escalation of extraction infrastructure and settlement projects in Alaska. In these conversations, they entertained the notion that Alaska Natives might have some rights in the land, though they routinely left the question unresolved. Instead, when Alaska Natives objected to proposed railways, timber harvesting, mining, and fishing developments without resolution of their land rights, lawmakers began structuring law and policy such that these projects could commence contingent on the possibility of a future settlement at the discretion of Congress and the courts. This maneuver relied on the ambiguous legal status of Alaska Natives that lawmakers and corporate interests mobilized in the legal definition of *tribe*. In the context of increasing Native activism around land rights, these lawmakers and corporate interests argued that Alaska Natives had not been recognized as tribes via treaty or other means that would convey that legal status. To them, this meant that Alaska Natives did not meet the criteria by which to be recognized as prior owners of land from which they had been or would be dispossessed. To settlers, corporate interests, and lawmakers, "tribe" had customarily been the eligible entity for retroactive attribution as prior owner of the land. Thus, if Alaska Natives did not qualify for this retroactive status, then there was no need for redemptive purchase. If there was no need for redemptive purchase, then there was also no need for prior consent from or negotiation with Alaska Natives regarding the sale or transference of their lands. Lawmakers defended this logic with language from the 1884 Organic Act that protected both "Indians" and "other persons" on an equivalent basis from being disturbed in the possession of lands used, occupied, or claimed by them. As we have seen, the courts did not interpret the 1884 Organic Act as affirmation of Aboriginal title, casting additional uncertainty on what constituted "use and occupancy," how much land could be claimed under that provision, and if such claims could be made on an individual, clan, village, or other basis.[5] This suspended the recursive component of the dispossessive process, situating Alaska Natives as potential future prior owners of the land so long as lawmakers continued to question and debate their legal status and the existence of "tribes" or the equivalent in Alaska.

In this context, Alaska Natives walked a fine line as they sought to establish sufficient parallels in their legal status to tribes such that lawmakers would recognize their land rights or concede to a settlement, while simultaneously distinguishing themselves enough to evade BIA oversight and sustain their own land regimes. These efforts resulted in two significant pieces of federal legislation that buttressed the legal basis for collective Alaska Native land rights: the 1935 passage of the Tlingit and Haida Jurisdictional Act and the 1936 Alaska Reorganization Act (ARA). The former recognized Tlingit and Haida peoples as members of a tribal entity eligible to bring land claims against the federal government in the US Court of Claims. The latter recognized groups of Alaska Natives as eligible to establish tribal governments and request Indian reservations per the 1934 Indian Reorganization Act (IRA). Neither resolved the ambiguities embedded in the 1884 Organic Act, but they are significant examples of how Tlingit and Haida activists infused various tenets of their own legal and political orders into US law and federal Indian policy in their efforts to achieve a palatable affirmation of their Indigenous land rights. In advocating for both, they took advantage of the shift in continental Indian policy from assimilation toward the recognition of tribal sovereignty reflected in the IRA and their anomalous legal status to convince Congress to accommodate their clan- and village-based political organizations and the adaptations those entities had made over the previous seven decades of US occupation.

The passage of the Tlingit and Haida Jurisdictional Act and the ARA occurred within a broader shift in Indigenous–US relations in Alaska and the contiguous states and as part of an important reorientation in US empire leading up to the Second World War. Throughout the 1930s, the Roosevelt administration sought new ways to manage the boundaries of incorporated "properly national" space during the deepening crisis in Europe leading up to and throughout World War II. In 1934, President Franklin D. Roosevelt created the Division of Territories and Island Possessions as part of a rapid and drastic reorganization of the executive branch of the federal government. This new division consolidated the administration of all noncontiguous territories, incorporated and unincorporated, into one central agency, and in the following years the federal government experimented with the ways these noncontiguous territories could be used to define and reify the parameters of national space and national identity while facilitating US imperial ambitions. Alaska's transition to incorporated status had utility in this regard, as the frontier narrative maintained a firm boundary between national settler space and unincorporated territories, while territorial status maintained sole federal authority, which facilitated imperial objectives without the interference of a state government.

Indigenous Land Rights as Rights of US Citizenship

At the same 1920 ANB convention where Andrew Hope reported the success of Tlingit voting, Tlingit attorney William Paul Sr. (Tlingit, Tee-Hit-Ton) gave a presentation on federal law and Indian lands. A survivor of the Sheldon Jackson Presbyterian mission school and the Carlisle Indian Industrial School, Paul had attended the Banks Business College in Philadelphia and Whitworth College in Spokane, Washington, and earned a law degree from La Salle University. He was the first Alaska Native admitted to the Alaska territorial bar, and he gained fame when he successfully defended his mother, Tillie Paul, after she was arrested for defying poll workers and assisting Native voters.[6] He was the first Alaska Native elected to the territorial legislature in 1924, and while some experienced him as controversial and combative, he is celebrated for his tireless efforts in the courts and elsewhere on behalf of Alaska Native citizenship and land rights and is remembered as the "Father of Alaska Native Land Claims."

Addressing the convention, Paul read a letter he had received from the Land Office in Washington in which federal officials conceded that

FIGURE 3. Group portrait of the Paul family. *From left,* William Paul Jr., William Paul Sr., and Frederick Paul. Courtesy of Alaska State Library, Alaska Native Organizations Collection, ASL-P33-31.

per the 1884 Organic Act, "Indians shall not be disturbed in the possession of their lands," with the "terms under which they might obtain title . . . reserved for future legislation by Congress." He informed the convention that despite this promise, legislation regarding Alaska Native land rights had never been passed and that Indigenous Peoples in the contiguous states had laws that protected Indian property. He explained how the Supreme Court rulings in *Cherokee Nation v. Georgia* and *Johnson v. M'Intosh* mandated that "the government must protect Indian property," implying Alaska Natives were due the same protections. The minutes reveal that he elaborated that these rights were vested in tribal units and held in trust rather than in individuals regardless of citizenship status and "any contract to sell land by any *Indian is null and void* and of no effect [unless authorized by Congress]." While these protections might be useful to employ, Paul also cautioned that *Cherokee Nation* "says that the [relationship of the] Indian [to the United States resembles that of] a ward [to his guardian]" which limited the authority Indians in the contiguous states could exercise over their own land (brackets in original). Perhaps advocating for an outcome in which

Alaska Natives could leverage federal protections for their land as Indians but avoid being treated as wards, he suggested that the ANB ought to petition Congress to pass a law affirming Alaska Natives as full citizens of the United States. His brother Louis Paul endorsed this strategy, whereby Alaska Natives could then "stand on their rights of citizenship and demand title to their property."[7]

The Pauls, and likely a number of their colleagues at the convention, did not think of citizenship and its attendant property rights or the guardianship structure of protections for Indian land as a substitute for their own land regimes, legal orders, and the social and political relationships that regulated them. Rather, the legal maneuvering of Paul and other ANB and ANS members in the 1920s suggests that they had identified the ways the US legal system protected citizens in the possession of property and regulated the purchase of Indian land as critical points of departure from which to protest, prevent, or be compensated for the theft of their own lands. Citizenship guaranteed their ability to assert ownership of land and other property by acquiring individual fee simple title to certain lands, whereas Indian or tribal status meant that they could also potentially seek recognition of Aboriginal title with land rights and protections vested in their collective sovereign polities. Together, the two formulations of what the US legal system recognized as valid title presented methods by which they could challenge the settler, corporate, and federal presumptions to ownership of land in Alaska and achieve a patchwork of recognition status that supported their own objectives. The persistence of their status as potential future prior owners undoubtedly facilitated dispossession across Southeast Alaska at an accelerated rate, but in the 1930s and 1940s, the ANB, ANS, and other land rights organizations began to threaten the possibility of costly future land claims settlements in their protests of large-scale timber and fishing operations that commenced without their consent. In this way, ambiguity opened up an important space in which Alaska Natives might define any land and settlement arrangement on more agreeable terms.

While some aspects of trust lands and federal protections were attractive, many ANB and ANS members were wary of the reservation system, and this shaped their developing strategies and thinking on citizenship. Peter Simpson (Tsimshian, Killer Whale Phratry) echoed Paul's concerns regarding the restrictions on landownership should the recognition of land rights in Alaska mirror that in the contiguous states.

He related to the convention his dismay upon discovering that after migrating from British Columbia and building a sawmill, he "was told that, since he was an Indian, he was not entitled to a mill site."[8] Simpson had relocated to Southeast Alaska in 1889, along with a number of other Tsimshian peoples and an Anglican minister by the name of William Duncan. Once settled on Annette Island, Duncan petitioned the federal government for a permanent Indian reservation for the community, and in 1891 Congress fulfilled the request, creating the Metlakatla (Annette Island) reservation. Soon after, Simpson and his counterparts learned that they could not exercise autonomy over their own property and economic operations, thus Simpson speculated that he would be better off "to escape the reservation" and therefore have the ability to own his home.[9]

Simpson continued to speak on the problems of federally controlled land arrangements in his presentation, "The Failure of the Reservation System," at the Wednesday evening session. Again, he cautioned against what he perceived as an underhanded ploy to take Tsimshian property. He argued that in Metlakatla, British Columbia, his community had "owned their own sawmill, a cannery, clam cannery, and a clothing factory," but they were informed by the provincial courts that "they did not own the ground on which their houses, stores, and homes were built." He continued:

> They gave up their property and came to Alaska to get away from a reservation. Father Duncan went to Washington, knowing the desires of the Tsimshian people. He went to Washington for that purpose. He came back with what he claimed to be the solution to the desire in their hearts, which was the right to own their own homes. At New Metlakatla in Alaska, my people recreated a fine business comparable to their former possessions. But they discovered that, contrary to Father Duncan's first announcement, they were on land owned in common or a reservation . . . and all of their sacrifices were all in vain. I left my home, which I had built, and it is still standing there, rotting I guess, on that reservation. This system is now being promoted by the officers of the Indian Bureau System in Hydaburg, Bayview, and Howkan. The result will be the same—no ownership of homes because the title is reserved to the Government.[10]

To Simpson, the reservation system was being used to steal Native land, livelihoods, and autonomy. He, like the Pauls, understood that Indigenous Peoples, as members of sovereign nations that predated the United States or British Canada, had rights in the land and that the legal mechanisms that both the United States and Canada had employed in the supposed protection of Native lands in the form of reservations was undermining those very rights. They also understood that in order to avoid punitive oversight by a colonizing government, they needed to chart a different path. If the federal government could not claim them as wards, they could potentially work out a more agreeable land arrangement.

The combination of citizenship and Indigenous land rights also represented important strategies for Native regulation of the fishing industry, especially in terms of abolishing the fish trap. Both Native and non-Native people in Alaska were hostile to the fish trap, and numerous other territories had banned its use. For this reason, the corporate canneries that relied on fish traps had successfully lobbied against the transfer of fishing regulations to the territorial government in 1912, despite the fact that other territories, including Hawaiʻi, regulated their own fisheries.[11] The canneries also lobbied aggressively against Indigenous fishing rights; the uncertainty around Alaska Native tribal status and land rights permitted the canneries to assert that Alaska Natives had no Aboriginal fishing rights that the canneries were bound to respect, let alone any claim of exclusive access to streams or tidelands.[12] Samuel Jackson (Tlingit, Sitka) spoke on the problems of the fishing industry, in which he argued that "the blame" for the devastation of Tlingit salmon economies lay "primarily on the fish traps." He reported that between Tenakee and Hoonah, he counted forty-eight fish traps capable of catching over a million fish because the traps, unlike a seiner, fished twenty-four hours a day. The traps reduced the number of salmon available for Native subsistence, and the efficiency of the traps also reduced the number of Native fishermen the canneries would employ, thereby limiting the ability of the fishermen to supplement their livelihoods with a cash income. Additionally, Native fishermen were more heavily policed for violations of fishing regulations, while "white fishermen" could frequently be observed "throwing away over 3,000 humpies on the bank and taking only the reds."[13]

Like the Tlingit leaders two decades prior, the ANB was appalled at the behavior of those operating the non-Native canneries. Not only was the corporate implementation of the fish trap a threat to their own access to salmon, but it also encouraged tremendous wastefulness that disrupted and offended human and nonhuman kinship relations that ordered Tlingit cultural and spiritual life.[14] Taking salmon without permission was an egregious offense, though leaving the carcasses of discarded humpies on the banks of the rivers represented an equally serious transgression in its repugnant treatment of salmon as resources rather than relatives. Tlingit poet and linguist K̲eixwnéi Nora Marks Dauenhauer (Tlingit, Lukaax̲.ádi) articulates this relationship in her poem "How to Make Good Baked Salmon from the River." She describes that after filleting a salmon, the innards are to be fed to the seagulls and ravens "because they're your kin," and the same is to be done with the bones instead of throwing them back into the water "because salmon have spirits and don't like to see the remains of their kin thrown in by us among them."[15] For many Alaska Natives, witnessing the violent commodification of relatives and kin, notwithstanding the dumping of three thousand humpies on the beach, constituted an egregious violation of multiple, layered, and cascading reciprocal relations, the maintenance of which had sustained their societies for thousands of years. The simultaneous overharvesting and discarding of catches by commercial fisheries reflect the transactional rather than relational valuation of salmon and the carefully cultivated habitats they require to thrive. Despite this, none of the speakers overtly advocated for an outright expulsion of the canneries. Instead, they appear to have envisioned that as citizens and Indigenous people with extensive knowledge of salmon habitat management they might influence federal regulations such that both Native and non-Native needs might be met. Echoing the significance of Tlingit permissions protocols and relations to nonhuman kin, they perceived citizenship as a way to gain access to the legal spaces in which decisions about cannery operations were made such that they might ensure the persistence of their subsistence practices and values.

These strategies crystallized at the historic 1929 ANB and ANS Convention in Haines when members voted to formally pursue passage of a congressional jurisdictional act. If passed by Congress, such an act would allow Tlingit and Haida to sue the United States in its Court of Claims for money damages for the taking of Tlingit and Haida lands. Convincing Congress that such legislation was warranted required the ANB to provide evidence of federal liability for a legal taking, thus demonstrating their status as prior owners of lands for which they had not yet been retroactively redemptively compensated. By this time, former territorial judge James Wickersham had been appointed to serve as Alaska's territorial delegate, and he worked with William Paul Sr. on drafting the proposed jurisdictional act. In the interim between the ANB's resolution and the introduction of a jurisdictional act to Congress, the Alaska responsibilities of the Office of Education were transferred to the Bureau of Indian Affairs by secretarial order in 1931. This decision drew objections from a number of territorial and federal officials and lawmakers, with Alaska's congressional delegate Dan Sutherland protesting the move on the racial and thereby legal distinctions that lawmakers had historically drawn between Indigenous Alaskans and Indians in the contiguous states. He implored Congress not to make the change, arguing in session that "primarily, the people of Alaska, the aborigines, are not considered Indians. We have . . . various races there and sometimes we speak of them as Indians, but officially they are recognized as the native people of Alaska. . . . They are native people, and it is a serious question whether they are Indians or not."[16] The interior solicitor disagreed, issuing an opinion in 1932 that "it is clear that no distinction has been or can be made between the Indians and other Natives of Alaska so far as the laws and regulations of the United States are concerned whether the Eskimos and other natives are of Indian origin or not, as they are all wards of the Nation and their status is in material respects similar to that of the Indians of the United States."[17]

Advocacy for passage of the jurisdictional act reveals the ways the ANB and ANS drew on this recent change in administrative jurisdiction to render themselves legible to federal Indian law that governed land rights while also seeking a settlement structure that might avoid the restrictions associated with the solicitor's designation of Indigenous Alaskans as wards of the government. In support of the former objective, when Congress considered the bill, they sent James Wickersham, then serving as Alaska's territorial delegate, with a petition in which they drew explicit parallels of themselves as Indigenous nations and their experience of dispossession to those of tribes in the contiguous states. To this end, they employed the term *Indian* to assert a specific legal identity that would resonate with lawmakers, and they identified material losses they had suffered as a direct consequence of governmental actions that had been implemented "without giving us a hearing." They intentionally petitioned "in the name of the Alaska Native Brotherhood," an organization of "over 5,000 native Indians," on behalf of "the native Indians of southeastern Alaska" whose condition had been "getting worse and worse" since "the United States Government took over Alaska from our forefathers." As Native "Indians," they levied charges on the federal government, which they alleged "has locked up the forests" and "taken . . . our ancient fish streams" without consultation, in the end "giving us nothing for it."[18] The wording of the petition sought to dislodge the ambiguity around Alaska Natives as potential future prior owners of land in Alaska and establish them as actual prior owners of the land for which they had not yet been redemptively compensated. This also served as a warning that if the courts recognized Tlingit and Haida as prior owners of lands from which they had been dispossessed, then by implication all Alaska Natives were current owners of the lands they still used and occupied in the territory.[19] If successful, their petition and passage of a jurisdictional act would establish that all lands in Alaska were subject to redemptive purchase and therefore potentially subject to negotiation prior to any additional theft.

Several senators and government officials balked at this possibility, demonstrating that BIA jurisdictional administration would not be read as the recognition of land rights or political sovereignty for Alaska Natives. Instead, many argued that Alaska Natives had no justifiable claims because there had been no formal negotiation for land cessions resulting in reservations, nor had there been large-scale collective dispossession in Alaska. The commissioner of Indian Affairs suggested that those tribes in the contiguous states for whom Congress had adopted a jurisdictional act allowing them to bring suit against the United States had asserted claims "based on some treaty obligation or on some express or implied understanding between the United States and the Indians affected." Conversely in Alaska, "Congress took no particular notice of these natives" and "never undertook to hamper their individual movements, confine them to a locality or reservation, or to place them under the immediate control of its officers, as has been the case with the American Indians." Absent the trappings of what lawmakers considered formal dispossession by treaty or another recognized agreement, many concluded that a jurisdictional act for Tlingit and Haida claims was "without precedent" and therefore unnecessary.[20]

In response, Wickersham reiterated the racial and therefore legal similarities he had previously drawn between Alaska Natives and Indians of the continent, arguing that "they are American Indians in the strictest ethnological sense" and "the situation in Alaska is exactly the same as it is in the United States with respect to bills of this kind."[21] Drawing on his conclusions in *United States v. Berrigan* and *United States v. Cadzow* regarding the distinctions between "uncivilized" and "settled" tribes, he contended that the language in the Treaty of Cession with Russia guaranteed "the Alaskan Indians . . . the same assurance of citizenship in the United States as those in the Louisiana and Mexican purchases, and the uncivilized Indians came in with the assurance they would be treated exactly as the Indian tribes in the United States are." He continued that while Alaska Natives had not been removed or placed on reservations, the commercial fisheries, in the absence of any formal recognition of Alaska Native land rights, came into the territory from San Francisco year after year and depleted the fish, forcing Indigenous fishing operations out of their ancestral waters. He argued that this dispossession was "now just the same situation you would have if you had taken over the Sioux country, or the lands of any other Indians, and elbowed them out without paying them a cent."[22] Citing recent decisions of the Interior Department, Wickersham sought to establish that Alaska Natives were at least "within the spirit, if not within the exact letter, of the laws relative to American Indians" because Congress had committed the federal government to protecting Alaska Natives in the use and occupancy of their lands. To them, this statutory record had made it "clear that no distinction has been or can be made between the Indians and other natives of Alaska so far as the laws and relations of the United States are concerned."[23]

While the ANB had crafted a policy and supporting documents to draw themselves into the legal sphere of federal Indian law regarding land rights, they nevertheless took this opportunity to define the ways they might pursue claims. Section 2 of the bill gave the Court of Claims jurisdiction to hear "all claims of whatsoever nature, legal or equitable, which the said Tlingit and Haida Indians of Alaska may or claim to have against the United States for lands or other tribal, community, or individual property rights." The inclusion of "individual property rights" within the jurisdictional act's provisions likely represented important ways that the ANB sought to integrate a variety of possibilities for articulating damages and prompting compensation. In this way, they sought settlement structures that reflected their own definitions of valid claims within their own land and property regimes and the adaptations they had made since US occupation, including their vision of US citizenship.[24] In this sense, it also represented a departure from the jurisdictional acts adopted for tribes in the contiguous states, provoking sharp criticism from the Department of Justice (DOJ). In a memorandum in March of 1934, attorneys for the DOJ warned that the far-reaching possibilities for claims under its provisions set a dangerous precedent. Specifically, they argued that if the bill "confined itself strictly to authorizing the Tlingit and Haida Indians of Alaska to prosecute their (*i.e.* tribal) claims . . . it would be unobjectionable."[25] They expressed alarm that "the bill goes further than this" and "apparently authorizes not only suits by the tribes for tribal property, but suits by individuals of the tribes for the taking of individually owned property." According to DOJ attorneys, "this is something which has never been done heretofore" and would "establish a bad and dangerous precedent" that could encourage "individuals of other tribes" to seek "similar treatment" in addition to their tribal claims.[26] Interior Secretary Harold L. Ickes likewise objected in a letter to the Committee on Indian Affairs that "the bill, as drawn, is wide open" and "provides for the adjudication of individual property rights."[27]

The ANB's assertion of individual property claims exemplifies the ways they sought to achieve a settlement structure that could accommodate the dynamic and complex nature of Tlingit and Haida land and property regimes. As mentioned above, they were also suspicious of the legal implications of how the federal government defined tribal property in relation to wardship status. This is further evident in Paul's objection to Interior Department approval of attorney contracts in the pursuit of claims under the jurisdictional act's provisions.[28] He argued that this requirement "was designed for non-citizen Indians," and that "Alaska Indians are fully competent to represent their own interests without the intervention of the Sec. of the Interior." He continued that as citizen Indians, "there is no way to extend the jurisdiction of the Secretary of the Interior or the commissioner of Indian Affairs" over Tlingit and Haida matters. Additionally, the political geography of Tlingit and Haida people was so complex that the requirement for each community to seek Interior Department approval of their attorney would all but "defeat our appearance [in court] by making conditions which our people . . . physically cannot meet." This was because there "is a wide difference between the . . . tribes of the states organized as tribes and living in small, restricted areas and the Indians called Tlingits and Haidas living in 18 villages separated . . . over [hundreds of] miles."[29] To Paul and many other ANB members, the political geography of Tlingit and Haida society and their status as citizens rendered Interior Department approval of attorney contracts obsolete.

Congress passed the Tlingit and Haida Jurisdictional Act in 1935, authorizing "Tlingit and Haida Indians of Alaska" to bring suit against the United States for communal or tribal property rights taken by the US government without compensation. Absent, however, was the right to sue to vindicate individual property claims. Nevertheless, the debates preceding its passage reveal the ways Tlingit and Haida people sought to articulate their land regimes into US law in ways that more accurately reflected their relationships to each other, the land, and US economic and political institutions. The objections of lawmakers and government officials demonstrate how they sought to prevent the Court of Claims from recognizing and compensating anything other than tribal or communal property to the exclusion of individual property or other claims. In doing so, they may have anticipated that the courts would sustain the long-held belief that tribes as they had been legally defined in the contiguous states did not exist in Alaska, and therefore Tlingit and Haida people would not meet the threshold for retroactive compensation for tribal or communal property. It would be twenty-four years before the Court of Claims issued a judgment acknowledging federal liability for the taking of Tlingit and Haida land and another ten years before it determined the amount of monetary damages. In the interim, lawmakers, corporate interests, and government officials continued to debate the legal status of Alaska Natives and the applicability of federal Indian law to the territory, continuing to focus on the legal definition of *tribe* as the criteria by which Indigenous Peoples could claim collective land rights and assert collective nation-to-nation negotiation for the alienation of those lands.

Importantly, the enactment of the Tlingit and Haida Jurisdictional Act followed on the heels of the passage of the Indian Reorganization Act, and the ANB along with other Alaska Native organizations leveraged this national policy shift to shape the recognition of their land rights. The IRA brought an end to allotment policy and sought to encourage

Indigenous people in the United States to use reservations as homelands for purposes of economic development and self-government. Largely the product of Commissioner of Indian Affairs John Collier, the IRA aimed to "conserve and develop Indian lands and resources" through the restoration of remaining Indian lands that had been slated for allotment and the extension of loans and credit systems that tribes could utilize in pursuit of economic development. The act stipulated that, while not generally applying to US territories, Sections 9, 10, 11, 12, and 16 "shall apply to Alaska." Sections 9–12 included provisions by which tribes, incorporated as Indian chartered organizations, could qualify for loans that could be used for education and other economic endeavors, while Section 16 authorized "any Indian tribe, or tribes, residing on the same reservation" to "organize for the purpose of receiving" the charters.[30]

The Alaska provisions in the IRA offered another opportunity for the ANB and other Alaska Native organizations and villages to articulate their practice and theory of nationhood and sovereignty and influence the ways the federal government delineated their land rights. To do so, they leveraged the distinctions lawmakers and government officials had long employed to deny them nation-to-nation negotiating status in their favor, seeking amendments to the IRA that might reflect the current and historical political organizations and property laws of their communities. To this end, William Paul Sr. worked with Territorial Delegate Anthony Joseph Dimond to remind lawmakers that the federal government did not consider Alaska Natives "tribes" as the term had been defined in federal Indian law. As such, restricting eligibility for IRA incorporation to "tribe or tribes" would be effectively prohibiting many if not all Alaska Natives from utilizing even those specific sections of the legislation that Congress had extended to the territory. They contended that because there are "no recognized Indian reservations, tribes or bands in Alaska . . . it would be undesirable to carry over . . . the requirement . . . that organization be restricted to the Indians of a single tribe, band, or reservation."[31] Additionally, as Alaska Natives adapted to US occupation, many villages had come to consist of members from a variety of localities who had developed a range of economic, social, and political relationships within and outside of the customary clan structures. In this vein, they sought ways by which the IRA might recognize historical political relationships and accommodate ongoing adaptations. To achieve this, they proposed the following amendment to the IRA, which they "based upon the language of section 9 of the Federal Credit Union Act" of 1934: "Provided, That groups of Indians in Alaska not heretofore recognized as bands or tribes, but having a common bond of occupation, or association, or residence within a well-defined neighborhood, community or rural district, may organize to adopt constitutions and bylaws and to receive charters of incorporation and Federal loans under sections 16, 17, and 10 of the Act of June 18, 1934 (48 Stat. 984)."[32]

Although Congress initially excluded Alaska Natives from Section 7 of the IRA, which addressed Indian landholdings, the final version of the Alaska Reorganization Act of 1936 included Paul's recommendations, which the Interior Department and members of Congress ultimately conceded would only function appropriately if Alaska Natives were included in the IRA's land provisions. The application of Section 7 to Alaska was of particular importance, as it authorized the secretary of the interior to "proclaim new Indian reservations . . . or to add such lands to existing reservations," and in a letter to the Senate Committee on Indian Affairs, Interior Secretary Harold Ickes argued that without Section 7, the remainder of the IRA was incompatible with Alaska. He contended that for "Indians in Alaska" who "are to set up systems of local government," it was "necessary to identify [them] with the land [they] occup[y]" such that the "geographical limits of their jurisdictions" might also be defined. Furthermore, Ickes suggested that by providing for reservations in Alaska, "the United States Government will have fulfilled in part its moral and legal obligation in the protection of the economic rights of Alaska's Natives."[33] Congress concurred, adopting the ARA with nearly all of Ickes's recommendations.

The inclusion of Alaska Natives in the IRA was not an admission of the existence of Aboriginal title in Alaska, nor did it constitute recognition of Alaska Native nationhood or sovereignty. Rather, the Interior Department, along with other government officials and lawmakers, likely worried that Congress's passage of the Tlingit and Haida Jurisdictional Act the previous year had potentially opened up the entire territory to litigation that could foreclose access to fishing, timber, and mining extractables. To minimize this threat, the Interior Department rejected the flexible spirit in which the ANB had sought their amendments and began restricting the ways Alaska Natives might organize, incorporate, and petition for reservations. According to protests from

William Paul, the Interior Department began rejecting petitions for charters of incorporation from all entities except villages. Paul refuted this interference in a long letter to Ickes in 1937 in which he warned that such restrictions would "mix the Alaska business up so badly that the very purpose of the law will be defeated." To Paul, the Alaska Reorganization Act had been crafted to specifically accommodate the variety of historical, customary, and changing conditions and affiliations of Alaska Native people. He argued, "These people are held by a common bond of association based on a common language, legends, custom, clan system, totemic system, house system, membership in fraternal societies, religious societies, schools, and by residence. The ramifications are endless and are of such a nature that by careful selection an organizer could accomplish any given purpose."[34] Importantly, limiting eligible groups to village membership threatened to cut across clan and house lines, and while he conceded that "Indian villages should be encouraged to organize as one unit," it "is more important that groups so organized are harmonious." Paul's intended interpretation of the phrase "common bond of association" included any "number of persons or things" without restriction. He attributed the Interior Department's interpretation of tribal and village organization in Alaska as the result of "a total lack of information on that subject" and believed that in order to render the IRA effective in Alaska, the Interior Department needed to allow for selective organization.

The implementation of the IRA in Alaska was contested and controversial, as many Alaska Native communities debated the efficacy of reservations in actualizing their land rights. The process by which they prompted federal officials and lawmakers to debate and consider the possibility of collective tribal land rights in Alaska was nevertheless crucial. In the following decades, the ANB, ANS, and other emerging land rights organizations across the state injected these possibilities, born of uncertainty and ambiguity, into numerous plans for settler infrastructure and commercial extraction projects to the chagrin of lawmakers and corporate interests. In this way, they mobilized their identities as citizens to articulate the values, land regimes, and legal orders of their clan-structured societies into federal Indian law in ways that fundamentally informed their ongoing strategies. This became increasingly relevant in the years leading up to World War II, when the role of Alaska in global geopolitics added new and unprecedented pressures to these struggles for Alaska Native land and ways of life.

The Pivot of Empire

The struggle over the Indigenous land and citizenship rights in Alaska was part of a much broader contest over the meaning and function of territories in US empire. As mentioned briefly above, the Interior Department transferred the administration of Alaska Native affairs from the Bureau of Education to the BIA in 1931, apparently signaling further integration of Alaska and Alaska Natives within the scope of national territory and national policy following formal territorial incorporation at the turn of the century. This move toward the appearance of uniformity of law and policy in Alaska was hardly a seamless transition and drew objections from a number of government officials and lawmakers. Likewise, formal designation of Alaska as an incorporated territory did not resolve tensions around how government officials understood the relationship of Alaska to the nation proper. Many envisioned Alaska not as a settler space but rather as an auxiliary appendage that functioned in support of domestic and international projects for a national collective to which it was not entirely integrated. These paradoxes in Alaska's relation to the nation proper informed and influenced new techniques of dispossession and Alaska Native resistance to US occupation and thus need to be understood in the larger context of increasing international tensions in the decade prior to World War II. While government officials were working diligently to weave Alaska into the broader narrative of US frontier expansion, they were also theorizing the ways territories could facilitate imperial projects that furthered US interests and hardened boundaries between what was part of and proximate to the US settler nation.

Alaska, as a quasi-inside-outside space, provided an important geographic and narrative locale for these experiments in boundary-making in two important projects in domestic and imperial administration. The first was the Matanuska Valley Colony, a New Deal initiative in which the federal government relocated roughly two hundred families from Minnesota, Wisconsin, and Michigan to Southcentral Alaska in the heart of Dena'ina homelands. By 1934, the turmoil of the Great Depression had ravaged farm families across the Midwest, and the Roosevelt administration sought ways to alleviate destitute Americans. The second was the proposal to populate Alaska with refugee colonies in the wake of increasing antisemitism in Europe. Government officials envisioned the territory, its agricultural potential, and its stores of natural resources as having the ability to facilitate economic stability in the midst of the Great Depression by providing employment opportunities and new markets for American manufactured goods through government-supported development projects that would establish a permanent base of white settlers. These settlers and the infrastructure they helped establish could, in turn, support military objectives across the Pacific. To this end, President Roosevelt, through executive order, established the Division of Territories and Island Possessions in 1934, under which he consolidated the administration of Puerto Rico, the Virgin Islands, Alaska, Hawai'i, and the Philippines, along with a number of Pacific islands and atolls. These areas became critical to US strategic interests, and in the mid-1930s federal officials considered Alaska especially significant to national security and global ambitions. Both the Matanuska Colony and the proposals for refugee colonies failed—the former largely due to poor planning and the abandonment of the colony by colonists and the latter due to the xenophobic and antisemitic sentiments of Congress and Alaska Territorial officials. Together, they nevertheless reveal the elaborate process of boundary management at the edges of empire.

By the mid-1930s, lawmakers had become increasingly concerned that Alaska's low population of US citizens would make the territory difficult to defend in the advent of global war. The Homestead Act had failed to attract large numbers of permanent settlers, thus Alaska Territorial Governor John Weir Troy agreed to plans by the Federal Emergency Relief Administration's Division of Rural Rehabilitation to solve the problem of Alaska's low population of white settlers through government-funded colonization efforts. In 1898, the federal government had established the first agricultural experiment station at Sitka, followed by several more in the Interior after the turn of the century. These included the Matanuska Experiment Station, established in 1915, which amid the Great Depression was selected to host the Matanuska Colony. To this end, the federal government gave "provincial colonization" a frontier facade, framing the project as the continuation of a distinctly American tradition in which independent, yeoman farmers would pioneer into the wilderness, converting it to productive farmland. Though public framing for the endeavor aimed to inspire nostalgia for frontier settlement, the Matanuska Colony reveals the important ways the Roosevelt administration perceived the utility of territories in mitigating both domestic and international tensions. Lawrence Westbrook, the director of the Division of Rural Rehabilitation, wrote that the inspiration for the colony had come from the 1847 English pamphlet "Systematic Colonization" by Arthur Mills. Mills had advocated that colonization projects were the solution to the problems arising from large numbers of "poverty-stricken people of England." Rather than the last chapter in United States westward expansion, Westbrook instead considered the Matanuska Colony to be America's "first venture into provincial colonization."[35]

Despite the fanfare accompanying the departure of the families of colonists from their homes in the Midwest to Southcentral Alaska, the Matanuska Valley Colonization Project was plagued by constant difficulties. Clearing the land took much longer than anticipated, and the two hundred families soon became disillusioned. Like the extension of the Homestead Act to Alaska, the Matanuska Colony failed to encourage any notable migration of white settlers to the territory. As early as June of 1935—just a few short weeks after their arrival—a number of colony families were requesting that they be returned to the United States, and monthly reports of the colony reveal that it was hemorrhaging members.[36] By 1940, only 106 of the original families remained, confirming for many that the colonists were nothing more than a group of "subsidized and deluded trekkers" and that the government's attempts at colonization were interfering with the interests of those who considered themselves to be proper settlers.[37]

Despite marketing Alaska as the nation's new, albeit last, frontier, the anticipated waves of US citizens eager to perform their settler homesteading birthright failed to materialize, and government officials began to explore the possibility of enacting legislation that would permit the immigration of select groups of European refugees to US territories. In November of 1938, the Foreign Policy Association released a report calling for international loans to finance emigration in the wake of rising antisemitism in Central Europe, and the Conference on Jewish Relations reached out to Felix S. Cohen concerning a possible refugee colonization project in Paraguay. In response, Cohen and other Interior

Department officials began exploring options to resettle European refugees in Alaska by creating a new category of nonquota immigrants who could reside in US territories. They imagined that doing so could alleviate domestic economic pressure by establishing new markets for American manufacturers while also buttressing national defense through increasing Alaska's population.[38] They also imagined that territories could be spaces in which to establish new tiers of citizenship and immigration status that would achieve these goals while barring entry of those awarded these new citizenship categories to the United States proper.

The Interior Department investigated the feasibility of this proposal and released a report in 1940 entitled *The Problem of Alaskan Development*. Often referred to as the Slattery Report, it cited factors such as the high cost of living and lack of employment opportunities as preventing significant numbers of Americans from emigrating to and remaining in Alaska; however, it concluded that the most significant deterrent was "the effects of Immigration laws."[39] Interior officials pointed to the Immigration Act of 1924 and the system of quotas that restricted immigration into the United States as having a disproportionate effect in Alaska "whose future well-being depends on new immigration and new capital."[40] They supported these findings by comparing "two styles" of "planned immigration" by which the federal government had facilitated the relocation of two different communities to Alaska: the Matanuska Valley Colonization Project and the Metlakatla Indian Community. Whereas the Matanuska Colony had been largely unsuccessful, the report argued that colonists who had remained since their arrival in 1935 had yet to establish a self-sustaining agricultural community and that even their intermittent seasonal success had come at great expense to the federal government. They argued that Metlakatla, however, was a more appropriate model. The Metlakatlan Indian community consisted of Tsimshian peoples who had migrated from British Columbia and settled on Annette Island in Southeast Alaska, along with an Anglican missionary who petitioned the federal government for an Indian reservation for their benefit. Father Duncan claimed the community had fled Canada under threat of religious persecution. When Congress created the Indian reservation in 1891, they justified doing so on account that the Metlakatlans were a category of "foreign Indians" who, despite living a "civilized" and industrious life as "god-fearing people" in Canada, had been dispossessed and abused by the Church of England such that they fled to a territory of the United States in search of refuge. Indeed, even Senator Henry L. Dawes, the architect of allotment policy, conceded that their experience and what he considered to be their elevated level of "common sense in the matter of civilization than any Indians I ever saw anywhere" warranted a permanent Indian reservation.[41]

In the decades following the establishment of the Annette Island Indian Reservation, Metlakatla had developed a thriving timber industry, and its community members represented what Interior Department officials considered to be an "outstanding example in recent times of a successful refugee colony."[42] They mused in the report that successful colonization in the territory was perhaps more probable with "a group of human beings bound together by a common tragic experience and by common ideals" rather than those, like the Matanuska colonists, "who can go back to a more or less comfortable existence if they tire of Alaska."[43] They proffered a solution in which public purpose development corporations would be formed to facilitate relocation and settlement in Alaska and that, while sincere attempts should be made to "find qualified American citizens," it was inevitable that they would "have to look for skilled workers in foreign communities."[44] To do so would require legislation allowing for exceptions to the stringent immigration regulations in the 1924 Immigration Act.

To convince Congress to approve the immigration of people whom the 1924 Immigration Act had sought to exclude, the architects of the legislation proposed that Alaska's territorial status made it ideal for housing colonies of noncitizens who would not be permitted to enter the United States proper. These efforts led to the consideration of two bills by Congress: S. 3577, A Bill to Provide for the Settlement and Development of Alaska, known as the King-Havenner Bill, and H.R. 2791, A Bill Providing for the Utilization of Unfilled Immigration Quotas in Order to Colonize Alaska for Purposes of National Defense and as a Market for Surplus Production.[45] Both bills represent the ways the Roosevelt administration sought to use territories to manage the boundaries of national space, mobilizing them as places where new categories of legal residency might facilitate military and economic objectives. In both Alaska and the Virgin Islands, the administration proposed establishing "restricted alien settlements" to which the refugees would be confined in order to prevent their migration to the contiguous states. Specifically, the Alaska legislation provided for the establishment of Alaska development corporations that, with the approval of the secretary of the interior, "certify as settlers persons not ineligible to citizenship . . . as non-quota immigrants . . . solely for entry into and residence in the Territory of Alaska."[46] The bill stipulated that any nonquota immigrants admitted under its provisions must reside in Alaska for a period of five years, at which time they would be eligible to apply for reclassification as a quota immigrant "if the quota for that year has not otherwise been filled."[47] If any person who entered Alaska as a nonquota immigrant attempted to travel to the contiguous states, they would be subject to imprisonment, fines, and deportation. Secretary of the Interior Harold Ickes argued in Senate hearings that the settlement of Alaska with chartered communities of nonquota immigrants would first and foremost "be promptly reflected in a proportionate expansion of the Alaskan market for American products."[48] Importantly, he referred to similar provisions that had already been established, for example, to provide admission to the territory of Hawaiʻi for immigrants not entitled to enter the continental United States.[49] Likewise, President Roosevelt had entertained the idea of allowing, through both Congress and executive order, the migration of Jewish refugees to the Virgin Islands and potentially Alaska to solve labor shortages while responding to the growing humanitarian crisis in Europe.[50] In this vein, territories could be useful in the project of defining and maintaining, along lines of race and national origin, the desired national character of lands considered within the nation proper as reflected in the 1924 Immigration Act.

Ultimately, both bills failed to become law. Those who objected consisted mostly of white settlers and territorial officials in Alaska who feared that if federal officials could set Alaska apart as "an area to which aliens may be admitted, but cannot come to other parts of the United States," it may very well compromise their own citizenship status.[51] Territorial Delegate Anthony Dimond lamented that the abridged rights of nonquota immigrants along with the burden the bill would place on Alaskans who were US citizens would set a dangerous precedent. He protested that "anyone traveling from Alaska to the States would be obliged to show that he was not a member of one of the restricted alien settlements" and that current residents of Alaska opposed turning the territory into a "semipenal colony."[52] To them, the designation of Alaska as a place in which variations in citizenship categories distinguished the territory from the contiguous states ran headlong into the implications of incorporated territorial status and the frontier narrations that lawmakers and judges had employed to distinguish Alaska from those they considered to be unincorporated territories forty years prior. To federal officials, Alaska, along with other territories and island possessions, represented critical spaces of empire on which the federal government relied to advance military and economic interests. To those ends, the proposed variations in the citizenship status of nonquota immigrants functioned similarly to the withholding of Indian status and federal Indian law from Alaska Natives in that both were part of a broader settler imperial apparatus that sought to establish and maintain territories, regardless of incorporated status, as places outside the borders of properly national territory and therefore outside the scope of the Constitution.

The Spanish-American War and the initiation of possessory claims by the United States to additional noncontiguous territories ushered in a new and important context for the ways Alaska Natives sought to negotiate increasing settler presence. In this context, Native leaders pursued citizenship and voting rights to increase their say in regional and territorial affairs and federal legislation and to assert their land rights in court. Importantly, they staked their claim to US citizenship on their status as Indians and their assertion that federal Indian policy applied to them. As US citizens and Indigenous Alaskans, they then mobilized elements of the US legal system that protected Indian land and the property rights of citizenship in seeking federal legislation that would recognize this spectrum of land rights. They did this by drawing on the ambiguities that lawmakers had ascribed to their legal status, situating themselves as potential future prior owners of Alaska whose rights in the land hung over any proposed infrastructure or extractive projects and white settlement. In their efforts, they seized on a moment in which the meanings of citizenship, US–Indigenous relations, territories, and national space were in tremendous flux, devising strategies that they hoped would achieve an outcome that sustained their own long-standing legal, political, economic, and cultural orders and the land regimes that supported them.

4

Denying Sovereignty

The Corporate-Military Crucible and the Erasure of Native Nationhood

In the years immediately following passage of the Tlingit and Haida Jurisdictional Act and the Alaska amendments to the Indian Reorganization Act (IRA), Alaska Natives leveraged the implications inherent in both types of settlement structures to assert and exercise their Indigenous land rights and to define their roles in Alaska's future as US citizens.[1] The Alaska Native Brotherhood formed the Central Council of Tlingit and Haida Indian Tribes of Alaska (CCTHITA) in 1939 to pursue the federal lawsuit *Tlingit and Haida Indians of Alaska v. United States,* and villages and other Native organizations across the territory began the process by which to incorporate under the IRA, secure loans for economic development, and file petitions for the establishment of Indian reservations with the Department of the Interior.[2] As part of this vision, some villages in Southeast Alaska sought to open their own canneries and fishing operations, and an increasing number of Alaska Natives in Southeast and Southcentral Alaska sought to supplement their subsistence economies through wage work. To them, citizenship guaranteed their participation in local and national politics where they might influence regulations that affected their lands and livelihoods and that offered opportunities to diversify their economies. Affirmation of their land rights through the IRA amendments buttressed these objectives and provided a means by which they might sustain the cultural, social, and political values and reciprocal attachments between themselves, the land, and nonhuman kin. Together, citizenship along with land rights recognized through IRA reservations could allow Alaska Natives to accommodate and negotiate settler and corporate commercial presence in less disruptive ways, allowing for their collective continuance as Indigenous Alaskans.

At the same time, settlers, corporations, government officials, and lawmakers sought to curb these efforts and responded by escalating the systemic racial exclusion of Alaska Natives from housing, education, employment, and public accommodations and by lobbying against federal protections for Alaska Native lands. World War II exacerbated these tensions as the rhetoric of democracy and equality employed by the Roosevelt administration to garner and sustain support for the war effort gave Alaska Natives leverage in combating discrimination while bolstering settler and corporate claims that IRA reservations in Alaska gave Alaska Natives an unfair economic advantage on account of their race. Just three weeks after the United States entered into the war, Alaska Native Brotherhood (ANB) and Alaska Native Sisterhood (ANS) Grand Camp Leaders Roy Peratrovich (Eagle, Flicker House, Naasteidi, Kooyu K̲wáan) and Elizabeth Peratrovich (Lukaax̲.ádi) wrote to Alaska's territorial governor, Ernest Gruening.[3] In their letter they requested his aid in their struggle to eliminate racial segregation and discrimination against Alaska Natives. They wrote, "Our Native boys are just as willing as the White boys to lay down their lives to protect the freedom that he enjoys." They continued, "We were shocked when the Jews were discriminated against in Germany. Stories were told of public places having signs, 'No Jews Allowed.' All freedom loving people in our country were horrified at these reports, yet it is being practiced in our own country."[4] Like their African American counterparts, Alaska Natives keenly understood that a war waged abroad in the name of freedom and democracy was not reflected in the realities at home.[5] These contradictions were especially glaring for Alaska Natives who had volunteered in the Alaska Territorial Guard, patrolling two hundred thousand miles of tundra and five thousand miles of coastline only to return home and encounter signs advertising "We Do Not Cater to the Indian or Filipino Trade" and "Meals at All Hours—White Help Only."[6]

During World War II and in the postwar years, government officials and corporate interests also escalated their use of the Euro-American rhetoric of equal citizenship and emerging civil rights discourse against Indigenous land rights. As the Interior Department approved IRA reservations, Territorial Governor Ernest Gruening, along with corporate fisheries and timber interests, protested settler and commercial exclusion from lands they considered to be part of the public domain. Gruening would argue throughout his tenure as territorial governor that Indian reservations threatened economic development of Alaska and prevented Alaska Natives from becoming "equal citizens of the Territory—politically, economically, [and] socially."[7] In contesting reservations, he repeatedly appealed to the racial and legal distinctions whereby Alaska Natives and their lands had been excluded from federal Indian policy. In this way, he—like others before him—animated the ambiguity around Alaska Native legal status in order to prevent their recognition as Indigenous polities entitled to retroactive redemptive purchase for lands already appropriated by non-Natives and as owners of lands not yet transformed into property and for which the United States must negotiate.

Corporations and their attorneys and lobbyists likewise balked at the barriers that Alaska Native land rights posed to their operations, and they also voiced their opposition in the rhetoric of racial equality. They contended that Native reservations unfairly denied white-owned businesses equal access to what they understood as extractable commodities. They argued further that this race-based exclusion would undermine the war effort as well as postwar economic stability and national security by discouraging white settlers from taking up permanent residence in the territory. To this end, equal rights rhetoric buttressed the ways corporate interests aligned themselves with US strategic military and economic interests. While most historians remark on Alaska's military significance in terms of its strategic geographic location, federal officials, lawmakers, and military personnel also worried that Alaska's rich stores of so-called untapped resources would make it the target of potential aggressor nations. Throughout the nineteenth century, the region had been fraught with European and US competition over ocean resources such as whales, fur seals, and walrus. Indeed, one of the first acts of the federal government after establishing possessory claims had been to issue a contract for fur seal harvesting off the Pribilof Islands, a lucrative business from which, by 1943, the federal government collected revenues upward of $1 million annually.[8]

Corporate contracts for commodity extraction had long been an objective of US claims to possession of Alaska, and in the interwar years Congress took measures to protect the territory against the designs of hostile competitors. Policymakers and military officials understood wartime success and postwar economic stability and national security in terms of US military hegemony, and US territories were critical to these ends.[9] In anticipation of future military conflicts, Congress passed the Wilcox Air Base Act in 1935, which authorized the construction of numerous air bases in areas of the contiguous US west, the Panama

Canal Zone, and Alaska. During WWII, the bill and its underlying premises facilitated the transformation of the commercial airline now known as Alaska Airlines into the largest charter operator in the world by the end of WWII.[10] Prior to 1947, the United States had no official air force, and the federal government eyed the capabilities of Alaska commercial bush pilots to fly in and out of areas known for difficult terrain and unpredictable weather conditions. Through government contracts and the distribution of surplus military supplies, Alaska Airlines became a critical experiment in federal appropriation of civilian labor, logistics, and equipment capacities for executing military operations on the far side of the globe. To this end, Alaska Airlines pilots and aircraft participated in the Berlin Airlift of 1948 and Operation Magic Carpet, which populated Palestinian homelands with nearly fifty thousand Yemenite Jewish settlers in the fall of 1949. This entanglement of corporate airlines and national defense laid the foundation for the creation of a permanent Civil Reserve Air Fleet (CRAF), which most recently facilitated the evacuation of troops and refugees following the US withdrawal from Afghanistan in 2021.[11]

The ambiguity around Alaska's relationship to the nation proper and the legal status of Alaska Natives had facilitated these projects, and this chapter traces the ways government officials and corporate interests were quick to merge their opposition to Native land rights with postwar economic stability. As Alaska Natives doubled down on their status as polities eligible for both preemptive negotiation and redemptive purchase for their lands at the close of WWII, lawmakers sought access to the old growth spruce and hemlock forests that constituted Tlingit and Haida homelands. Territorial officials and logging interests conceived of these forests as untapped timber resources with the potential to support postwar Alaskan economic development as a matter of national interest. To achieve access to the Tongass, they worked with Congress to pass the 1947 Tongass Timber Act, which permitted the federal government to lease Tlingit and Haida lands for timber harvesting. Advocates for the bill's passage drew on the long-standing argument that Alaska Natives were not "tribes" and therefore had no collective land rights the government was required to negotiate for prior to issuing leases.[12] They argued further that if Aboriginal title had existed in Alaska, the territorial legislature's enactment of the Alaska Anti-Discrimination Act nullified such rights in lieu of equal citizenship.[13]

In their opposition to the bill, Tlingit and Haida people rearticulated the very ambiguities these officials hoped would secure access to the Tongass, arguing that failure to preemptively negotiate land rights presented a significant risk to investors should the CCTHITA prevail in *Tlingit and Haida Indians of Alaska v. United States*. These threats of legal uncertainty and the potential liability worried some corporate investors, thus Congress attempted to assuage these fears by including a clause in the Tongass Timber Act mandating that profits be held in escrow until the courts determined the nature of Alaska Native land rights. In this way, the Tongass Timber Act exemplified the utility of settler imperial ambiguities in extending the temporal window of the recursive function of dispossession. Holding profits in escrow would allow timber companies to strip Tlingit and Haida forests and destroy the habitat of salmon, moose, bear, otter, and other nonhuman relations while relocating the possibility of redemptive purchase to an unspecified date in the future. Ultimately, the ways Alaska Natives also leveraged these ambiguities and the risks they posed to corporate profits prevented unilateral foreclosing of their rights as Indigenous Alaskans.

The debates for and following passage of the Tongass Timber Act had implications beyond Alaska, as lawmakers contemplated the ease with which they could access land and commodifiable resources in the territory in the absence of tribes and tribal reservations. In this context, their focus expanded from repealing the IRA amendments in Alaska to the possibility of repealing tribal status in the contiguous states.[14] Many of the lawmakers that weighed in on the Tongass Timber Act predominantly represented states with sizable Indigenous populations and landholdings in the form of reservations. As they developed their arguments in favor of the bill, they did so by claiming that the absence of tribes and a reservation system in Alaska had contributed to Alaska Native assimilation into and capacity to contribute to the territorial economy. They suggested that the recent Alaska Native civil rights movement and passage of the Alaska Anti-Discrimination Act evidenced the expediency with which the lack of reservations and alleged absence of tribes in Alaska facilitated economic objectives while offering a testament to the benevolence of US democracy. This rhetoric came to buttress the arguments of lawmakers who posed tribal governments and tribal landholdings as barriers to settler access to land and extractable commodities in their own states, thus in the years preceding termination policy,

Alaska's legal landscape figured prominently, revealing the ways settler imperial logics occasionally tracked back toward the core of empire.

"Never Desired to Be Treated as Wards"

The rhetoric of equal citizenship and the ambiguities around Alaska Native tribal status escalated in 1943 when the ANB and ANS brought antidiscrimination legislation to the territorial legislature. That same year, the Interior Department approved applications for a 1.4 million–acre Indian reservation for the Venetie Neets'ąįį Gwich'in and the thirty-five-thousand-acre Karluk fishing reserve for the Alutiiq/Sugpiaq communities of Kodiak Island, the latter of which included offshore fishing waters.[15] The Karluk reserve included a ban on any non-Native fishing activities within three thousand feet of shore, reflecting recent Department of Fisheries regulations that prohibited the placement of fish traps in locations to "which any Alaskan native or natives has or have any rights of fishery, by virtue of any grant or by virtue of aboriginal occupancy."[16] The implementation of the IRA in Alaska was likewise bolstered by the 1942 opinion of Interior Solicitor Nathan Ross Margold, in which he likened Alaska Native land rights and legal status to the Aboriginal rights of tribal nations in the contiguous states. He argued that "aboriginal occupancy of particular areas of water or submerged land creates legal rights which, unless they have been extinguished, the Department is bound to recognize."[17] He informed federal officials that Alaska Natives occupied a similar legal status to "Indians of the continental United States" due to their dependency "upon the Federal Government for the vindication and protection of their property rights," concluding that the federal government could not deny "the present existence of these rights" simply because they had not "received adequate protection in the past."[18] Margold's opinion warned that despite the absence of treaties, formal recognition of Aboriginal title, or nation-to-nation negotiations with Alaska Natives, the federal government was constitutionally obliged to protect Alaska Native land rights in congruence with policies in the contiguous states and territories.

With a number of additional petitions for reservations pending in the Interior Department, white settlers, territorial officials, lawmakers, and commercial fishing and timber corporations began challenging the validity of Native land claims. The commercial fishing industry had long benefited from the unsettled nature of Indigenous land rights in Alaska, and after the passage of the Alaska amendments to the IRA, they worried that the Interior Department could "establish any reservation it might see fit." Furthermore, the act implied that the government would not be obliged to compensate cannery owners for the loss of the "large expenditure of private capital investments" made in areas with pending reservation applications should they be forced to close their operations at those locations.[19] Many bemoaned that "it is apparent that the Indians have it in mind to take over a large part of the fishing grounds of Alaska" and that the whole policy of the federal government was "directed toward transferring the ownership of fish traps from white owners to Indian owners and the general turning over of the fishery industry of Alaska from white to Indian operation."[20]

Challenging the application of the IRA in Congress, before the Interior Department, and in the courts, white settlers, corporations, and their allies in the territorial government argued that Indian reservations in Alaska ran contrary to the long history of legal distinctions between Alaska Natives and tribal nations of the contiguous states, undermined the premises of equal citizenship, and threatened national security. Attorneys for various commercial fishing entities refuted Margold's opinion and subsequent fishing regulations, claiming "there was not in Alaska the same tribal relationship which existed among the Indians with which we are more familiar in the United States proper. The Indians of Alaska were not dealt with as tribes. They became and are full American citizens."[21] Governor Gruening and other territorial officials agreed, concurring that the creation of Indian reservations did not reflect Alaska Native legal status, was incompatible with the ANB and ANS advocacy for antidiscrimination legislation, and undermined plans to develop Alaska economically. Gruening admonished Interior Department officials, warning that "Indian policy and practice which work well in the states" would not "do so in Alaska." He continued that "the establishment of reservations in a territory where . . . there have been none, will among other numerous consequences set us far back in the matter of discrimination. If large areas . . . are suddenly made the exclusive prerequisite of one race, retaliation in some form or other . . . will accentuate race prejudice and cleavage."[22] He likened Indian reservations to "inverted Jim Crowism" that would be "as tragic for the 'natives' as it is for whites" in that reservations would interrupt "an orderly and sound development of the Territory by inciting racial animosity . . . by strictures setting aside widespread areas of 'no trespassing-by-whites.'"[23] While Gruening did not support ongoing exploitation of Alaska's resources by absentee corporations, he nevertheless advocated for access to fishing waters on the basis of equal citizenship. To this end, he suggested that because Alaska Natives constituted nearly half the population, "it follows that they would, and should, under such a policy receive corresponding benefits."[24] To him and the corporate fishing interests, citizenship rendered the federal obligation to reconcile Alaska Native land rights obsolete.

In the context of global war, citizenship carried additional currency, and opponents of Native land rights argued that Indian reservations in Alaska threatened to undermine national interests and American efforts in WWII. In the spring of 1944, William Paul Sr. filed petitions for the Tee-Hit-Ton of Wrangell, members of the Juneau Tlingit Alaska Indian Geographical Division, members of the Douglas Tlingit Alaska Indian Geographical Division, and members of the Sitka Tlingit Alaska Indian Geographical Division in which they claimed ownership of their lands in addition to "the fish that swim along the shores of said area within 3,000 feet."[25] In response, Juneau attorney H. L. Faulkner warned that disruption to the supply of canned salmon by way of Indian reservations constituted another "tragedy . . . that the administration at Washington in a time when the country is engaged in a war which assumes more and more every day the aspects of a life-or-death struggle, should continue its assaults on all those engaged in the production of the things the country and the world so desperately need."[26] By framing Native fishing rights and landholdings as adversarial to the war effort, he implied that Alaska Natives and the Interior Department officials who supported them were in dereliction of their patriotic responsibilities as US citizens "at a time when we should all be bending every effort to save our country from impending disaster."[27]

The nature of the petitions filed on behalf of Tlingit communities refuted both Gruening's claims that citizenship nullified Native land rights and Faulkner's charges that Native land and fishing rights impugned Native citizenship. Rather, the petitioners suggested that their ancestral rights to "exclusive possession of land, submerged land, and waters" constituted the means by which Alaska Natives could establish an economic foothold in developing capitalist markets. Alaska Native communities had taken up seining, blending their subsistence practices with capitalist endeavors in ways that would allow them to contribute to the salmon supply as US citizens engaged in the national economy. They alleged in their petitions that the federal government's failure to protect their ancestral rights had allowed corporate fish traps to impede the salmon runs "in complete derogation of the property rights of the petitioner and its members" and "in such large numbers that said seining grounds were rendered valueless." This in turn "forced [them] to obtain a livelihood elsewhere."[28] In other words, their land rights as Indigenous people were what provided them the means to exercise their rights as citizens in a settler-capital legal order that valued and protected property. Alaska Natives perceived their US citizenship not as an exchange of one set of rights for another but rather as coconstitutive identities and political statuses that mutually reinforced one another. Their status as Indigenous people within a US incorporated territory had qualified them for citizenship, and their ability to express and exercise their citizenship rights was a direct function of their rights as Indigenous people.[29]

Gruening and his counterparts in the fishing industry continued to situate US citizenship as incompatible with Native land rights and political sovereignty generally and argued that citizenship for Alaska Natives was the outcome of the history of legal distinctions between Alaska Natives and tribes in the contiguous states. In his statement to the 1944 ANB Annual Convention, Gruening warned that policies that excluded white people from certain areas of the territory constituted the same kind of racial discrimination that Alaska Natives experienced in their exclusion from housing, education, and public accommodations. He coupled this with the reminder that unlike Indigenous people in the contiguous states who required protection from the government, the situation in Alaska had been significantly different; thus, the rights of Alaska Natives had historically been mitigated through eligibility for US citizenship instead of government wardship. He stated that "in southeastern Alaska the Native peoples have never desired to be treated as wards in the same sense that Indians have been in other parts of the United States" and that "certain restrictive legislation which applies to Indians in the United States does not apply to them here."[30] By this logic, Gruening situated wardship as both a precondition for the recognition of tribal land rights and a status incompatible with citizenship, which allowed him and his counterparts to posit two conclusions that suspended recognition of Alaska Native land rights as eligible for preemptive negotiation or redemptive purchase in the logic of dispossession. The first conclusion foreclosed preemptive purchase on the assumption that nation-to-nation negotiations not only made property out of land but also made wards out of tribal members by confining them to reservations following the cession of other portions of their territory to the federal government. The second conclusion foreclosed redemptive purchase on the assumption that because Alaska Natives had never been wards of the government or confined to reservations, they had never been dispossessed. Contrary to policies in the contiguous states, Gruening argued that Alaska Natives had been permitted to "live pretty generally in the villages where they have always lived" and could "be counted upon to continue to live there" and therefore had not been dispossessed or removed in similar fashion to Indigenous people of the contiguous states and territories.[31]

Attorneys for the fishing industry echoed Gruening's arguments. Juneau attorney H. L. Faulkner scoffed at the attempt by Alaska Natives to assert exclusive fishing rights, and his objection also rested on the contention that Alaska Natives had not experienced dispossession from their homelands similarly to that experienced by tribal nations in the contiguous states. In a letter to the Alaska Packers Association, he contended that "so far as fishing for their own use is concerned, they have never been deprived of that right and they can still hunt and fish where they please." He also rejected the argument put forth by Paul in the petitions for fishing rights that protection of exclusive Native possession of their ancestral lands and fishing grounds was a function of their proprietary rights as citizens. Faulkner fumed that because he perceived Alaska Natives as having retained subsistence rights, "we must conclude what they want today is something in excess of that and the right to absolute dominion over the fisheries in certain areas so they may use them for commercial purposes."[32]

Alaska Natives lobbying for passage of antidiscrimination legislation rejected settler expectations of citizenship that would require the forfeiture of their land rights along with the social, cultural, economic, and legal orders the land supported. Native leadership in the ANB and ANS had worked closely with Gruening and other members of the territorial legislature for years on civil rights legislation, and they understood the logic by which non-Native people conceived of citizenship in relation to Indigenous land rights.[33] They also understood the fear of government officials and corporate interests that their access to Native land might be curtailed by reservations and profits diminished by monetary settlements, and they situated those possibilities strategically. For example, when the territorial legislature convened to debate the Alaska Anti-Discrimination Act in January 1945, ANB member Roy Peratrovich testified that failure to pass the bill would leave them no choice but to pursue reservations. He insisted that Alaska Natives "were opposed to any form of special privilege" and that, without equal protection under the law, they could "not stand beside you and aid you in your fight against Ickes."[34] To non-Native people, these statements may have appeared as though Peratrovich and other ANB and ANS members were willing to abandon their land rights in favor of equal citizenship. However, Indian reservations were not universally accepted among Alaska Native communities as the most effective way to preserve landholdings, and while legislators and territorial officials may have interpreted Peratrovich's statements as a rejection of land rights generally, he was more likely expressing concerns many had with the nature and terms of IRA reservations.[35] For example, the Native village of Utqiagvik scoffed at the proposed size of their reservation, leaving solicitor Irwin Silverman with the impression that "no local sentiment favors the setting aside of any area smaller than . . . 30,000 square miles."[36]

Peratrovich, Paul, and other Alaska Native leaders sought a variety of methods by which to achieve the best outcome in terms of land rights and the negotiation of settler and corporate presence. While not entirely convinced that reservations were the most effective means of protecting land rights, Peratrovich also continued to seek potential alternatives to the IRA, requesting an opinion from interior secretary attorney at large George Folta in the fall of 1944. Folta responded to Peratrovich's request regarding the possibilities for the resolution of Native land rights, stating that his "inquiry whether the natives of Alaska could be compensated in money for the loss of their aboriginal rights, must be answered in the affirmative." He continued to suggest that a combination

FIGURE 4. Governor Gruening signs the Alaska Anti-Discrimination Act. Witnessing are (*left to right*) O. D. Cochran, Elizabeth Peratrovich, Edward Anderson, Norman Walker, and Roy Peratrovich. Courtesy of Alaska State Library, Alaska Territorial Governors Collection, photographed by Amy Lou Blood for Ordway's, ASL-P274-1-2.

of "compensation alone [or] reservations" might be possible and that "adjudication of such rights" would likely need to proceed "in the Court of Claims."[37]

As WWII drew to a close and the Alaska Territorial Legislature passed the Alaska Anti-Discrimination Act in 1945, the ANB, ANS, and other Native organizations continued to press for land rights as corporate interests intensified their opposition to the IRA in Alaska. To this end, the corporate-military relationships forged in wartime defended these efforts, and Alaska Natives faced increasing assaults on their roles as Indigenous citizens in the context of postwar economic recovery and a tenuous peace to which territories became critical sites of US global hegemony.

"He Who Holds Alaska Holds the World"

In their attacks on Alaska Native land rights and citizenship during WWII, corporate interests had seized on the momentum of the interwar years in which federal officials and lawmakers had identified the strategic importance of Alaska in terms of both its geographic location and its stores of what they considered to be vast, untapped resources that would contribute to US military and economic security. In 1935, sandwiched among passage of the Indian Reorganization Act, the Tlingit and Haida Jurisdictional Act, and the Alaska Reorganization Act, Congress passed the Wilcox Air Base Act. The bill authorized the secretary of war to establish ten military posts known as "frontier defense bases" located around the perimeter of the contiguous states, the Rocky Mountains, the Great Lakes area, the Panama Canal, and the Territory of Alaska. These "frontier defense bases" would host one bombardment fleet and one coast defense fleet each, capable of accommodating "in an emergency, at least one thousand airplanes."[38] The bill reflects increasing concerns among lawmakers and military officials about the defensibility of US territories, the extractable raw materials in Alaska, and the transportation routes necessary for military and economic efficacy in mobilizing those resources and utilizing Alaska's strategic location. While historians have cataloged the strategic advantages of Alaska's northern location, along with the role that access to extractable resources played in strategizing for national defense, the ways these plans were contingent on access to Native land is less frequently addressed.[39] In this context, national defense interests provided an incentive to maintain the settler imperial ambiguities around the legal status of Alaska Natives and the nature of their land rights, making Alaska critical to understanding the entanglement of corporate and military objectives in the rise of US hegemony.

In congressional hearings for the Wilcox Air Base Bill, Brigadier General William Mitchell argued compellingly for a rigorous military buildup of Alaska. He claimed that Alaska was crucial in the successful development of any air defense program, both for its geographic location and for the territory's northern oceanic climate that would allow for training pilots to navigate the kinds of dangerous conditions they would encounter should the United States find itself at war with an adversary across the Pacific. He urged lawmakers at length to focus primarily on Alaska in terms of any air defense program, stating, "Alaska is the most central place in the world for aircraft, and that is true neither of Europe, Asia, or North America. I believe in the future he who holds Alaska will hold the world, and I think it is the most important strategic place in the world."[40]

While Alaska's strategic geographical location proved paramount for Mitchell in terms of the ability of the United States to reach far-off, overseas targets in the event of war, other lawmakers and military officials raised concerns about the vulnerability of the territory given its sparse Euro-American population and its millions of resource-rich acres that might prove desirable to other empires. Indeed, the bill's namesake, J. Mark Wilcox, began his introduction of the bill with an argument about the urgent need to safeguard Alaska's mineral resources from the designs of the Japanese empire. He warned that "another fact . . . that we cannot overlook . . . is that the Empire of Japan is entirely without metals" and that "Alaska is a veritable storehouse of minerals, and that it is closer to Japan than it is to the center of the Continental United States." Referring to the recent Japanese invasion of Manchuria, he continued that not only minerals but also the forests of Alaska "must be protected in case the ambitions of the Japanese should lead them to attempt to extend her Empire by appropriating some of our territory."[41] Other lawmakers and military officials agreed, proffering the fact that mineral and forest resources were not only vital for economic development but also "essential to any war program," with General Mitchell concurring that "any military effort against another nation must be an effort against its population and resources."[42]

Also advocating in favor of the bill was Alaska Territorial Delegate Anthony Joseph Dimond. He agreed with his counterparts regarding Alaska's strategic location for both defensive and offensive purposes, though after stating his concurrence he continued that "there is another sound reason . . . for the establishment of an air base . . . in Alaska; and that is to give training to the Army flyers." He recounted the tragic death of Colonel Carl Benjamin Eielson a few years prior, who, despite his skill as a pilot in Alaska and having been the first to fly a plane over the Arctic Ocean, had crashed during a subsequent flight. He recalled that when territorial officials requested aviators from the military to assist in the search for Eielson, they were informed that the military didn't have planes or pilots suited for Alaskan conditions. As a solution to this lack of capability, Dimond suggested that Alaska had another valuable resource to aid in developing and buttressing US military preparedness. He stated: "Now, our pilots fly up there. The commercial pilots fly almost every day, or every day, summer and winter. The flying conditions, of course, are not the same as in the United States. But we fly in the winter. We fly in fogs. It is very seldom that we have any difficulty. Let me say that if we had our base in Alaska . . . they could give every pilot some training in fog flying, in cold-weather flying, an experience that would be very difficult for them to get continuously anywhere else."[43] Dimond understood the need for pilots and aircraft capable of navigating Arctic conditions, and his lobbying for increased military presence in Alaska and his characterization of commercial pilots as poised to facilitate national defense initiatives would find traction in the transformation of a small regional private airline into the largest charter operation in the world in the years immediately following WWII. This merger of private enterprise and military utility was not entirely new, but it demonstrates the role of Alaska in facilitating experimental relationships between private corporations and military interests in the rise of US hegemony throughout the twentieth century and into the present.

By 1942, the military had begun utilizing commercial airlines—namely, Consairway and United Airlines—in shuttling crews, freight, mail, and key personnel across the Pacific as part of the air transport command, a unit of the army mobilized to transport equipment under the United States' lend-lease program. It is in this context that Alaska became critical to WWII and later Cold War international policy. Alaska served as a crucial delivery route of eight thousand lend-lease aircraft to aircrews in the Soviet Union, and the air bases and routes the military had constructed proved imperative when, as lawmakers and military officials had predicted when passing the Wilcox Air Base Bill, Japan did in fact invade Alaska. In 1942, commercial airlines "logged 90 percent of the air transport miles flown worldwide," leading military officials to consider "the impact of wartime decisions on the postwar situation of the airlines." The dependency of military operations in Europe on the employment of a civil air fleet revealed that the military had "no management structure available to organize or operate the far-flung enterprises required. The airlines, however, did, and contracting was a way of harnessing that management know-how."[44]

It is in this context that airlines in Alaska sought to expand their operations. Alaska Airlines originated as a small charter airline servicing remote villages under Linious McGee. Throughout the 1930s, McGee would sell what was at the time called Star Air Service to a group who renamed it Star Airlines, who then pursued a number of small mergers and buyouts within the territory. The new conglomerate would become Alaska Airlines in 1944. Shortly after WWII ended, the new airline's president James Wooten sought out and purchased war surplus Douglas DC-3, DC-4, and C-46 aircraft, converting them into full freighter aircraft. These purchases allowed him to secure military contracts to carry cargo in the 1948 Berlin Airlift, forging an important relationship between the private Alaska Airlines and the US military. The following year, Alaska Airlines pilots and aircraft transported nearly fifty thousand settlers from Yemen to the newly created state of Israel as part of the Zionist settler expulsion of Palestinians from their homelands.[45] In pursuit of postwar economic objectives and amid Cold War tensions, Israel became a key "aspect of U.S. militarization of the entire Middle East" and was, and remains, imperative to achieving and sustaining US hegemony.[46] To this end, the relationship between commercial airlines and the US military would become a permanent feature of this endeavor and its attendant projects as the federal government came to recognize "the employment of strategic air transport as an effective element to project national power."[47] During the war and in the years immediately after, domestic airlines achieved increasing utilization rates and expanded routes, and more firms transitioned into international carriers. Bolstered by the acquisition of surplus military aircraft and increasing world routes secured through Civil Aeronautics Board awards, commercial airlines had become so engrained in strategic defense that ATC Commander Maj. Gen. Robert Wells Harper commented in 1946 that "there is no military organization known to me that has, as a civil counterpart, an industry so closely parallel in organization, management, and operations as the Air Transport Command has in the United States Civil Air Transport Industry. This similarity is of great significance when considering the role which the United States Civil Air Transport Industry will play in the ultimate maintenance of our National Security."[48]

In the years following the Berlin Airlift and Operation Magic Carpet (a.k.a. On Wings of Eagles), the federal government codified the coupling of commercial airlines and Cold War international policy and military strategy. In 1951, the Truman administration finalized an agreement drafted by the Department of Commerce and the Department of Defense by which participating commercial airlines would commit a percentage of their aircraft and personnel to military operations to be called up as needed for strategic airlifts. According to Commerce Secretary Charles W. Sawyer, the Civil Reserve Air Fleet was "based on the belief, which was borne out by experience in the last war, that the most efficient use of that part of your fleet" would "give the armed forces the use not only of your airplanes but also of your management ability, your experience, your organization, your know-how, and your personnel." CRAF gave authority to militarize allocated equipment and personnel to the recently created air force and allow for "a specific number of 4-engine transport aircraft" to be earmarked for assignment to the reserve fleet and undergo modifications enabling them to engage in "military support operations on 48 hours notice." While the CRAF program went into effect in 1951, no portion of it was ever mobilized until US oil imperialism culminated in the military response to Saddam Hussein's 1990 invasion of Kuwait. Under the authority of the Military Airlift Command, CRAF aircraft and personnel had forty-eight hours to respond to activation, and from August 7, 1990, to January 15, 1991, CRAF carriers assisted in moving 400,000 troops and 355,000 tons of cargo to the Arabian Peninsula. When Operation Desert Shield became Operation Desert Storm with the commencement of bombing operations, Secretary of Defense Dick Cheney called up additional CRAF reserves, bringing the total number of activated aircraft to seventy-six passenger and forty cargo planes participating in the airlift. By May 1991, they had completed more than 5,400 missions.[49] CRAF would prove to be an essential piece of the US imperial apparatus in the Middle East, most recently having been activated to facilitate the chaotic evacuation of American troops along with Afghani allies and civilians when the Taliban retook control of Afghanistan in late summer 2021, proving the ways the US corporate-military machine is necessary to sustaining a global empire.

As a strategic location for overt defense objectives and as a storehouse of extractable resources, the theft of which filled the coffers of corporate entities while solidifying federal claims to possession, Alaska functioned as an important nexus of imperial geographies and economies. Both the utilization of Alaska's strategic location and access to extractable raw materials were contingent on the appropriation of Native land. To facilitate the former, the US government initiated the creation of what became the Fort Richardson army base and Elmendorf Air Force Base (now Joint Base Elmendorf-Richardson), which resulted in the rapid expansion of Anchorage into Alaska's largest and most populated metropolitan area. To facilitate the latter, lawmakers sought legislative solutions to suspend the recognition of Alaska Native land claims in the form of reservations or monetary compensation. While some lawmakers, government officials, and corporate interests advocated for a speedy settlement, others continued to insist on legal distinctions between Alaska Natives and tribal nations in the contiguous states, thereby using ambiguity to proceed with dispossessive projects without preemptive negotiation or redemptive purchase. Nevertheless, by exploiting the divergent legal categories among Indigenous Peoples in noncontiguous territories claimed by the United States, the federal government established and sustained critical nodes of empire. In this way, Alaska functioned as a space in which government officials could work out the form and function of Indigenous–US relations and global empire outside of the confines of federal Indian law and federalist legal structures that could undermine unilateral federal authority.

Timber and Termination

While military air bases were critical to the ways government officials envisioned Alaska's role in facilitating US hegemony, so too were initiatives that would likewise bolster post–World War II economic development. Since the early twentieth century, federal officials in various agencies had worried about how to best approach the "development of our great Northern Empire," and as WWII ended, those concerns were heightened by ongoing contests over Native land rights.[50] In August 1945, the House Committee on Territories conducted hearings in Ketchikan, Juneau, and Anchorage to investigate what they considered to be the unusually slow incorporation of land and extractables into corporate markets and the construction of settler infrastructure in Alaska. In these hearings, representatives for the fishing, mining, and timber industries and government officials openly fretted that there was "no such thing as clear title in Alaska" because of the unresolved nature of Alaska Native land rights.[51] The Juneau Chamber of Commerce lamented the potential consequences for Alaska's postwar economic development, complaining that "so long as the controversy remains unsettled tremendous uncertainty exists as to the rights of Alaskans and of those who wish after the war to come to Alaska to settle on lands, to fish and navigate waters, and to develop Alaska's natural resources. While the controversy remains open to dispute, no one can predict whether . . . he may not find himself subjected to the superior easement of aborigine right."[52] Representatives of the mining, fishing, and timber interests concurred, arguing that Native land claims constituted "a cloud extending over the entire Territory" that not only "would destroy the canning industry of Alaska" but also would prohibit harvesting of "the largest timber cuts used to feed the lumber mills at Ketchikan, Juneau, and Sitka."[53]

In the preceding decades, these same officials and corporate interests, like their predecessors, relied on the legal ambiguities around Alaska Native land rights in their appropriation of Native lands. By mid-century, their hesitancy to proceed with extractive and settlement endeavors demonstrated the ways Alaska Native land rights activists reframed those ambiguities as a potential barrier to further dispossession and disruption to their livelihoods. And like their predecessors at the turn of the century, Native activists advocated for a patchwork of possibilities for land rights that would ensure the continuance of their dynamic economies and social and legal orders. Frank Peratrovich (K̲aa X̲'oos Hít Taan, Kaagwaantaan), ANB member and president of the Alaska Seiners Union, refuted claims that federal protections for Native rights undermined the economic pursuits of non-Native people. To the contrary, he argued that supporting Native business enterprises through the various provisions of the IRA and the elimination of fish traps would benefit "everyone who has seen fit to adopt this country for his home." Peratrovich testified that prior to the crowding of streams with fish traps, he had been able to support his five siblings and his mother throughout the year through seasonal fishing and that most families and communities could earn enough to send their children to school and to purchase winter supplies. He noted that the corporate-owned fish traps had destroyed smaller operations, Native and non-Native alike, and insisted that the federal government owed Native communities "protection of some sort." While not an advocate for Indian reservations in every instance, he nevertheless reasoned that for many communities "such a set-up" had been a "wonderful opportunity for the native people to organize under this act and take advantage of the benefits" that allowed them to compete with non-Native businesses. Their ancestral rights guaranteed this, and he concluded that because "[we] have always hunted and fished these areas," we "are still entitled to it."[54]

Several members of the House Committee on Territories and the representatives of non-Native business interests challenged Peratrovich's vision for resolving Native land rights through a combination of reservations and industry regulations in cooperation with non-Native interests. As before, they argued that the IRA and its potential to reserve Native lands constituted "privileges that white people do not have" and as such "leaves uncertainty in every phase of Alaska life." Juneau Chamber of Commerce representative R. E. Robertson railed that Alaska Natives "are citizens" and as such "they can develop the same rights and opportunities and not be given special opportunities" above and beyond those white settlers exercised or what Congress had recognized for tribes in the contiguous states. He charged that Alaska Native village or group organization for purposes of the IRA was not a "tribal relationship" the "way it is in the states" but rather allowed any number of possible Indigenous claimants to seize any piece of ground in Alaska. As such, any potential individual or business could never be assured that any title they might obtain was free and clear of any "superior easement of aborigine right."[55] He advocated for legislation that would extinguish all Aboriginal title in Alaska and permit the Court of Claims to hear and decide any liability and compensation.

No such bill came to fruition. However, the following year an alleged pulp and paper shortage intensified interest in the old growth forests of Tlingit and Haida homelands. In June 1946, Assistant Interior Secretary Oscar L. Chapman inquired with the Interior Department's solicitor regarding the "active interest of a group which proposes to establish a large pulp and newsprint mill in southeastern Alaska." He argued that if the project came to fruition, it would mean the infusion of $20 million into the territorial economy. He warned, however, that potential investors were "concerned about the unsettled status of Indian claims in the area" and thus lamented that "it would be most unfortunate if the proposed development, undoubtedly the most significant potential activity on the Alaska horizon, should be blocked by reason of any such uncertainty."[56] While a number of federal examinations had been conducted to determine the extent of Indigenous land rights in Southeast Alaska, lawmakers debated their validity and disagreed on potential methods for recognition or compensation.[57] Furthermore, many argued that the studies revealed that Alaska Natives had made an adjustment to so-called modern conditions and incorporated commercial fishing and wage labor into their economies. Because of this, they concluded that Alaska Natives had failed to maintain possessory rights to the majority of their homelands through use and occupation. Despite this readiness to reject the plurality of economies and land regimes suggested by Frank Peratrovich and other Native activists, the persistence of Alaska Native land rights advocacy continued to give lawmakers and businessmen pause.

To allow timber companies access to Southeast Alaska, the Department of Agriculture, Governor Gruening, and Alaska Territorial Delegate Bob Bartlett advocated for a legislative pathway that would further extend the temporal window between the transference and transformation of land into property and potential redemptive purchase. The resulting House joint resolution, the Tongass Timber Act, would allow the Department of Agriculture to contract for the sale of timber in the Tongass National Forest "notwithstanding any claim of possessory rights." Any profits from the timber sales would be held in an escrow account "until the rights to the land and timber are finally determined by or under future legislation."[58] The proposal threatened to indefinitely postpone the recognition of their ancestral land rights while irreparably altering Tlingit and Haida homelands, thereby threatening the persistence of Tlingit and Haida cultural, spiritual, and legal orders. When Congress convened for hearings on the bill in 1947, a number of Southeast Alaska Natives testified in opposition to its passage, protesting that no timber projects be permitted to proceed without settlement of their land rights. Nonetheless, the Tongass Timber Act and the debates surrounding its enactment exemplified the structure of settler imperialism and its contingency on legal ambiguity. The bill represented a method by which lawmakers could maintain uncertainties in the legal status of Native land and suspend the resolution of those uncertainties indefinitely. But in response, Native opposition sought to leverage those uncertainties in forcing a settlement, venturing that the potential liabilities the government and corporate interests might face in the future would prove an effective incentive.

Their testimony reflected this strategy. Tlingit and Haida representatives reiterated the history and substance of their ancestral land regimes and emphasized how their theories and practices of diplomacy could accommodate US interests, while their attorneys stirred up anxiety among pulp and paper investors over the clouded nature of land titles in Alaska. ANB member and former Territorial Legislator Frank L. Johnson spoke first, invoking Tlingit protocols of property regimes and permissions before explaining how they might be satisfied and allow timber projects to proceed. He began by situating Tlingit as one of the nations of first Alaskans who "have lived in that country all their lives." He then reminded lawmakers that "when the Russians occupied the area, we were never bothered about our ownership of the land" because "they came in there with our permission." Johnson went on to explain the patterns of clan mobility for trading and political purposes and that while "we went wherever we pleased . . . we respected one another's property." They had "very definite boundaries" and always understood "certain areas as belonging to certain families," and it was expected that "if you came in there you asked permission first." Johnson concluded his statement by informing the committee that the communities he spoke for were willing to permit timber harvesting operations if their land rights could be settled "and not be allowed to drag on for 10 or 20 years." He and his communities knew that timber corporations were hesitant to proceed without Tlingit permission, and he articulated those protocols into the rights rhetoric of the US legal system and synthesized them with their identities and rights as citizens. He confirmed that they understood "if we opposed the bill . . . we would be doing not only ourselves and our people an injustice, but the Territory as a whole," and while "they would like to see the place developed," they felt "their property rights should be protected" and their permission to use the land granted on terms acceptable to them.[59]

Frank Peratrovich spoke next, reinforcing the principles of Tlingit Indigenous land rights, diplomacy, and their vision for Tlingit and Haida futures as citizens of the United States and the Territory of Alaska. Like Johnson, he began by situating himself within Tlingit frameworks of kin, clan, and land, informing the committee that he "happened to originate in one of the three islands that Mr. Johnson referred to here. I was fortunate enough to see my great grandmother. She told us about the rights our family had on that particular island. Those are the things we base our arguments on, and our possessory rights." Emphasizing the legitimacy of Tlingit oral histories in establishing and sustaining Tlingit land regimes, he elaborated, "According to our belief . . . handed down through generations, we own all of the area. You understand . . . there are at least five or six different tribes in this particular area that I am living in and each one of the tribes claims certain other areas, salmon streams, and so forth."[60] He reiterated Johnson's description of clan boundaries and the ways they respected the ownership of those areas. Importantly, he situated Tlingit–US relations within long-standing practices of Tlingit diplomacy and the dynamic nature of their social and political orders, informing the committee that "it is not our intention to block . . . any industrial development in the Territory." Rather, "it is traditional that the native people of Alaska want to see a new industry come to the Territory," and they were "willing to help to develop that Territory" if Congress would reconcile the conflict over Native land titles.[61]

By asserting the precise nature of their land rights to the committee and expressing their willingness to work with timber interests and the federal government, Johnson and Peratrovich were translating their ancestral, Aboriginal land rights into the framework of property ownership. In doing so, they were informing lawmakers and timber and pulp interests that they were the ones to determine the conditions under which they would lease their lands. To this end, they hoped to maintain Tlingit authority over their homelands rather than conceding to the restrictions on Indian property that the Bureau of Indian Affairs and Interior Department exercised over Indian lands in the contiguous states. James Curry, the legal counsel for a number of Tlingit and Haida communities, had pursued this strategy on behalf of his clients from the outset of interest in Southeast Alaska for timber as a way to prompt federal recognition of Native landownership. He reasoned that "Indians should negotiate directly with pulp and fish interests and bankers as well as through the government," speculating that "if private interests and Indians get together, government will probably have to go along."[62] Curry succeeded in raising alarm among some pulp and paper investors, who voiced concern that "no pulp and paper company could afford the risk to the establishment of a plant in Alaska until the cloud represented by possessory Indian claims has been removed," but drew rebuke from lawmakers who balked at this insistence that Congress reconcile Native land rights prior to issuing timber contracts.[63]

Rather than concede that the uncertainties of Indian titles demanded reconciliation before timber and pulp paper operations could commence, committee members contended that the persistent ambiguity around Alaska Native land rights was what necessitated passage of the Tongass Timber Act. Territorial Governor Gruening warned of the losses to the territory if the "wholly nebulous state" of "aboriginal claims" prevented timber development, especially because "no one knows whether they have a claim at all." Others agreed, refuting the notion that Alaska Natives might have Aboriginal land rights similar to those recognized on behalf of tribes in the contiguous states. Many concurred that the "aboriginal rights of Alaska Indians were extinguished by our treaty with Russia for the Purchase of Alaska" and that all that remained after 1867 were the "the same rights that any citizen might have."[64] To them, Alaska Natives were US citizens who had never been recognized as tribes and for that reason did not share the legal and historical circumstances by which to qualify for preemptive negotiation for or redemptive purchase of their homelands.

Despite the overwhelming opposition of Alaska Natives, Congress passed the Tongass Timber Bill just five days after testimony concluded, opening up the Tongass National Forest to long-term corporate logging leases. While lawmakers and timber, pulp, and paper interests had achieved a legislative method by which to suspend the recognition and reconciliation of any Native land rights in Southeast Alaska, the potential for future conflicts or liabilities prompted them to pursue additional action against Indigenous rights in Alaska. Specifically, they worried about the Interior Department's ability to create Indian reservations under the Alaska amendments to the IRA, potentially blocking access to additional timber, mineral, and oil extractables. To disable this authority, the US Senate advanced two bills that had far-reaching implications for Alaska and came to inform congressional approaches to federal Indian policy in the contiguous states. In 1948, Congress considered Senate Joint Resolution 162 and Senate Bill 2037: The former would have repealed the authority of the interior secretary to create reservations in Alaska and rescinded the orders for those that had already been established, while the latter sought to "transfer to the territorial government of Alaska the administration within such territory of laws relating to Indians" to the territorial government of Alaska, removing Alaska Natives affairs from federal jurisdiction.[65]

S.J. 162 and S. 2037 embodied many of the underlying principles of termination policy that would coalesce in federal legislation five years later, demonstrating how struggles over Native land rights at the edges of empire influenced continental Indian policy. Proponents of the bill drew on policy distinctions between Alaska Natives and tribal nations in the contiguous United States, referencing the fact that Alaska Natives had never been forced onto reservations as evidence that tribally based landholdings were unnecessary in Alaska. For example, Senator Hugh Butler contended that equal US citizenship was antithetical to the "wardship status" for which he alleged reservations and services provided by the Indian Bureau had relegated tribal members in the contiguous states. He argued that these tribes looked forward to their "emancipation" from reservations, thus to perpetuate the policy in Alaska would be an injustice to the territory and Alaska Natives alike.[66] Interior Secretary Julius A. Krug, while not an enthusiastic supporter of the IRA, nevertheless understood the ways the bill would undercut Alaska Native economic stability. In the written statement he submitted as part of the Committee on Interior and Insular Affairs hearings on S. 2037, he argued that "S. 2037 would terminate any Federal assistance to the natives of Alaska in the conservation and development of Indian lands and resources, terminate authorization for the making of future loans to native communities, including the extension of further loans which are necessary to keep businesses operating, eliminate the right of native communities to develop home rule and form chartered corporations for the purpose of carrying on business activities, and repeal the procedures set up by Congress to safeguard native land rights within the Territory."[67]

In addition to drawing widespread criticism among Alaska Natives, the bill's potential to affect tribes in the contiguous states prompted several representatives from tribal organizations in the contiguous states to testify against them. Executive Secretary of the National Congress of American Indians Ruth Muskrat Bronson (Cherokee) spoke at length, calling "Senate Joint Resolution 162 . . . a vicious piece of legislation" that threatened to "wipe out any claim to land title which the Indians of Alaska have" and "threaten[ed] the security of all of the Indians of the United States." She agreed that the IRA was far from perfect, and while Alaska Natives "would prefer . . . to have the patents to their land rather than reservations, if they have to call it a reservation to get it, they will take a reservation." She contended that while Alaska Natives valued their US citizenship, voting rights, and role in territorial governance, "they want ownership of their land which they can protect just as any other citizen of the United States can protect against the marauding of the Forest Service and against the Fish and Wildlife Service and against other people who come in and grab off the resources which belong to them." Bronson also warned the committee about the dangerous precedent the proposals posed not only to Alaska Natives but also to tribal nations across the United States, cautioning lawmakers that destabilizing the legal principles of federal Indian law and Indian titles in Alaska could jeopardize their own claims to property in the contiguous states. She testified ominously that if "Indian titles can be wiped out in Alaska by congressional fiat, then Indian titles in all the States west of the Mississippi can be wiped out in a similar fashion." Rather than giving lawmakers and corporate interests easier access to Native land, Bronson warned that this unilateral disregard for the procedural recognition, reservation, and transfer of Indian land titles could put "millions of dollars' worth of mineral leases, timber contracts, and agricultural leases on Indian reservation lands" at risk. Bronson advised the committee that the "titles of white men which derive from Indian cessions—as most titles in our Western States do—are rendered uncertain if the validity of Indian titles is denied."[68]

Along with Bronson and the National Congress of American Indians, Native communities from Southeast Alaska sent letters opposing the bills to be incorporated into the congressional record. The Alaska Native Brotherhood in Wrangell argued that "the creating of reservations will act as a wonderful development for the territory," and the Hydaburg community likewise reaffirmed that "there is nothing to hinder timber development on reservations" and that they "want [their] rights settled in fair consideration without mere token settlement," protesting that the transfer of Alaska Native Affairs to the territory would disrupt any stability in economic development they had thus far achieved under its administration. Furthermore, realizing that both bills would deal a death blow to the availability of crucial IRA loans in addition to land rights, Alaska Natives at Hoonah warned against such action, stating that "the Wheeler-Howard Act means to the Indian what the Reconstruction Finance Corporation means to the whites."[69] While reservations remained controversial in many Southeast Alaska Native communities, these protests represented the ways that these communities had tailored elements of Indian policy to meet their unique needs and objectives. They saw the IRA as imperfect, but like citizenship it represented a tool by which they could potentially protect their homelands and pursue economic endeavors conducive to their communities and to the territory. In this way, they created important spaces for the articulation of their land relations and sovereignty within the uncertain legal landscape that lawmakers were attempting to script onto their homelands.

Proponents of the bill rejected these arguments and instead sought to further entrench their position that Alaska Natives had never been dispossessed of their lands because they had been placed on a path to citizenship rather than restricted to reservations as wards of the government. They used this false narrative to elide the ways their predecessors had mobilized ambiguities around Alaska Native racial classification and legal status in the absence of treaties and other statutory frameworks of contiguous westward expansion. In doing so, they aligned the federal government's refusal to recognize Alaska Native nationhood and tribal land rights in support of their opposition to the IRA in the contiguous states. Echoing Senator Butler's sentiments regarding the principles of equal citizenship and wardship status, Senator Zales Ecton of Montana argued that "before they were put on reservations, those Indians, as I understand it, were citizens of Alaska, . . . they weren't wards of any government."[70] Likewise, the Ketchikan Chamber of Commerce reflected the position of many white settlers in the territory, arguing that land rights in the form of IRA reservations would leave "the Indian . . . deprived of his individual rights of inheritance, private ownership of property," with the result "that our Indians will be forced back into a primitive state."[71] The proponents of these bills failed to accept the ways Alaska Natives synthesized citizenship and tribal landholdings, insisting that the lack of reservations in Alaska up until the Alaska amendments to the IRA supported their assimilatory logic that US citizenship was an adequate and necessary substitution for tribal sovereignty and the recognition of and negotiation for Aboriginal title.

Importantly, these discourses of assimilation and equal citizenship as incompatible with tribal landholdings in Alaska bolstered opposition to the IRA more broadly. Similar to the ways Alaska lent purchase to the development of the doctrine of incorporation with regard to the classification of US territories, it also gave leverage to those seeking to frame federal Indian policy in favor of repealing the IRA and dissolving the federal relationship between tribal nations and the US government. In Alaska, the distinctions lawmakers and government officials had cultivated in the eighty years since the Treaty of Cession with Russia had allowed them to avoid the constitutional requirements of preemptive negotiation and redemptive purchase for Alaska Native lands. In the post–World War II era, the debates over these distinctions represented an important opportunity to those looking for justification to rescind nationhood status and liquidate tribal lands and assets across the contiguous states as well. While neither S.J. 162 nor S.B. 2037 became law, the tensions they reflected dominated the confirmation hearings for Oscar Chapman as the new secretary of the interior three years later. When asked his position on IRA reservations in Alaska, Chapman responded that "I would like to answer the question a little more broadly than just to mention the matter of Alaskan reservations." He continued that "the question of setting up reservations for the natives of Alaska is . . . like dealing with the total Indian problem of America, quite complex. I have felt for some time, and I feel more strongly about it every day, that we should take an entirely new look at this whole question, not only at the matter of reservations for the Indians of Alaska, but also at the entire policy of dealing with the Indians."[72]

Encouraged by Chapman's suggestion that the current policy around Native landholdings ought to be reconsidered, Senator George W. Malone from Nevada chimed in, stating that he had just such "a bill . . . to make the Indians people and treat them like people." Agreeing that a widespread reversal of policy was necessary, he concluded, "I think it is time that we review them all." To this, even Chapman cautioned, "Remember, when you do that you repeal more than 5,000 laws," to which Malone replied, "That would not be a bad idea."[73] Under further questioning by Senator Arthur V. Watkins, the sponsor of the bill that became the legislative expression of termination policy, Chapman refused to fully acquiesce to Watkins's plans for "the final release of the Indians as wards of the government . . . as rapidly as possible." Instead, he favored a more gradual approach, nevertheless advocating for the ultimate dissolution of tribal nations in the United States and thereby opening up Native lands to corporate extractive endeavors.

S.J. Resolution 162 and Senate Bill 2037 failed to pass, though the congressional debates regarding them and the successful passage of the Tongass Timber Act reveal the ways that sustaining the ambiguous legal status of Alaska Natives operated within the logic of dispossession. By insisting on the lack of tribal organization in Alaska, and therefore negotiating the status of Alaska Natives as nations, lawmakers and government officials utilized the ambiguity around Alaska Native legal status to relieve constitutional requirements for preemptive negotiation and suspend redemptive purchase indefinitely. This also facilitated deepening corporate-military entanglement in the post-WWII orientation of federal domestic and foreign policies around economic and military hegemony in the Cold War. Alaska Governor B. Frank Heintzleman characterized the Tongass Forest bill as "not only the first plan of its kind in Alaska, but also . . . the largest single industrial investment ever made here."[74] By coupling the rhetoric of equal citizenship to post–World War II economic sustainability, lawmakers devised a method by which to thwart the recognition of Alaska Native land rights and support their objectives for terminating tribal status and landholdings in the contiguous states. The narrative that Alaska Natives had "never been dealt with as tribes" and had never been "wards of the government" mobilized the legal ambiguities and their historical contexts in ways that came to inform policy in the nation proper while facilitating the development of global imperial structures. Less than two years after Oscar Chapman's nomination hearings, Congress adopted House Concurrent Resolution 108, officially ushering in the disastrous policy of termination. In the years that followed, the utility of Alaska as a territory without formal recognition of Native nationhood or land rights nor state sovereignty to impede federal projects would underscore the debates over statehood.

5

Domesticating Empire

Alaska and the Conundrum of Statehood

In September of 1957, Gertrude Smith, an Iñupiaq woman living in Spenard, Alaska, penned an angry letter to Alaska Territorial Governor Mike Stepovich concerning the dubious means by which developers and statehood proponents were swindling Indigenous Alaskans out of their ancestral homelands. Smith demanded an investigation into her family's land, writing that "when it was decided to sell lots at Kotzebue, the people who have lived on a lot for many years were to have first chance to purchase that lot without opposition." She reported that when her sister attempted to purchase her lot, she was denied and informed that her land was in the middle of a proposed roadway and that they would offer her another. However, Smith and her sister later learned that instead of having been selected for a roadway, their family lot had in fact been purchased by a settler businessman by the name of John Cross who then proceeded to order Smith's family off their land. For her family to be evicted from their homelands, where "our great, [grandfather] have met the first white man there and welcomed him," was a startling rebuke of the ways many Alaska Natives had negotiated settler presence.[1] Smith knew John Cross was "one of the men who wrote the constitution for the State of Alaska," which was under consideration by territorial officials and Congress, and that he had been distributing pro-statehood propaganda throughout Kotzebue and the surrounding area.[2] She threatened that if Cross's actions represented what Alaska Natives could expect from "the statehood gang," then it was "high time" Alaska Natives "were waking up." She further warned that if Stepovich failed to investigate this fraud, she would "see that non-statehood publishers will learn of this before it is too late."[3]

Smith, along with Alaska Natives across the territory, recognized statehood as another attempt in the long history of legislative dispossession by which lawmakers, corporate interests, developers, and settlers could undermine Native land rights. Businessmen and developers like Cross knew they had much to gain if statehood became a reality, as the new state government would be poised to seize millions of acres of Native land that could then be leased, sold, or otherwise contracted for resource extraction, infrastructure projects, military expansion, and settlement. These projects were contingent on access to Native land, the legal status of which remained contentious and unresolved in Congress and in the courts following passage of the Tongass Timber Act. In this context, lawmakers sought passage of statehood legislation that omitted customary disclaimers by incoming states of any right to Native lands. Such disclaimers were established precedent in most statehood legislation in the contiguous states. But in the case of Alaska, lawmakers were drawing on the long-running argument that the distinctions in the legal status of Alaska Natives rendered such protections obsolete in the formation of the proposed state of Alaska. Doing so reveals the ways lawmakers sought to reconcile Alaska's relation to the nation proper while maintaining the settler imperial ambiguities of Alaska Natives and land, extending the function that legal ambiguity played in dispossession into the statehood era.

Alaska Natives objected to statehood legislation that did not contain explicit protection of their land rights. In statehood debates, they insisted on a settlement and land arrangement that might accommodate settler, military, and corporate interests in ways that ensured the persistence of their Indigenous political, legal, economic, and social orders, as well as the land relations that sustained them. They grounded their land rights activism in their formulations of Indigenous citizenship and nationhood, which they argued reflected their vested interests in the success of the future state of Alaska. They were also aware of the contingencies plaguing the efforts of statehood proponents, in which the Dwight D. Eisenhower administration, military officials, and corporate fisheries also opposed the transition from incorporated territory to state. Many federal officials understood noncontiguous territories as fundamental in the practice of boundary management for what they considered territory of the nation proper. For this reason, Eisenhower and military officials hesitated to relinquish federal authority in Alaska. Territories were fundamental to national interests as spaces absent a state authority that might interfere with federal objectives, especially in terms of US post–World War II hegemony building and the military exigencies that characterized US policy in the Cold War.[4] Likewise, the corporate fisheries and other extractive industries were some of the most vocal opponents of statehood, as they too rued the possibility of state regulatory bureaucracy that could stymie their operations. Because Alaska's long tenure as a territory had enabled these corporate and imperial projects to proceed with little intervention, statehood was not a foregone conclusion; thus Alaska Natives leveraged this uncertainty to influence the impact Alaska statehood might have on their legal status and land rights.

The global implications for Alaska statehood and the ways Native leaders influenced this transition are part of a much larger restructuring of US empire. In the years following the close of the Second World War, the United States reconfigured the statuses of several of the noncontiguous territories to which it maintained possessory claims. In 1946, President Harry S. Truman formally recognized the independence of the Philippines, and Alaska held a referendum in which a majority voted in favor of statehood; in 1947, the US Congress passed legislation establishing the right of Puerto Ricans to elect their own governor and formalized US administration of the US Trust Territory of the Pacific Islands, which included the Caroline, Mariana, and Marshall Islands; in 1950, the United States transferred the administration of Guam and American Samoa from the Department of the Navy to the Department of the Interior while rejecting incorporated status for both; Puerto Rico voted in favor of commonwealth status in 1952, and Congress revised the Virgin Islands Organic Act to allow for an elected governor. At the culmination of the decade, Alaska and Hawai'i would be awarded statehood status, and tiny Palmyra Atoll would remain the lone incorporated territory of the United States, a status it retains today.

This geopolitical remapping was symptomatic of the increasing pressures Indigenous Peoples in noncontiguous US territories were applying to the federal government and the ways the United States sought to assert and maintain imperial hegemony. It is no coincidence that the federal government also sought to restructure Indigenous–US relations internally as well, shifting federal Indian policy away from the recognition of tribal nations and tribal landholdings reflected in the Indian Reorganization Act (IRA) toward terminating tribal rights and assimilating Indigenous people into so-called civilized settler American society. At the height of the Termination Era, Alaska Natives challenged the ongoing dispossession from their homelands in the courts, pursuing numerous lawsuits, including *Tee-Hit-Ton Indians v. United States*,

Natives of Palmer, Alaska v. United States, and *Tlingit and Haida Indians of Alaska v. United States*. Each case sought recognition of Native land rights in distinct and important ways, reflecting how Native lawyers and activists understood and wielded these mid-century shifts in the legal categories and geopolitical boundaries that constituted the settler state and its imperial capillaries. Alaska Natives also fought the numerous statehood bills that sought to extinguish their land rights and their status as Indigenous nations, mobilizing around a vision of statehood that included Native land rights as a fundamental component of statehood economic development and as function of their status as Alaska's first citizens. Ultimately, the Alaska Statehood Act embodied aspects of both termination policy and Indigenous lobbying, as it both established a process by which the new state could select land to be transferred to state ownership while also recognizing the rights to lands "which may be held by any Indians, Eskimos, or Aleuts." In doing so, it carried forward settler imperial ambiguity into the statehood era.[5]

Native Land Rights and Statehood Politics

Settlers in Alaska had been agitating for statehood since the early twentieth century, but during WWII and the early Cold War period, territorial officials started lobbying for statehood in earnest. The first statehood bill to garner palpable attention from Congress was brought by Alaska Territorial Delegate Bob Bartlett in 1947 amid the contest over the Tongass Timber Act. It reflected the ways government officials, lawmakers, and corporate interests understood the intertwined and contingent nature of statehood, extractive development projects, and Native land rights. Like the Tongass Timber Act, statehood proposals were framed around the rhetoric of equality that undergirded both termination policy and Cold War diplomacy generally, with proponents of both arguing that Alaska Natives ought to be considered on an "equal" basis with white settlers and that Alaska ought to be incorporated into the Union on equal footing with other states. Thus, statehood might accomplish in Alaska what termination policy sought to achieve in the contiguous states. In this vein, Bartlett's 1947 bill mirrored the objectives of the Tongass Timber Act by seeking to bypass Alaska Native land rights in the statehood process and thus prompted Alaska Native land rights activists to leverage the ambiguities around their land rights to undermine statehood legislation. As National Congress of American Indians (NCAI) Executive Secretary Ruth Muskrat Bronson had warned, the Alaska Native Brotherhood (ANB) also implied that without clarification of their land rights, all land selections by the future state of Alaska could be called into question.[6]

In a letter to Congress from their attorney James Curry, the ANB explained that even if Congress passed the Tongass Timber Bill, they had no intention of withdrawing their land claims in the Tongass National Forest, thus sustaining ambiguities over the validity of title. Curry warned that the Tongass bill could not resolve "a disagreement based on doubt" and that "when title is in doubt, third persons have difficulty dealing with either of the two rival claimants." The ANB wagered that in the event Congress passed the Tongass bill, most pulp and paper companies would remain hesitant to commence operations if Native leaders and their attorneys challenged US Forest Service claims to Southeast Alaska. This risk was not lost on lawmakers and statehood proponents, who begrudgingly conceded to the reality that the unresolved nature of Alaska Native land rights undermined land titles across the entire territory. H. L. Faulkner, a Juneau-based attorney representing mining interests, realized as much, lamenting in hearings before the House subcommittee in 1947 that "the threat of those Indians' claims is still held over the territory" and that "they are the threat that is held over anybody who wants to go up there . . . whether it is a paper company, mining company, or any other company."[7] The possibility of this threat caused other committee members to question long-standing interpretations regarding Aboriginal title in Alaska, with Congressman William Lemke from North Dakota anxiously inquiring "if those claims are valid, then we really did not get anything from Russia? . . . If they claimed the whole thing, then even the money we paid to Russia was given away, because it belonged to the Indians, not Russia? . . . We bought it from the wrong party." Faulkner replied, "Yes; we bought it from the wrong party."[8]

By insisting on their Aboriginal land rights and casting doubt on federal claims, the ANB weaponized the legal fictions government officials and lawmakers had relied on in refusing to resolve the legal status of Alaska Natives and their land, and they applied this leverage in opposition to statehood legislation. In his letter, Curry balked at Bartlett's bill and its "lack of any provision similar to those which are universal in western statehood bills providing for the protection of Indian property rights." Drawing Alaska Natives into the customary recognition of Native land rights in the contiguous states, he continued that "it goes without saying that the Alaska Native Brotherhood and the National Congress of American Indians, and all of the various local organizations affiliated with both central groups will be opposed to the adoption of this bill."[9] In this vein, the ambiguity lawmakers had relied on for eighty years of US possessory claims to Alaska threatened to undermine their objectives as Alaska Natives rearticulated these same ambiguities as barriers to statehood, disrupting the ways lawmakers and corporate interests sought to actualize the materiality of dispossession and the making of property out of Native land.[10] Specifically, Alaska Native insistence on similar recognition of their land rights to that of tribal nations in the contiguous states prompted these lawmakers and corporate interests to harden their position that Alaska Natives had never been negotiated with as tribes, ultimately reifying the ambiguities that were coming to haunt their statehood efforts. Many scoffed that "the Indians in Alaska are different from the Indians in the States . . . , they were not divided into distinct tribes . . . and the right to citizenship was extended to them."[11] In this way, the ANB had succeeded in making their legal status as nations with Aboriginal land rights that required preemptive negotiation and redemptive compensation a central issue in ongoing statehood debates.

The response of ANB and Alaska Native Sisterhood (ANS) members and lawmakers alike demonstrates that the success of statehood legislation hinged on the question of Native land rights. Bartlett's 1947 statehood proposal failed; however, a subsequent bill, H.R. 5666, included the following, which satisfied Alaska Natives but drew objections from lawmakers: "That said State and its people do agree and declare that they forever disclaim all right and title to any lands or other property, the title to which is retained in or ceded to the United States by the provisions of this Act and to all lands lying within its boundaries owned or held by any Indian, Aleut, or Eskimos hereinafter called natives, or by any native tribes the right or title to which shall have been acquired through or from the United States or any previous sovereignty."[12] Upon review in the Committee on Public Lands, Senator Wesley D'Ewart of Montana deleted the phrase "or by any native tribes," reflecting ongoing efforts to carry over the legal distinctions in the status of Alaska Native land into statehood. The committee reasoned that this deletion kept the "terminology of the bill consistent" with "terminology customarily used in describing native groups in Alaska," concluding it would simply maintain the status quo.[13] This alleged aim for consistency implied that the committee was only willing to concede to the vague individual protections of the 1884 Organic Act, and the committee's actions drew swift rebuke from the ANB and ANS. In an onslaught of petitions, they argued that the omission was a ploy to continue denying their tribal land rights, warning Congress that "it has been the unbroken policy of the United States for more than 60 years to require each incoming State of the Union to agree to recognize Indian possessions of every charter, tribe, as well as individual." They reminded lawmakers that in other instances, Alaska Native land rights had been occasionally recognized on a tribal basis and that "approximately 126 native reservations have been established in Alaska in which title to land is vested in tribes or other communities."[14] They warned that this obvious departure from precedent would cost statehood advocates the support of the ANB, ANS, and NCAI in the territorial vote for statehood.

To this end, the ANB and ANS continued to pressure territorial officials in the Interior Department to support the IRA as an important method of recognizing their land rights and rights to self-governance, insisting that they could resolve the stymie of uncertainty by acquiescing to their claims. In December of 1948, ANS President Amy Yax Yeidí Hallingstad (Tlingit, Eagle, Tsaagweidí, and Aan Yakawlitseixi Hít) wrote letters to territorial delegate Bartlett and to Interior Secretary Julius A. Krug, criticizing them for their attempts to swindle Alaska Natives out of their lands in the process of statehood. To Krug, she urged him to "keep faith with the Alaskan Indians and sign the reservation proclamations without trying to pull the wool over our eyes by saying you need further legislation." She continued that his failure to act prolonged the "legal recognition to our rightful claims. We do not wish to hold up the progress of the Territory of statehood." But without his approval of the reservation petitions pending before him, Native communities in Alaska lacked the "right to dispose of the resources currently being stolen" from them by settlers, the Forest Service, and the corporate fisheries. Hallingstad similarly pressured Bartlett, accusing both him and Krug of stalling any recognition of Alaska Native land rights and therefore allowing the theft of Native timber and fish by the pulp and fishing industries. She emphasized again, "We want a just settlement according to the authority of the Wheeler-Howard Act . . . whereby Indians . . . will get the proper investments and title to their lands and waters."[15] She and others echoed Curry's arguments that the Forest Service and any other faction could resolve clouds of uncertainty that stymied their statehood and development plans if they would negotiate with Alaska's Indigenous nations.

Despite Alaska Native opposition, lawmakers continued to argue in debates over subsequent statehood bills that Indian reservations impaired Alaska Native citizenship and undermined statehood. They continued to insist that Aboriginal title in Alaska, if it had ever existed as it had in the states, had been extinguished. In hearings before the Committee on Interior and Insular Affairs in 1950, Senator Hugh Butler, who would become a major proponent of termination policy in the following years, interrogated Alaska District Judge and former Territorial Delegate Anthony Dimond as to the nature of Native land rights. He challenged Dimond on the legal status of Alaska Natives, stating, "There is a reservation problem developing for Alaska. . . . The Indian [in the states] has been a ward of the Government continually, and that has not been the case up to date in Alaska." His fellow Senator Zales Ecton, from Montana, mused that "it seems . . . that it would be a mistake to deliberately place some of these natives on reservations when to all appearances they are perfectly able . . . and willing to take their places as citizens of Alaska and of the United States on equal terms with every other State." He warned further that "if we go ahead and grant Alaska statehood and you get the Indian reservations fastened upon you . . . you will find that you will have even more complicated problems." Butler concurred, raising fears that the statehood bill as written would force the future state to acknowledge "that there is an aboriginal right and that in fact parts of Alaska, if not every foot of Alaska actually belong to a few natives that were there when we took it over from Russia."[16]

Frank Peratrovich testified in opposition to these claims, articulating the ways the ambiguity around Native land rights functioned to undermine Alaska Native citizenship and economic endeavors in addition to impairing statehood objectives. Importantly, he began by orienting his listeners to the broad spectrum of relations from which he understood and advocated for the mutuality of citizenship and Indigenous political status and land rights. He introduced himself as hailing from Klawock, where he was a small businessman, former mayor, a member of the

Alaska Territorial Senate and the Alaska Statehood Committee, and the current president of the Alaska Native Brotherhood, before exposing the ways that corporate interests had manipulated the unresolved status of Alaska Native land rights to their benefit. Contrary to the claims of Butler and other lawmakers, he argued that the IRA "has given Indian communities and Indian fishermen . . . a chance to earn their way and become good citizens of Alaska, the future State." In fact, he argued that the fishing corporations were guilty of scaring off "other investors looking to Alaska" by "rais[ing] the old cry of ancestral rights for Indians," while saying "nothing about the grandfather rights they hold in fish traps."[17] Furthermore, "these same trap and cannery owners . . . have opposed Government loans" like those available through the IRA "to the Indian communities to establish or purchase small canneries" and have lobbied intensely for "an end of the Alaska amendment to the Wheeler-Howard Act" to stymie competition from Native fishermen. Peratrovich contended that continued implementation of the IRA would be a tremendous boon for the future state, as statehood and the recognition of Alaska Native fishing rights and land claims could bring an end to the corporate exploitation that threatened salmon populations and the economies of Native fishermen and white settlers alike. He pointed to the "successful little cannery at Hydaburg, a plant financed and paid for through Wheeler-Howard loan funds," located on a small reservation established under the IRA the previous year. In closing, he again situated himself as a US citizen, "a Veteran of World War I," and lifelong fisherman, representing the ways many Native leaders had advocated for the integration of citizenship and national belonging into the defense of their Indigenous, ancestral land rights.

Despite Peratrovich's testimony regarding the centrality of Alaska Native land rights and the IRA to the economic success of a future state of Alaska, the committee moved to attach an amendment to H.R. 331 that rescinded the reservation orders that the interior secretary had established on behalf of the Native communities at "Akutan, Karluk, Wales, Unalakleet, and Venetie, or any other Indian reservations in the Territory of Alaska." The amendments also sought to repeal Section 2 of the Alaska amendments to the IRA that had granted the authority of the interior secretary to approve and establish reservations on behalf of Native communities. These amendments were adamantly supported by W. C. Arnold, a well-known attorney for a number of fish-packing operations. Like his counterparts, he relied on the long history of legislation and case law that had distinguished between Alaska Natives and tribal nations of the contiguous states, arguing that "no Indian wars were fought, such as characterized the development of the western domain," and Alaska Natives "were never segregated or placed on reservations," and "the United States never treated with them."[18] To him, these differences invalidated Alaska Native land rights, and he and his contemporaries in the mining and forestry industries sought to sustain these distinctions to exempt Alaska from the purview of preemptive negotiation with Alaska Native nations and to buttress future denials of redemptive purchase.

The final version of H.R. 331 included provisions similar to those that had been proposed in committee, prompting swift rebuke from the ANB, which passed a resolution at their annual convention in Craig opposing the ways statehood legislation was being employed to deny them their ancestral land rights. They also resumed their strategy of situating their land rights as a barrier to statehood. Following the convention, their attorney, James Curry, penned a letter to Senator Arthur V. Watkins in which he cautioned that "the Indians are more than a fourth of the voting population" and that "most of them favored the Statehood Bill until the 'joker' Section 5 (1) was inserted, cheating them of their right to reserve for their own use any part of the lands that they inherited from their aboriginal ancestors." He also advised the senator that Governor Ernest Gruening's attempts to convince the convention to accept the statehood bill with the antireservation clause had been disastrous. "He was unable to convince a single delegate! He left town immediately, a day ahead of schedule."[19] Curry's letter was followed by dozens of others from organizations both inside and outside of Alaska, Native and non-Native, berating their representatives to vote against the bill unless the antireservation clause was removed.[20] Their efforts were successful and the bill failed, though government officials and lawmakers continued to insist on the contingency of statehood for Alaska and the extinguishment of Alaska Native land rights.

Litigating Dispossessive Ambiguities

Following the demise of H.R. 331, lawmakers responded to the leverage Alaska Natives were wielding in their opposition to statehood when

Bartlett introduced a bill "to settle Native land claims in the territory of Alaska" in 1951.[21] The bill proposed the creation of a special committee to hear Alaska Native claims before the Indian Claims Commission, which would determine whether and to what extent Alaska Natives could be compensated for any legal taking of their lands. Bartlett argued that "if we go into statehood with that uncertain status [of Alaska Native land rights], it is not going to be too good." Acknowledging his intention to circumvent nation-to-nation negotiations, he continued that by passing his bill, "we will have cleared the way for the new state, and we will have done so sort of uniquely, because in the last 10 states they did not succeed in doing that very thing."[22] Bartlett recognized the ways Alaska Natives had complicated statehood legislation by suspending the unresolved nature of their land rights over potential state projects, thus he sought to remove land issues from the legislative realm and relocate them in the courts. In this way, he animated the ambiguity in settler imperial dispossession to elongate the temporal window between extralegal seizure and redemptive purchase. Similar to the Tongass Timber Act, Bartlett's land claims proposal sought to facilitate the passage of statehood legislation that would enable a new state government to initiate land selections by eliminating the potential for preemptive negotiation for Native land cessions and locating the possibility of redemptive purchase, once again, to an unspecified and uncertain date in the future.

The ANB, ANS, and representatives from the NCAI criticized this move as an unconstitutional bypassing of Indigenous possessory rights and an unacceptable usurpation of the rights of Alaska Natives as sovereigns to negotiate directly with federal officials. At committee hearings held in Juneau in November of 1951, ANB Secretary William L. Paul Jr. exposed the bill as a veiled attempt to rescind the IRA and to undermine the alignment of Alaska Native political status with the constitutional status of tribal nations in the contiguous states. He began his testimony by entering into the record a number of resolutions the ANB had adopted the previous year in which they had demanded the "immediate designation of land reservations under the Indian Reorganization Act" and had vehemently opposed "any legislation which contains provisions limiting or abolishing the authority of federal officials to confirm Native land titles in Alaska." Paul continued that the bill shifted the onus of proof onto Alaska Natives, forcing them to "prove we own what we own," which was "contrary to established principles of [the] trust relationship." As such, H.R. 4388 ran contrary to "the law of our country that Indian possessory rights are perfectly good legal title" and was thus "unsatisfactory, and at several points clearly unconstitutional."[23]

Paul and his counterparts were all too familiar with the ways lawmakers had long relied on the ambiguities they narrated into Alaska Native legal status to enact legislation and policies that excluded Alaska Natives from preemptive negotiation for their land and delayed redemptive purchase. Specifically referencing the Tongass Timber Act, he informed the committee, "We believe that this bill is a recognition that previous attempts by Congress to settle the Indian possessory claims problem, such as the Tongass Pulp Timber Sale Act, were inadequate to the extent that they were unconstitutional." He also criticized the ways lawmakers and corporate interests threatened Alaska Natives with the possibility that they might "be placed on reservations, be placed under trusteeship, wards of the government, rather than being fully competent citizens," if they insisted on land settlements through the IRA. Rather, he and other Native leaders instead saw the provisions of the IRA as the "preservation of property" necessary for Alaska Natives to make a living on equal footing and believed that "if the process of being first class citizens will also deprive us of our property then we would prefer to have reservations."[24] Importantly, he criticized the way the wording of the bill undercut Alaska Native subsistence rights, deliberately omitting "hunting and fishing grounds from the definition of community and individual lands" that Alaska Natives could potentially claim and also excluded "rights in coastal waters beyond low water mark." Paul contended that these provisions were particularly objectionable because they undercut Native ownership of "capital assets" from which they earned their living. He argued that "we have always owned the fisheries" and that "we expect to stay here the rest of our lives." Like Peratrovich, Paul objected to the ways the corporate fisheries had used the uncertainty about Native land rights in edging out Native fisherman, charging that "if these interlopers in the absentee canning corporations think they have any legal or equitable rights, let them be put upon their burden of proof, first."[25]

Bartlett's bill failed to pass, and subsequent deliberations over Alaska Native possessory rights, Aboriginal title, and extinguishment legislation were briefly put on hold in 1954 when the Department of the Interior reported that the US Supreme Court had agreed to hear *Tee-Hit-Ton*

Indians v. United States. William Paul Sr. (Tee-Hit-Ton) had filed the case on behalf of the Tee-Hit-Ton clan with the US Court of Claims back in 1951 after the Department of Agriculture harvested timber under the provisions of the Tongass Timber Act from Tee-Hit-Ton lands in what federal officials call the Tongass National Forest. The Supreme Court issued its decision in 1955, ruling against the Tee-Hit-Ton. The court, however, not only denied the Tee-Hit-Ton the compensation they had sought but also ruled broadly that no tribes had land rights that were compensable under the Fifth Amendment unless Congress had recognized them first. In his infamous opinion, Chief Justice Stanley F. Reed concluded that "the taking by the United States of unrecognized Indian title is not compensable under the Fifth Amendment" because "Indian occupation of land without government recognition of ownership creates no rights against taking or extinction by the United States protected by the Fifth Amendment or any other principle of law."[26] In what has been characterized as "one of the most glaring misrepresentations of fact ever uttered by a Supreme Court justice," he resolved that tribes "of this continent were deprived of their ancestral ranges by force and that, even when the Indians ceded millions of acres by treaty . . . it was not a sale but the conquerors' will that deprived them of their land." In concluding that Aboriginal title was not a function of inherent sovereignty and nation-to-nation negotiations, the ruling designated Congress as the sole arbiter of "Indian occupancy of Government-owned lands" and, in doing so, potentially jeopardized tribal lands across the United States.[27]

For Alaska Natives, the ruling left the status of their land rights and their political and legal status unresolved, but with an added layer of legal precarity. In declaring that Congress had no obligation to recognize Aboriginal title, the court avoided the question of whether the 1867 Treaty of Cession had extinguished Aboriginal title in Alaska, thereby affirming the ambiguities that structured the Tongass Timber Act.[28] Reed had argued that neither the 1884 Organic Act nor the 1900 amendments to the act had intended to grant to the Indians any permanent rights in the lands of Alaska but that it was rather intended "merely to retain the *status quo* until further congressional or judicial action was taken."[29] Reed concluded that the Tongass Timber Act signaled Congress's intention to continue a policy of nonrecognition of Alaska Native land rights, and his ruling affirmed Congress had the constitutional authority to do so. Legal scholars note that this "ambiguity left

Alaska Native aboriginal land claims in a precarious position" by leaving "open the question of whether Alaska Natives had any claim to the lands they occupied in Alaska."[30] By affirming congressional authority to deny Alaska Natives preemptive negotiation for and redemptive purchase of their lands indefinitely, *Tee-Hit-Ton* functioned as a critical node in the settler imperial formation that extended the temporal life of ambiguity while animating the legal theory that all tribes held their lands according to Congress's whim.

"It Is a State and It Is Not a State"

As *Tee-Hit-Ton* was working its way to the US Supreme Court, the ANB and ANS, along with a number of other Native organizations both inside and outside of Alaska, continued to wrangle with lawmakers over Alaska Native land rights in various iterations of statehood legislation. Lawmakers sought clauses that ranged from narrowing the scope and method by which Alaska Natives could protect their homeland from state land selections to rescinding the Alaska amendments to the IRA and releasing the funds accumulating in escrow per the provisions of the Tongass Timber Act.[31] Native activists and their attorneys objected to these proposals, maintaining their stance that they would protest any statehood bill that failed to protect their land rights as in earlier enabling acts. By 1955, their efforts to thwart statehood legislation that was not favorable to them became increasingly significant as the Eisenhower administration and military officials became more outspoken in their opposition to incorporating Alaska into the Union as a state. Since assuming the US presidency, Eisenhower had indicated he did not support Alaska statehood. Historians have suggested that partisan politics and economic concerns were the primary reasons for this resistance; however, concerns that a new state sovereignty might undermine the military utility of Alaska in an era of global Cold War informed much of Eisenhower's reasoning.[32] Territories were critical to US empire, and Alaska's function in twentieth-century imperialism rendered it indispensable to postwar US hegemony building, its narration as the last frontier and its status as an incorporated territory notwithstanding.

In July of 1954, Eisenhower admitted as much in a press conference in which he was pressed on his favorable response to the possibility of Hawai'i statehood and his reluctance to consider the same for Alaska.

Congress had joined the two statehood bills in an effort to have them pass together, causing the president to become more outspoken about his objections to Alaska statehood. To some, this represented a contradiction to the expected trajectory of an incorporated territory to statehood, and therefore a paradox of settler state narratives that emphasized US exceptionalism. Whereas Alaska had been naturalized as the last frontier at the turn of the century as a means by which to exclude other noncontiguous territories and inhabitants from citizenship and potential statehood, Eisenhower struggled to justify excluding Alaska from statehood despite the presumptions of incorporated status (i.e., that a territory's incorporation would inevitably lead to statehood). When asked to clarify "the Administration's position more specifically on Statehood for Alaska," he responded that he was concerned about the vulnerability of Alaska as a strategic location in the current Cold War hostilities, concluding, "These regions are of tremendous importance. And I don't think I should say more than that." When pressed on his "theory that a territory is necessarily easier to defend than a State," Eisenhower's answer revealed that, in his view, incorporated territories were not merely nascent states on an inevitable and predetermined path to inclusion in the Union. He responded with the following: "Well, I would say this: I don't say it's easier to defend, I say it's easier to use, because in one case it is under the absolute control of central government, and in the other case it is not."[33] The president's comments demonstrated how incorporated and unincorporated territories came to be configured in the US imperial matrix as sites from which to project and maintain imperial relationships and to manage the borders of properly national territory. Both territorial categories operate in specific ways within these coconstitutive projects of imperialism and national security, though the presumption of a pre-state character for incorporated territories conceals much of their function while naturalizing post-statehood narratives of inevitability and American exceptionalism.[34]

To many within the administration, it was "in the interest of national security that Alaska remain a Federal territory," and Eisenhower's responses further reveal the contingency of statehood and the imperial utility of incorporated territories.[35] Responding to these inquiries, the president wrote, "The admission of the Territory of Alaska to statehood . . . has a number of troublesome aspects," namely that "conversion of the Territory to a State cannot but raise difficult questions respecting the relationship of the military to the newly constituted State authority. Neither the nation nor Alaska could afford any impairment of the freedom of movement and of action by our forces in large areas of this critical region. I believe that it would be imprudent to effect so fundamental a readjustment unless a formula can be devised and approved by Congress which will adequately meet these defense needs."[36]

For these reasons, Eisenhower indicated that at most he might support plans to partition Alaska, with only the more populated Southcentral and Southeast regions considered for statehood.[37] Most lawmakers and statehood advocates in Alaska strongly opposed this, though some lawmakers conceded to including clauses in statehood legislation for military land withdrawals. The proposals would have allowed the president of the United States to establish "by Executive order or proclamation issued prior to the admission of the State of Alaska into the Union, one or more special national defense withdrawals." The withdrawals could not exceed 40 percent of the total acreage in Alaska and could only be established in the northern and western parts of the territory. Furthermore, thereafter such withdrawals could only be terminated by the president. In such areas, the United States would reserve "exclusive jurisdiction" with "sole legislative, judicial, and executive power" with such reserved powers "remain[ing] in effect . . . so long as such tract or parcel remains withdrawn, and the laws of the State of Alaska [would] not apply during the period of withdrawal."[38] These withdrawals represent one of many exceptions to statehood that lawmakers and Eisenhower's administration pursued for Alaska in the mid-1950s and further demonstrate the degree to which statehood was not a foregone conclusion for incorporated territories. In this vein, lawmakers also considered alternatives to statehood, including an elected rather than appointed governor and commonwealth status, designations similar to those conferred on Puerto Rico just a few years earlier.[39]

White settlers in Alaska who favored statehood strongly opposed these proposals as underhanded measures relegating them to the status of second-class citizens and denying them access to the vast majority of Alaska's extractible resources and land. Invigorated by the anticolonial rhetoric of American exceptionalism that characterized the Cold War, these territorial advocates of statehood organized a constitutional convention under the so-called Tennessee Plan in which territorial officials would nominate delegates to form a state constitution without an enabling act from Congress and then demand admission to the Union. Nevertheless, statehood for Alaska continued to hinge on satisfying federal jurisdictional concerns by acquiescing to Eisenhower's insistence on presidential authority to withdraw land for military purposes. Many lawmakers argued that "with the withdrawal provisions in the bill, the State of Alaska could not come into the Union on a basis of equality with other States and that therefore the bill flies in the face of the Constitution."[40] Likewise, some worried that withdrawal provisions would allow the federal government to "go back into Alaska and withdraw anything that was absolutely needed for the national defense." Given the relationship of extractable raw materials to national defense priorities, many felt that the federal government would employ this power to plunder Alaska's economic resources.[41] This possibility led Senator James Eastland from Mississippi to exclaim, "That is exactly it. It is a State and it is not a State. Membership in the Union would not be as firm, even, as the membership of a college student in a college fraternity." He continued, "We are talking about a State which cannot even enforce sovereignty in half of its area. It is neither in the Union nor out of the Union."[42] While Eastland's concerns were constitutional, his statement revealed the function of incorporated territories in US empire and the ways Alaska's duration as neither wholly inside nor outside of properly national space enabled US imperialism.

While beyond the scope of this book, it is noteworthy that the last two states to enter the Union share similarities in their noncontiguity, distinct legal relationship between their Indigenous nations and the United States, and geographical articulations in statehood. Like Alaska Natives, Kānaka Maoli have continuously resisted US assertions of sovereignty, including recent attempts to bring Native Hawaiians under so-called federal protections as federally recognized tribes in the same legal category as American Indians.[43] Pitched as an attempt to protect state and federal programs for Native Hawaiians, Hawaiian activists have resisted the bill as an attempt to abrogate their sovereignty, which "was not lost via conquest, cession, or adjudication" in either the 1898 annexation or 1959 statehood. Therefore, "those rights to self-determination are still in place under international law."[44] Likewise, Indigenous land and sovereignty constituted contested issues in Hawaiian statehood, when administration of the Homes Commission, the federal administrating body of Native Hawaiian lands held in trust, was transferred from Congress to the new state of Hawai'i as a condition of admission to the Union. Many Native Hawaiians understood this as an act of "forcible inclusion that is currently contested by Hawaiian sovereignty activists who challenge the very legitimacy of statehood."[45] The resistance of Native Hawaiians to US colonialism and forced inclusion within the legal frameworks of US federal Indian law reveal the irreconcilable nature of noncontiguous, incorporated territories with the assumptions and frameworks of US westward expansion.

In addition to the distinct relationship of Alaska Natives and Native Hawaiians to federal Indian law, the Hawaii Admission Act articulated similar geographical peculiarities to Alaska with regard to maintaining federal jurisdiction over noncontiguous territories as the intermediary nodes that manage the space between the nation proper and US imperial geographies. To this end, the Hawaii Admission Act defined the new state as "all the islands, together with their appurtenant reefs and territorial waters, included in the Territory of Hawaii on the date of enactment of this Act, except the atoll known as Palmyra Island, together with its appurtenant reefs and territorial waters."[46] Palmyra Atoll had been claimed by the United States as a guano island in the mid-nineteenth century and subsequently abandoned before being claimed by the Kingdom of Hawai'i. It was then illegally annexed by the United States along with Hawai'i, included in the statute "incorporating Hawai'i into the United States, and then ultimately excluded when Hawai'i became a state." Today, Palmyra Atoll remains the sole incorporated territory of the United States and as such reflects what legal scholar Christina D. Ponsa-Kraus describes as "a wobble in the elaborate process of combined inclusion and exclusion, expansion and retraction, projection and limitation, intended for territories at the margins of the nation."[47] The constellation of statutes, case law, and policy that constitute the settler imperial geography in Alaska likewise reflect this process.

Following the Tongass Timber Act, Alaska Natives used the settler imperial ambiguities around their legal status that the act had codified in their opposition to statehood proposals that sought to similarly delay reconciliation of their Indigenous land rights. As government officials and lawmakers deliberated the implications of Alaska Native legal status and land rights, Alaska Natives recognized the contingency of statehood and used the uncertainty around the issue to augment their influence as a political force in the territory. They identified statehood as a potential extension of the ambiguities inherent to the Tongass Timber Act that could further entrench the logic by which officials and lawmakers refused preemptive negotiation for and delayed redemptive purchase of Alaska Native homelands. In this vein, they reminded statehood advocates, settlers, and corporate interests that perpetual ambiguity also threatened these objectives, and as stakeholders in the future state, the recognition of Alaska Native land rights and proper negotiation with Alaska Native nations for consent was the only path forward by which future endeavors for settlement and development could be securely pursued.

In addition to reflecting the long-standing ambiguities and uncertainties in Alaska Native land rights, the ways government officials and lawmakers charted Alaska's crooked and tenuous path from a customs district to statehood demonstrates the utility of liminal spaces in conceiving, defining, and executing US imperialism. From the late nineteenth century, government officials, jurists, and lawmakers positioned Alaska as either inside or outside the boundaries of properly national territory in response to the exigencies of empire. Designation of Alaska as an incorporated territory at the turn of the nineteenth century functioned to establish a boundary between national space and imperial possessions. This in turn allowed the United States to justify perpetual territorial status and the denial of citizenship and constitutional rights to the millions of inhabitants it sought to exclude from the nation proper. Following WWII, white settlers and territorial officials presumed incorporated status implied that Alaska would proceed to statehood, inciting objections among federal officials and the military. The Eisenhower administration's resistance to statehood and the various proposals for partition or commonwealth status belie the distinctions between incorporated and unincorporated territorial status, revealing the doctrine as a method by which US interests could manipulate and maneuver the imperial geography. Statehood and new state jurisdiction threatened these objectives and prompted federal officials to insist on the inclusion of provisions by which they might retain or establish areas of federal jurisdiction.

As discussed in the next chapter, both the ambiguities over Alaska Native land rights and the role of Alaska in US empire would carry over into the statehood era. The latter became evident in ongoing militarization, proposals for nuclear experimentation, and tensions between the new state entity and the federal government. The former provoked a statewide response among Alaska Natives as the new state entity commenced with land appropriation and Congress extended the termination policy–era Public Law 280 to Alaska upon admission into the Union. By extending Public Law 280 to Alaska, Congress transferred civil and criminal jurisdiction over Alaska Native lands to the new state of Alaska, undermining Native sovereignty and complicating Alaska Native efforts to govern their homelands. In this context, Alaska Native nations mobilized a formidable response to the increasing pace of dispossession that culminated in their successful blockage of the proposed trans-Alaska pipeline after the discovery of oil at Prudhoe Bay and the passage of the Alaska Native Claims Settlement Act in 1971.

6

Disrupting Dispossession

Post-ANCSA Landscapes and the Myth of the Last Frontier

In October of 1969, Peter Ezi, treasurer for the Native Village of Eklutna, testified before the House of Representatives Subcommittee on Indian Affairs in support of land claims legislation for Alaska Natives. In his testimony, Ezi argued that "not too long ago" Eklutna people and other Indigenous Alaskans had "the pride of self-sufficiency," though "our once proud subsistence way of life has been replaced by the wardship way of life." He continued, "As wards of the BIA we had no control over our land . . . and as we struggled for a living, the very land we lived on was being taken bit by bit."[1] The Native Village of Eklutna is situated in the heart of Dena'ina territory along what is now called Knik Arm, roughly thirty miles north of Alaska's largest and most populated city of Anchorage. A critical waterway for Dena'ina salmon subsistence relations, the area became a strategic location for US and State of Alaska interests following World War II. In this context, Ezi argued that until recently, "Eklutna people . . . roamed widely over the whole Cook Inlet area and beyond," relating how the father of one of his childhood friends "used to set rabbit snares right about where Fourth and Gambell cross."[2] The rapidly increasing numbers of white settlers had been especially disruptive, and Ezi explained that the development of Anchorage into a bustling urban center had come at a devastating cost for Dena'ina people. To support urban expansion, state and federal agencies had repeatedly appropriated Dena'ina land to construct the infrastructure necessary to support the growing population. He recounted that in 1936 the secretary of the interior withdrew a tract of 328,000 acres for the Eklutna Industrial School with the intention that it would become an Indian reservation under the provisions of the Alaska amendments to the Indian Reorganization Act. This reserve was short-lived, and because of the ambiguity surrounding Alaska Native legal status, "our rights in the reserve were never made clear, and as a result everyone took the opportunity to take some land from us."[3]

Like many other Native activists, he keenly understood that the refusal of the federal government to recognize Alaska Native land rights through treaties or nation-to-nation negotiating status had facilitated dispossession. He and his community had been forced to relocate their villages and fish camps as settlers, corporations, and state interests proceeded to seize Native land under the auspice that Alaska Native nations were not tribes. He contended that the lack of clear land rights allowed "our supposed guardian, [the] BIA," to sit "idly by" as the state constructed highways through their hunting grounds and overtop their walking paths, built hydroelectric dams in their salmon streams, and severed their access to thousands of acres when the federal government began construction of the Fort Richardson army base and Elmendorf Air Force Base.[4] He echoed the sentiment of Native organizations across the state when he advocated for a settlement of their land rights that would not leave them "under the thumb of the BIA or any other guardian or Government agency" while recognizing their status as citizens capable of governing their own affairs.[5]

Eklutna, along with many other Alaska Native nations, had experience with the ways lawmakers had wielded the settler imperial ambiguities against the recognition of their status as sovereign nations and the status of their land. Nearly twenty years before Peter Ezi appeared before Congress members to testify in favor of a land settlement, another member of his family, William (Bill) Ezi, had filed one of the largest land claims suits in US history in 1951. The 2,500-square-mile claim garnered national attention when *The New York Times* published an article reporting on the enormity of the area claimed in the suit, which included the "rich Matanuska Valley farming area and a $25,000,000 power project" that had been the source of electricity for the growing city of Anchorage.[6] Ezi filed *Natives of Palmer, Alaska v. United States* in the Indian Claims Commission (ICC), where it lay dormant until May of 1964 when the US Assistant Attorney General Ramsey Clark filed a motion to dismiss the suit.

Clark reasoned that the ICC did not have jurisdiction to hear the case on two important points that demonstrate how settler imperial ambiguity had transmuted from a matter of unresolved uncertainties in racial and legal status and congealed into a systematic and circular logic of dispossession. The former was characterized by the utility of the temporal pause animated by indefinite anticipation of "future legislation by Congress" that would resolve Alaska Native land rights. The latter is characterized by the codification of a legal argument whereby government officials were provided an ongoing method by which to deny the recognition of any Alaska Natives as prior owners of land from which they had been dispossessed in the event they are deemed racially non-Indian. This chapter argues that the crystallization of this dispossessive logic was a product of the simultaneous victory of the Central Council of the Tlingit and Haida Indian Tribes of Alaska (CCTHITA) in *Tlingit and Haida Indians of Alaska v. United States,* in which the courts found their status identical to Indian tribes, and the admission of Alaska to the union as the forty-ninth state, after which government officials established new census categories to delineate and limit categories of Alaska Natives that the federal government would recognize as racially, and therefore legally, Indian.

While Ezi's lawsuit languished in the ICC, *Tlingit and Haida Indians of Alaska v. United States* worked its way through the United States Court of Claims, where attorneys for the CCTHITA faced similar challenges to their status as a tribal nation eligible to sue the federal government. Filed following passage of the Tlingit and Haida Jurisdictional Act, *Tlingit and Haida* ultimately prevailed, reflecting the strategy to mirror back to the commission the expectations and qualifications of a "tribe." This rendered their claims legible to the US legal system in ways that lawmakers, territorial and federal officials, and corporate interests had sought to prevent since the late nineteenth century. They knew that situating themselves within the "strict terms and conditions" of US legal framings of tribal nations might allow them to avoid the "pitfalls" of other unsuccessful land claims suits by Alaska Natives.[7] This chapter traces the trajectories of these two cases, revealing how multifaceted strategies of Alaska Native nations determined the character of the legal landscape in Alaska and influenced federal Indian policy in the late twentieth century. *Natives of Palmer* and other suits filed in the ICC succeeded in clouding title until the passage of the Alaska Native Claims Settlement Act (ANCSA), which in large part was made possible by the success of *Tlingit and Haida* in the Court of Claims. By claiming nearly all of Southeast Alaska by Aboriginal title before being dispossessed of their lands via "acts of the United States," CCTHITA strategy in *Tlingit and Haida* proved crucial for dislodging the settler imperial ambiguity that had stalled redemptive purchase for Alaska Native land.[8] By forcing the federal government to retroactively recognize them as prior owners of "property," the CCTHITA established the basis by which Alaska Natives would demand preemptive negotiation as a condition of land appropriation across what is for now called the state of Alaska.

Scholars have long recognized that *Tlingit and Haida* represented an important pivot point in the broader struggle for Alaska Native land rights and Indigenous land claims writ large. Attorney Chris McNeil (Tlingit, Haida, Nisga'a) argues that the case was a crucial moment, reflecting a shift from strategies that pursued monetary compensation for lands from which tribes had been dispossessed to seeking settlements that would also result in restoring lands back to tribes. In his analysis of *Tlingit and Haida,* McNeil asserts that during early organizing for land claims rights in the 1920s and 1930s, the Alaska Native Brotherhood (ANB) and Alaska Native Sisterhood followed a course of action characteristic of congressional policy in the late nineteenth and early twentieth centuries. This model limited settlements to monetary compensation from the United States for fair market value for lands at the time of their alleged taking and never contemplated that lands would be returned to Native tribes.[9] Between securing a liability judgment in 1959 and an award for damages nearly a decade later, the petitioners in *Tlingit and Haida* and Alaska Native leaders across the state had come to envision an alternative settlement that ultimately culminated in a combination of land and monetary compensation. In this vein, many Native leaders saw a corporate model as one way to assert political and governing autonomy over their homelands and to ensure their collective continuance as Native people and nations.

With these objectives in mind, and under intensifying pressure from the new State of Alaska's ongoing process of land selection and the discovery of oil at Prudhoe Bay, Alaska Natives from across the state formed the Alaska Federation of Natives in 1966, ultimately forcing a statewide reckoning of Alaska Native land claims and rights to self-determination, economic and political autonomy, and rights as US citizens. ANCSA was by no means universally championed among Alaska Natives, and the subsequent outcome of the settlement has not yielded proportional outcomes in terms of economic development across the twelve regional corporations and the many village corporations.[10] Nevertheless, the cases of Eklutna Inc., a Dena'ina village corporation created under ANCSA, and Sealaska, the Southeast regional corporation created under ANCSA, demonstrate the ways village and regional corporations leveraged the possibilities anticipated in the settlement. For example, Eklutna Inc. is now one of the largest private landholders in the Anchorage borough, and Sealaska has mobilized resources from ANCSA to fund multiple economic, educational, and political initiatives and programs.[11] While the settlement reflected the legacies of settler imperialism and the ways Alaska Natives worked to achieve recognition of their Indigenous land rights within that legal framework, ANCSA had broad implications for federal Indian policy in the contiguous states. ANCSA and the Native activism that mobilized for its passage were fundamental to the shift in national policy reflected in the Indian Self-Determination and Education Assistance Act. Furthermore, ANCSA marked a commencement as much as it marked a culmination in Alaska Native Affairs, as village and regional corporations grappled with the radical changes the settlement brought across the state and worked to implement its provisions. This process brought new and complex questions to the courts, Congress, village councils, the new Native corporations, and the state legislature as multiple parties sought to define the terms and parameters of Indigenous rights within the scope of the legislation.

"Natives in Alaska Are Not Exclusively Indian"

In 1959, Alaska became a US state and the US Court of Claims ruled in favor of the CCTHITA in *Tlingit and Haida Indians of Alaska v. United States*. These two events solidified Alaska as part of the national territory and confirmed that those whom Congress and government officials would recognize as racially and legally Indian resided in the forty-ninth state and held their lands under Indian title. In many ways, *Tlingit and Haida* nearly dislodged the settler imperial ambiguity from the dispossessive process when the court concluded that Tlingit and Haida constituted "a homogeneous and interrelated group of Indians" with established Indian title to which they were owed compensation for an identifiable taking on behalf of the federal government.[12] Consolidated as the Central Council of the Tlingit and Haida Indian Tribes of Alaska, the court determined that Tlingit and Haida people of Southeast Alaska were eligible to sue the federal government on the same legal footing as tribes. It also concluded that the federal government's creation of the Tongass National Forest in Southeast Alaska constituted a compensable action by the federal government.[13] This victory reflects the longstanding practices of Tlingit and Haida diplomacy in which they articulated their legal and political orders in ways that resonated within the US legal system. The CCTHITA satisfied the federal government's criteria as a recognizable group of Indians, while accommodating clan and village structures, thus providing for an outcome that mapped more appropriately onto their political geographies even as those formations had changed and adapted to US colonialism.

The success of these strategies did not come without substantial challenges, and government officials and federal attorneys persistently disputed the legitimacy of the CCTHITA and their claims. Abiding by the mandate in the 1935 Jurisdictional Act, the ANB voted to establish the Central Council at their annual convention in 1939. This new entity was immediately rejected by the Interior Department as a valid representative body with authority to enter into an attorney contract. Despite this, the CCTHITA met and elected officers two years later at the ANB convention at Wrangell, and after years of slow progress they secured approval from the interior secretary to hire a law firm and file the suit on October 1, 1947.[14] As it had in the ICC cases, attorneys for the United States levied their defense in the form of an attack on the distinctions between Tlingit and Haida political organization and recognized tribal nations of the contiguous states. They argued that while the CCTHITA constituted an "identifiable group of American Indians" for the purposes of bringing a claim under the Tlingit and Haida Jurisdictional Act, they were not a legal "tribe," and therefore they were "incapable of owning tribal or community property."[15] The court rejected this argument, ruling in favor of the Tlingit and Haida. Thus, nearly a century after the United States signed the Treaty of Cession with Russia and began its occupation of and extraction of commodities from Tlingit and Haida homelands, the Court of Claims affirmed collective, tribal land rights in Alaska.

This opened new and compelling conditions of possibility whereby Alaska Natives across the state could leverage their status as future prior owners of land against further settler encroachment by compelling the federal government to negotiate for their lands. As such, it threatened the presumptions of settlers, government officials, and corporate interests that tribes and tribal lands did not exist in Alaska, thus prompting a realignment of racial and legal categories in the new state. This process is reflected in poststatehood and post–*Tlingit and Haida* land claims suits filed by Alaska Native nations who resided outside of Southeast Alaska and for whom lawmakers had prescribed racial categories of Indigeneity that were not "Indian." The response of the US attorney general's office to petitions filed by these tribes in the ICC exemplify the process by which government officials incorporated the Indian status of Tlingit and Haida peoples into the settler imperial formation as a boundary by which they could exclude Indigenous Alaskans they designated as non-Indian from claiming a similar legal standing. They reified this boundary with their previous arguments that the federal government had not signed treaties with Alaska Natives, therefore they had not been formally dispossessed or removed from their lands.

This fused the legal and racial distinctions in Alaska into an operative dispossessive logic, which operates as follows: Only those recognized as racially Indian could claim Indian title and tribal status; Indian racial identity produces an Indian legal status in which land is vested, therefore establishing a legal capacity for dispossession; this legal capacity for dispossession is reflexively affirmed through what lawmakers and government officials designate as an identifiable legal taking (a treaty or other documented act of the federal government) that acknowledges (preemptively or retroactively) the legal/racial status of those on the land; the legal taking requires either preemptive negotiation or redemptive purchase depending on the temporal recognition of Indian racial/legal status. Thus, because "not all natives in Alaska are Indian," not all land in Alaska is held under Indian title. Therefore, not all Alaska Natives have the capacity for dispossession. Thus, preemptive negotiation or redemptive purchase are sometimes, but not always, operative in Alaska, and their animation is contingent on recognition of Indian racial identity, which is constituted and confirmed through an identifiable taking of land—an action that is only possible for those awarded an Indian racial/legal designation. This racialization is likewise reflected geographically, whereby Alaska is somewhat, but not entirely, considered integral to the nation proper, and the conference of Indian racial identities on those located in the southeastern portion of the state functioned as a spatial boundary that lawmakers and government officials sought to buttress in subsequent land suits.

Government officials sealed the contingencies of this logic into Indigenous–US relations in Alaska as part of their efforts to reassert the authority of US institutions to define the racial and legal limits of Indigenous nations. Poststatehood, they wielded this logic against petitioners in land claims suits brought by Alaska Natives in the ICC. As illustrated by Peter Ezi's testimony that opened this chapter, Dena'ina peoples of Southcentral Alaska faced a drastic increase in US settler colonial and imperial pressures in the early twentieth century. Like the Tlingit, Haida, and Tsimshian had experienced in the Southeast, the dual ambiguities around the legal status of Alaska Natives and the relationship of Alaska to the nation proper had facilitated their dispossession and displacement. Eklutna lies roughly thirty miles northeast of what is now Alaska's largest city of Anchorage. The population of Anchorage and the surrounding area increased substantially when President Woodrow Wilson authorized the construction of a five-hundred-mile railroad route from Seward to Fairbanks. The project carved a path through Alutiiq, Upper Inlet Dena'ina, Ahtna, and Tanana homelands, snaking through fishing, hunting, trapping, and berrying grounds and severing the walking paths that connected them.[16] Railroad construction crews peaked at roughly 4,500 workers in 1917, with the rapidly expanding tent town of Anchorage serving as the central construction hub.[17] The increase in white railroad workers from outside the territory had profound and immediate impacts on Dena'ina life, with the 1918 flu epidemic ravaging dozens of villages.[18] In the wake of the devastation wrought by the flu, the Bureau of Education established an orphanage for Native children, which was soon after converted into a vocational school. At the time, only Congress had the authority to create Indian reservations in Alaska, though an act on February 23, 1925, did permit the secretary of the interior to establish public purpose reserves for the "vocational training [of] the aboriginal native people of the Territory of Alaska."[19] Under this authority, Interior Secretary Hubert Work established the Eklutna reserve as one of several public use reserves. The reserve totaled 1,368 acres, and by 1930 the Eklutna Industrial School was the largest of the territory's three Native boarding schools. According to congressional documents provided to accompany Peter Ezi's testimony regarding the rapid dispossession of Dena'ina peoples in the 1930s and 1940s, the interior secretary added to the initial reserve when he "temporarily withdrew a tract of 328,000 acres" in 1936. The expansion came in response to recommendations made by the Bureau of Indian Affairs, likely after protests and complaints from Dena'ina that the increasing settlement on account of the railroad expansion and the construction of the Anchorage-Matanuska Valley Highway had impinged significantly on their subsistence economies.[20] These construction projects compounded the effects of the flu epidemic, and in the late 1920s several Dena'ina villages had consolidated, with many Dena'ina relocating to Eklutna, Kenai, Tyonek, Pedro Bay, Nondalton, and Lime Village or seeking work in Anchorage.[21]

To facilitate the growth of Anchorage and the accompanying transportation infrastructure, developers dammed the Eklutna River in 1928, devastating the salmon habitat that Dena'ina at Eklutna had stewarded and regulated for generations, compounding the effects of displacement and disease. As Peter Ezi would testify forty years later, the municipality and utility corporations, in concert with the railroad, commenced with these projects without any consideration or consultation with Dena'ina people. Records indicate that the only land rights dispute that Anchorage Light and Power negotiated was the purchase of 161.42 acres of land from a disgruntled homesteader for $1,500 in 1929.[22] In the 1930s and 1940s, the Matanuska Valley Colonization Project and the militarization of Alaska accelerated Native dispossession across Southcentral Alaska, and the Interior Department revoked the 1936 expansion of the Eklutna reserve except for 9,200 acres under the auspice of "increased pressures from the Anchorage community for use of woodland within the larger [reserve] area" and "the establishment of the Fort Richardson military reserve." In 1946, the same year the Harry S. Truman administration established the Indian Claims Commission, the Bureau of Indian Affairs (BIA) closed the Eklutna school and sold the condemned buildings and land to the Alaska Railroad.[23] The Alaska Railroad, Glenn Highway, and the appropriation of Dena'ina waterways for hydroelectric dams and shipping purposes, and the squatters that accompanied them, constituted illegal countermobilities that cut through Dena'ina geographies. In response to these disruptions to their legal and political orders and their relations to each other, the land, and nonhuman nations, William Ezi, known as "Walkin' Bill" for his effective use of Dena'ina walking paths that connected Southcentral Native communities, filed a claim on behalf of a consortium of Dena'ina people. Referring to themselves as the "natives of Palmer, Alaska," they argued that they had "been deprived of the continuous use" of their lands and waters that "surrounds Palmer, Alaska, and takes in the greater portion of the Matanuska Valley, and adjacent areas."[24] Indeed, the area claimed totaled roughly 2,500 square miles, encompassing nearly the entire region north of Anchorage along the Knik Arm of the Cook Inlet.

Their petition reflects how government officials and lawmakers used the ambiguous legal status of Alaska Natives to deny the recognition of land rights by rendering land claims as contingent on race and obfuscating the means by which Alaska Natives could establish a clear and identifiable legal taking. In this way, Assistant Attorney General Ramsey Clark's response reflected this transmutation of ambiguity into a self-reflexive logic of dispossession. Clark filed the motion for summary judgment to dismiss the *Natives of Palmer* on the basis that the "racial identity of the petitioner" and the "subject matter of the claim" failed to confer jurisdiction on the ICC.[25] Regarding the first point, he emphasized that the ICC could only adjudicate claims brought by "any Indian tribe, band, or other identifiable group of American Indians." He noted that the petitioners identified themselves as the "Natives of Palmer, Alaska," and therefore the commission could not presume jurisdiction. He argued that from the late nineteenth century, the legislative and judicial history of Alaska clearly reflected the ways government officials and lawmakers had intentionally demarcated the racial and legal distinctions that characterized Indigenous–US relations in Alaska. He reminded the commission that "Congress has consistently recognized and preserved Alaskan racial distinctions in its acts respecting Alaska" and "that Congress has for many years been aware of the distinction between Indians and other natives of Alaska." Clark continued that Congress had defined Indigenous Alaskans as "native Indians, Eskimos, and Aleuts of the whole or part blood inhabiting Alaska at the time of the Treaty of Cession and their descendants." These distinctions had been codified in the US census, which in 1940 listed the category "native stock" to enumerate "races indigenous to Alaska" and distinguish them from the category of "American Indian."[26] Tellingly, these categories were modified immediately following Alaska's admission to the union in 1959, and the 1960 census identified "Aleut and Eskimo" separately from "American Indian" on census questionnaires used exclusively in Alaska.[27] By restricting ICC jurisdiction to Indian tribes, bands, or groups, Clark argued that Congress had intended to exclude those it recognized as Native but considered racially non-Indian. Because "natives in Alaska are not exclusively Indians," the ICC could only exercise jurisdiction over claims in which the petitioner had proven Indian racial classification. He concluded that "native is not synonymous with Indian" and that those relegated to non-Indian racial categories did not have similar legal standing to those recognized as Indians.[28]

Clark's second rationale in filing for dismissal in *Natives of Palmer* draws on the premise of the first and fused Indian racial status with the capacity for dispossession. In their petition, the Natives of Palmer, Alaska, claimed that the construction of settler towns and cities along with the railway and road infrastructure had "deprived [them] of the continuous use of lands and waters" to which they held "on the grounds of continuous prior use and occupancy" from "time immemorial up to the present time." Clark concluded that in the absence of any evidence demonstrating illegal seizure or the violation of the terms of any preemptive negotiations, the "petitioner does not specifically allege loss of any described lands or taking of its lands by defendant."[29] The Natives of Palmer asserted that they had been displaced from their homelands without any negotiation or compensation even though they had never "given up said lands," nor had they "sold or abandoned our lands." They concluded that because no "action whatsoever [had been] taken to protect [their] rights," they were "now in danger of losing all the rest of [their] land."[30]

Clark took the opportunity to interpret the petitioners' claims that they had never "sold or abandoned" their lands nor had their lands been the subject of any preemptive negotiation as evidence that no formal taking had occurred. Because the ICC was limited to "rendering money judgements only," petitioners must demonstrate and request compensation for a specific taking inflicted by the federal government. He refused to interpret the petitioner's allegations that the settler townsite of Palmer and the railroad and roadway construction and clearing of farmland associated with it had deprived those identifying as Natives of Palmer, Alaska, of the use and occupancy of their lands as a taking. Clark thus concluded that "the petition does not specifically allege loss of any described lands or a taking of its lands by defendant." Implicit in this section of his motion is that a petitioner must deliver evidence of a formal taking, which, according to Clark's logic, they would only have if they had been acknowledged as Indians by the federal government. To him, their questionable status as Indians precluded any preemptive negotiation that would have taken place. These implications generated the self-reflexive, looping character of the settler imperial logic of dispossession by which proof of a legal taking was contingent on racialization as Indian, as an identifiable taking was itself anticipated by the Indian racial category of the occupants.[31]

William Ezi and the Dena'ina who filed the Palmer land claim were not the only community of Alaska Natives who sought a settlement through the ICC, and there are a dozen dockets detailing claims of Alaska Native villages and other organizational entities from across the territory.[32] Filed amid the escalating conflict over statehood and Native land rights, and under mounting pressures from corporate timber, mining, and fisheries interests, and an increasing settler population, many Native nations sought redress in the ICC as one method to protect their lands. These filings also reveal the ways many Alaska Natives sought to provoke recognition of their land rights by aligning their Indigenous identities with those reflected in federal Indian policy. In many cases, the petitioners were careful and deliberate to characterize themselves as tribes or other "identifiable groups" with the authority to bring such claims against the United States before the ICC. To do so, each community drew on its distinct relationship to the legislative and judicial history that Congress and the courts had scripted into Indigenous–US relations in Alaska. For example, the Yup'ik of Gambell on St. Lawrence Island had incorporated under the Alaska amendments of the IRA. They thus argued in their petition that they, as the Native Village of Gambell, "maintain a tribal organization recognized by the Secretary of the Interior." While the application of the IRA to the Alaska context recognized villages as the operative political unit, Gambell insisted on land rights as members of a tribe, thereby further aligning their collective nationhood status. They urged that the "members of the Native Village of Gambell constitute a part of that tribe of Eskimos known as the St. Lawrence Island Eskimos," with tribal claims to the entirety of the island.[33] Furthermore, they anticipated the race-based objections the federal government would likely employ in denying their land rights. They were explicit in their legal Indian status by contending that "although Eskimos are considered anthropologically a race apart from other American Indians, they have always been treated by the Defendant as American Indians and fall within the jurisdiction of the Act of August 13, 1946."[34]

The collective responses of the ICC commission and the US attorney general's office to the Gambell petition and other filings by Alaska

Natives further reveal that the settler imperial ambiguities had congealed into a logic of racial-spatial-legal contingencies. In all Alaska Native suits brought before the ICC, the attorney general drew on the long history of the distinctions between Alaska Natives and Indians in the contiguous states. For example, in the case of the Native Village of Gambell's petition, the attorney general's office argued that despite the legal status of the petitioners as coeval with what the government defined as an Indian tribe, they did not satisfy the "basic statutory requirement of the Act that a petitioner be a member of the Indian race," nor could they provide evidence of a formal taking. Some petitions sought redress for lands taken by "industries and other people" while also requesting a formal determination of their land rights to prevent future losses.[35] Like *Natives of Palmer,* US attorneys took the opportunity to dismiss these petitions on the grounds that the petitioners could not point to "a direct cause of action against the United States" resulting in dispossession or removal.[36] While the ICC only had jurisdiction to award monetary judgments and could not affirm the boundaries of lands "presently used" by the plaintiffs, dismissal on this technicality ignored white settler and corporate encroachment while buttressing the correlation of Indian racial identity and the possibility of preemptive negotiation on a nation-to-nation basis for land cessions. These pro forma responses demonstrate how government officials had translated the ambiguities around Alaska Native legal status into a prescribed logic that allowed them to deny the recognition of Alaska Natives they categorized as non-Indian as the prior owners of their homelands indefinitely.[37]

While *Tlingit and Haida* confirmed the existence of Aboriginal title in Alaska for those racialized as Indian, it also established the legitimacy of incorporated central council entities to represent the interests of diverse Alaska Native villages and clans located across vast geographic landscapes on the same footing as tribes in the contiguous states. Achieving a legal status equivalent to tribal nations was an important strategy; however, Central Council members continued to seek modifications to that status that would facilitate greater autonomy and lessen interference from the Interior Department or the BIA. While awaiting the court's decision on damages, members of the CCTHITA pursued changes to the 1935 Jurisdictional Act that would allow them to administer the settlement and manage Tlingit and Haida affairs in ways that reflected the profound changes their nations had adapted over the previous decades of US occupation. Specifically, they challenged the ways Congress had imposed restrictions on beneficiary eligibility, the prohibition on per capita payment structures, and the authority the interior secretary would have in managing the funds. The act limited beneficiaries to those "persons of Tlingit or Haida blood, living in or belonging to any local community of these tribes" in "the region known and described as southeastern Alaska" and limited the use of settlement funds to what the interior secretary might approve as "productive economic instruments and resources of public benefit" that, "under regulations he may prescribe," would contribute to "the future economic security and stability of said Indian groups."[38] To the CCTHITA, these restrictions were incongruent with their own criteria for belonging and represented an unacceptable imposition of federal authority and wardship status that they had worked diligently to avoid.

In 1965, the CCTHITA presented a series of amendments to the 1935 Jurisdictional Act before the US Senate that reflected their ongoing efforts to leverage settler imperial ambiguity in defining their own relationship to the federal government and the new state of Alaska. This strategy promised to redefine the ways tribes interacted with federal and state agencies and ultimately informed much of their approaches to a statewide land claims settlement. The proposed amendments would establish greater autonomy over the CCTHITA dispersal of settlement funds and allow them to define their own political geographies by including Tlingit and Haida people who had relocated from traditional villages to other areas of Southeast Alaska, other areas within Alaska, or outside the state entirely. Central Council president Andrew Percy Hope (Tlingit, Eagle, Kaagwaantaan) argued for CCTHITA authority to establish criteria by which Tlingit and Haida people could be accounted for on the rolls. He recounted the "substantial migration and resettlement of the Tlingit and Haida" whereby "large numbers . . . have left their traditional native villages and moved to modern towns in southeast Alaska which . . . were established by white persons." They did this for a number of reasons, including searching for wage work or "more advantageous educational facilities" for their children. He continued that substantial numbers of Tlingit and Haida had also relocated to other parts of Alaska and other states, such as California, Oregon, and Washington. Because the 1935 Jurisdictional Act had been construed to mean that only "traditional Tlingit and Haida tribal villages of communities may prepare rolls and only persons living in or belonging to those traditional tribal villages may be listed on those rolls," he and others worried that this would exclude substantial numbers of Tlingit and Haida people.[39]

Hope also pressed Congress to afford more authority to the CCTHITA in managing the settlement award in ways that would likewise accommodate Tlingit and Haida diversity and geopolitical complexity without paternalistic BIA oversight. He argued that "there are differences of views among the Tlingit and Haida Indians as to the ultimate use of the judgement monies," as they are "not a single compact people . . . [but] rather live in widely separated places" with differing "economic and social conditions." He contended that these differences should not be contingent on congressional, Interior Department, or BIA mandates but rather be resolved through legislation reflecting what Tlingit and Haida people determine is most effective and beneficial to their communities. He and his counterparts emphasized their status as US citizens, for whom "the last thing we want is to be regarded as wards or charges," reflecting the ways that Tlingit and Haida people sought to achieve federal recognition of an Indigenous governing body that could operate without obstructive BIA oversight.[40] Congress adopted the amendments in August that same year, granting the Central Council the authority to "prepare plans for . . . and to exercise such further powers with respect to . . . distribution of said funds as may be authorized by Congress" while allowing the rolls of Tlingit and Haida to include those who lived not only in Southeast Alaska but also in other areas of the United States and Canada.[41]

Four years later, the Court of Claims issued its decision on the monetary value of the damages for the 17,601,288 acres for which it determined the federal government was liable. This acreage consisted of withdrawals made for the Annette Island reserve in 1891, totaling 86,730 acres; the creation of the Tongass National Forest in three presidential proclamations in 1902, 1907, and 1909, totaling 14,956,312 acres; and the creation of Glacier Bay National Monument in 1906, totaling 2,558,246 acres.[42] Despite the favorable ruling, the commissioners only awarded the Tlingit and Haida $7.5 million, relying on a method of valuation that only accounted for what the commissioners defined as the single most valuable use of the land. This method allowed the commission to parse out what it interpreted as having the greatest monetary value to the exclusion of all other uses of the land and base the compensation amount on the "fair market value" of that single usage at the time of taking. As part of their calculations, the commission ruled that there would be no recovery for the loss of Aboriginal fishing rights even though the liability phase of the suit found that fishing rights constituted a compensable taking. In his detailed analysis of the case, Chris McNeil describes the way the commission also devalued timber resources and established requirements that mandated that Tlingit and Haida provide proof of actual mining operations or probable profitability from mining in order to consider such uses in the valuation process. He concludes, "Bottom line, it was evident in 1969 and even plainer today that the valuations for the takings from Tlingits and Haidas was extremely low and far below fair market value."[43] Despite this outcome, *Tlingit and Haida* was pivotal in terms of its impacts on Alaska Native land claims strategies. It established, first and foremost, that the courts would potentially recognize Alaska Natives as the prior owners of lands held under Aboriginal title that had been transferred out of their possession, thus requiring redemptive purchase and implying the possibility for preemptive negotiation. The paltry monetary settlement and the refusal of the court to incorporate Tlingit valuations of their land and the complex human and nonhuman relations it sustained further motivated them, along with Alaska Native nations across the state, to pursue a preemptive settlement.

"The Whole State Is a Native Village"

By the time the Court of Claims closed the file on *Tlingit and Haida,* Alaska Natives across the state had come together to form the Alaska Federation of Natives (AFN), and in the wake of a Tlingit and Haida victory, they began wielding the recognition of their land rights against further dispossession. Alaska's constitution allowed the new state to select up to 102,550,000 acres of what the federal government determined to be "vacant, unappropriated, and unreserved" land without consent from or negotiation with Alaska Native nations, and the AFN immediately began strategizing to stop this process. To prevent the Interior Department from approving the state's proposed land selections, Alaska Natives filed a barrage of land claims petitions with the Department of the Interior, wielding the unsettled—and therefore uncertain—status of their land rights as a barrier to any further appropriation of their land without negotiation. This threat persuaded Interior Secretary Stewart Udall to freeze all land selections and title conveyances until Native land claims were settled. In response, the State of Alaska sued Udall on the grounds that the freeze violated the Alaska Statehood Act, and while the state secured a summary judgment in its favor in district court, the Ninth Circuit reversed, remanding the case back to the district court for trial.

Importantly, the Ninth Circuit's decision implied that lands in Alaska were subject to Aboriginal title, and they recommended that litigation be deferred until Congress passed legislation settling Native land claims in the state.[44] In response, Governor Walter J. Hickel agreed to establish the Governor's Task Force on Native Land Claims, which he charged with drafting a statewide settlement. The task force consisted of several dozen leaders of Native organizations, along with a handful of representatives from the State and the Interior Department. Headed by State Representative William Iġġiaġruk Hensley (Iñupiaq), the task force brought their recommendations to Congress the following year. The proposal, Senate Bill 2906, reflected not only the wide spectrum of Alaska Native ways of life as they had responded to increasing colonial pressures over the past hundred years of US occupation but also the ways they sought a settlement that recognized their Aboriginal rights as Indigenous Alaskans without acquiescing to the authority of the Department of the Interior or the BIA. In this way, they insisted on a formulation of Alaska Native–US relations that accommodated a pluralistic mutuality of land use, economic development, and Indigenous autonomy.

In February of 1968, Hensley addressed the Committee on Interior and Insular Affairs at hearings held in Anchorage in which he urged Congress to adopt the task force's recommendations. In his statement, he described the detrimental ways the unsettled nature of Alaska Native land rights had affected Alaska Natives, arguing that the task force's proposal offered a solution that could simultaneously ensure diverse Indigenous futures while accommodating settler livelihoods, state development agendas, and federal objectives. He argued that "unlike the Indians of the lower States, there are few officially recognized tribal groups in Alaska," and despite this lack of recognition, they "feel that the areas they inhabit and occupy still belong to them—under Indian title." He continued that Alaska Natives felt "that compensation would not be the answer to the problems that we are facing today—we feel that continued use and occupancy of large areas of land is necessary." The task force had concluded that "we own major portions of Alaska under Indian title" and "we have the right to request that the Government convey a certain amount of land to the Alaska Native rather than be paid completely in cash or financial considerations." Likewise, many on the task force agreed that reservation lands held in trust would impose barriers to Native economic endeavors. Instead, their settlement proposed the conveyance of forty million acres of land to Native villages in fee simple, while retaining usufructuary rights to ceded lands customarily used for hunting, fishing, and trapping for a period of a hundred years. To accomplish this, the proposal outlined a corporate structure for the settlement, calling for the creation of regional Native corporations and one statewide Native corporation to administer lands and monetary awards and called for a 10 percent royalty interest in Outer Continental Shelf (oil) revenues and an initial grant of $20 million from the federal government. In this way, the task force sought a settlement that would accommodate a diverse range of Indigenous livelihoods and futures while reducing interference from the BIA. In Hensley's words, "The Alaska Native seeks not to isolate himself from the State—but to become a moving and dynamic part of the State—and we feel that a resolution of land problems will enable us to participate."[45]

The Interior Department proposed a settlement of its own, the provisions of which reflected the efforts of government officials to restrain recognition of Alaska Native land rights within the limitations of settler imperial legislation that had insisted on narrow understandings of Native land use and occupancy. In stark contrast to the expansive and dynamic vision of the task force's proposal, the Interior bill would merely amend the 1926 Alaska Native Townsite Act to authorize the interior secretary to grant "in trust . . . to each tribe, band, clan, village, community, or group of Natives in Alaska . . . title to the village site . . . now occupied by such group." As trustee, the interior secretary would have complete authority to administer the trust with the assistance of a committee composed of five members, only one of whom "shall be appointed from nominations submitted by Alaska Natives."[46] The trust would expire after twenty-five years, and all other lands outside of the townsites for which Alaska Natives sought compensation would be consolidated into a single claim to be filed no more than six years from the date of the bill's enactment.

Members of the task force and Native organizations across the state offered quick rebuke to the Interior Department proposal. While it included the same 10 percent revenue payments from the Continental Shelf profits, the cession of all lands outside of Native village sites and the overreaching authority of the interior secretary and the BIA in Alaska Native affairs was unacceptable. Emil Notti (Koyukon), president of the Alaska Federation of Natives, railed against increased federal control in Native lives. He argued that federal and state interference had been catastrophic in terms of Native well-being, as federal policies allowed for the decimation of the salmon fisheries and the devastation of hunting and trapping livelihoods. He concluded, "Controls by federal agencies over the resources and lives of people in Alaska has not met with any success. . . . They have failed in every instance. . . . The Native people in Alaska . . . want to have control of their own destiny. And if there are going to be mistakes made, we want to make them, not let the bad decisions be made in Juneau, or even farther away, in Washington D.C."[47] He urged the Senate committee to pass S. 2906, advocating, like Hensley, for a settlement that would allow for the persistence of Alaska Native subsistence economies, cultures, and autonomy in ways that recognized Alaska Native rights to land and self-governance as Indigenous people outside of the purview of paternalistic federal Indian policies.

Several others testified in support of the task force's proposal, identifying how government officials and settlers had used ambiguity in the legal status of Alaska Natives to facilitate dispossession. Ruby Tansy (Tanana), a representative from Cantwell and an elected member of the National Indian Youth Council, confronted the committee about the dubious methods by which government officials had allowed settlers to displace her community from their Indigenous homelands. Like Frederick Moore nearly seventy years prior, she indicted the means by which miners and homesteaders had acquired title from a government that had never negotiated with any Alaska Natives for the land it claimed the right to sell. To her, title was merely a "white man's tool" that allowed "homesteaders and the State" to take "our lands that we own." This process had increased with "the opening of the highway," by which "more and more white people came." She recalled her recent outrage at a map provided by the Federal Field Committee that "had Cantwell [listed as] a white community" because "we don't have as many Indians as whites now." She protested this erasure, telling committee members, "I was so mad when I saw that because I know that it was an Indian community." To Tansy and her counterparts, it was absurd that Alaska Natives needed to confront Congress and the State "saying, give us back our land when in fact the land is ours." Her testimony reveals how the federal government's refusal to recognize Alaska Native land rights had facilitated these underhanded methods of dispossession, belying the fact that Alaska Natives owned the land and that the government, according to its own constitutional provisions and legal precedent, would need to negotiate for it. She warned that the refusal of government officials, corporate interests, lawmakers, and settlers to recognize Alaska Native land rights did not change the fact that "the whole State is a Native village. It really is."[48]

Congress took no further action on this slate of bills, though the testimony from members of the task force and other Native leaders from across Alaska reveals the ways they envisioned a settlement that would keep Native lands in Native possession and facilitate Indigenous autonomy over their participation in capitalist economic development, therefore securing the place of Alaska Natives as core policymakers in the state of Alaska. These objectives are reflected in the petitions of Native communities to the ICC or the Court of Claims in defense of their land. Their requests for a process by which they could establish recognition of their land rights and secure compensation for the losses they had already sustained reveal the ways they sought to maintain control over their futures as nations and as Alaska's first citizens who also had an inherent stake in Alaska's future. To this end, Alaska Native post-statehood efforts demonstrate that a settlement that did not include Native landownership in perpetuity was unfathomable. In advocating for a settlement of this nature, they traced the consequences they had borne as a result of government officials and lawmakers who framed their legal status as uncertain, ambiguous, and therefore irreconcilable for over one hundred years, and they indicted those who sought to deny and erase the existence and persistence of their nations by confining their land rights to allotments and townsites.

Tansy's declaration that the "whole State is a Native village" and her critique of legal title as a "white man's tool" used by those seeking to erase and deny Indigenous land relations and governance resonated through subsequent proceedings on settlement legislation. In this way, they continued to expose the ambiguity in their legal status as a method by which government officials, settlers, and corporate interests sought to subvert Alaska Native legal, political, and cultural orders and the rights to the land that sustained them. Tansy's description of the dispossession her community experienced in Cantwell illustrated this method of settler imperial dispossession and accompanying erasure, achieved through the legal ambiguity lawmakers and officials had employed in Alaska since 1867. By refusing to recognize Aboriginal title or Indian Country in Alaska, the federal government narrated a legal fiction in which these various interests could imagine Alaska as "vacant, unappropriated, and unreserved" public lands for which it had the authority to convey title. In this way, the hundred years of US occupation in Alaska represented a new approach to possessory claims in both logic and application that centered around the ambiguities sown in race, Indigeneity, and law by federal officials in the late nineteenth century. Upon statehood and the CCTHITA victory in *Tlingit and Haida,* these ambiguities cemented the contingency of land rights on Indian racial identity, severing land rights from Indigeneity. While Alaska Natives protested this legal legerdemain, these dynamics continued to provide a rhetoric by which government officials, corporate interests, and settlers would try to refute Alaska Native nationhood and land claims in the twentieth century and beyond.

In the years following the 1968 hearings, Congress debated several more bills in efforts to settle Alaska Native land claims. Alaska Natives held fast to their objective of securing a settlement that included both land and a monetary award, along with a structure that many felt allowed them the greatest amount of autonomy in relation to the United States and the State of Alaska. The AFN continuously reiterated that "historically, dependence and reliance on federal and state programs has effectively denied the principle of self-determination to the aboriginal people of the United States." In the context of this historical precedent, they sought an alternative that they argued could transfer "control of their destinies to the Native people" with the "creation of a statewide Native corporation and . . . twelve regional corporations," thereby providing "a maximum of local self-determination."[49] In these proposals, the AFN, Native members of the governor's task force, and Native organizations across the state generally concurred that this would require revenues from oil exploration, a minimum of forty million acres, and an initial settlement award of $500 million, with additional provisions that sought protections for Alaska Native subsistence use.

The bill that became law ultimately adopted the corporate structure of the AFN proposal, establishing the twelve regional corporations and over two hundred village corporations.[50] These ANCSA corporations served as the vehicles through which the land and monetary aspects of the settlement would be administered. In total, ANCSA included a land settlement for 45.7 million acres to be selected and owned in fee simple by the corporations and a monetary settlement of $962.5 million for the extinguishment of Aboriginal title to remaining lands in Alaska. Perhaps unsurprisingly, ANCSA was vague regarding Native subsistence rights. Section 4(b) declared that "all aboriginal titles . . . including any aboriginal hunting or fishing rights that may exist, are hereby extinguished."[51] However, Congress provided a detailed committee report that stated quite clearly that they expected the secretary of the interior and the State to protect Native subsistence rights, and other sections of ANCSA provided methods for land withdrawals by which the interior secretary could do so.[52] The Native subsistence protections that emerged from ANCSA took legislative form in the Alaska National Interest Lands Conservation Act in 1980, which ultimately granted a subsistence preference right to "rural" Alaskans.[53] Implied in this language was the fact that most rural Alaskans were Native, though the refusal to establish subsistence rights explicitly on the basis of Indigenous rights is telling and reflects long-standing efforts among lawmakers to avoid recognition of this political legal status.

ANCSA was also silent on the status of Alaska Native governance, and in this way it seemingly raised more questions than it answered. The regional and village corporations constitute for-profit corporations under Alaska state law; however, the language in ANCSA made clear that it was not intended to terminate any social or economic services for Alaska Natives or prevent Alaska Natives from participating in other federal programs designed for American Indians.[54] In this way, ANCSA is very much a product of the preceding hundred years of ambiguity that government officials crafted around Alaska Native legal status and the ways Alaska Natives navigated the impacts of settler imperialism on their lands and livelihoods. It also did not resolve these ambiguities, as is evident in ongoing legal battles since its enactment regarding a number of issues, including subsistence, the status of ANCSA lands in relation to trust lands, jurisdiction over Alaska Native allotments, and debates about the circumstances in which the ANCSA corporations may be considered tribes.[55] These complex dynamics persisted even after the assistant secretary of the interior for Indian Affairs added 226 Alaska Native village corporations to the federal register of federally recognized tribes in 1993, demonstrating the ways settler imperialism informs the ongoing form and function of US empire in Alaska. State and federal officials routinely employ this long history of ambiguity in their efforts to deny or undermine Native sovereignty in Alaska; however, these contests and the resources the state must marshal against tribes merely exposes the US imperial and settler colonial empire as incomplete and contingent. Most importantly, the persistence of Alaska Native nations and the legal, political, cultural, and social orders they sustain and enact daily is a testament to this reality and reveals how Alaska Native tribal governments, corporations, subsidiaries, communities, organizations, and individuals collaborated and mobilized to ensure Indigenous futures in their homelands.

Persisting Indigenous Land Relations

On February 1, 2024, the Interior Department Solicitor Robert Anderson issued an opinion declaring that Alaska Native tribes have jurisdiction on Alaska Native allotments. Considered Indian Country, Native allotments in Alaska are subject to state jurisdiction under Public Law 280, thus the opinion represents a significant increase in governing authority for Alaska Natives over their land.[1] As such, the decision has the potential to affect the ways Alaska Natives approach economic initiatives, develop and implement fish and wildlife regulations, and exercise law enforcement. Coming on the heels of the Interior Department's approval of applications from Alaska Native tribes to bring allotments and other tribally held lands into federal trust, tribal jurisdiction over allotments expands their eligibility for certain federal programs and services that typically exclude tribes without reservations.[2] Both decisions reflect the dynamic strategies of Alaska Native nations as they orient themselves in relation to federal Indian policy, state and federal officials, settlers, and corporate entities—including Alaska Native Claims Settlement Act (ANCSA) corporations—throughout the state.

The impacts of these decisions have been immediate and profound. For example, the Native Village of Eklutna had unsuccessfully sought to establish a casino-style tribal gaming hall on an eight-acre family allotment currently held in trust by the federal government. The National Indian Gaming Commission had initially rejected their proposal because Alaska tribes did not have jurisdiction over their allotments. In light of the Interior Department's recent opinion, the commission has approved Eklutna's resubmitted proposal.[3] Representatives of the tribe described how the gaming hall will deliver a much-needed infusion of funding to the community, citing that Eklutna is "in dire need of housing," a gathering center, and office space, and the tribe desperately needs to expand the infrastructure of their small community health clinic.[4] Similarly,

Alaska Native tribes across the state are deliberating on the ways these jurisdictional changes will affect their communities. Native Village of Beaver First Chief Rhonda Pitka (Koyukon Athabascan, Iñupiaq) spoke with reporters about the tremendous boon the solicitor's opinion could provide in terms of community safety. She described that in her village, which lies 110 miles north of Fairbanks, federal law enforcement is slow to respond to incidents of trespass and theft on Native allotments, thus tribal jurisdiction would allow the tribe to bring claims in tribal courts. Likewise, Joel Dáxhajóon Jackson (Tlingit, Kàach.àdi), president of the Organized Village of Kake, sees opportunities to use allotments and federal trust lands as one of many mechanisms to protect Tlingit ways of life and land relations as they continue to ward off development projects in the Tongass.[5]

In response, the State of Alaska continued the long tradition of objecting to recognition of Indian Country and the creation of trust lands in the state, accusing the solicitor of unilaterally reversing decades of policy and federal Indian law, thereby violating ANCSA's explicit provisions "prohibiting creating land into trust/reservations." Representatives for the state argued that "in two strokes of its Solicitor's pen, [the] Interior has changed how Alaska has operated for more than 50 years" and that, by creating "additional Indian Country," Alaska "has gone from minimal amounts of tribal territory jurisdiction to millions of acres" in which tribes, the state, and the federal government would exercise concurrent jurisdiction.[6] They warned that tribal jurisdiction would affect taxes and expand federal authority in environmental regulations, a topic state officials have contended with since Alaska statehood.

ANCSA has also complicated relationships between tribes, in which governing authority is vested, and the ANCSA corporations, which are separate legal for-profit corporate entities that the federal government considers as tribes for varying purposes. For example, when Congress passed the CARES Act during the 2020 Covid-19 pandemic, the US treasurer determined that ANCSA corporations qualified as tribes for the purposes of relief funds.[7] This prompted a lawsuit filed on behalf of six federally recognized tribes in Alaska and twelve federally recognized tribes in the contiguous states, citing the challenges the tribal governments would face if forced to compete with the corporations, which are not governing entities. Emphasizing the significance of these distinctions, the treasurer's inclusion of ANCSA corporations in the CARES

Act also compelled the Alaska Federation of Natives to pass a resolution at their 2022 annual convention affirming that Alaska Native Corporations are not sovereign tribes. Rather ANCSA, as a settlement with a corporate structure, established a legal and political landscape in which not all Alaska Natives are shareholders. Thus, when Alaska Native village corporations were designated as federally recognized tribes in 1993, it afforded tribal members who were not shareholders an important legal status by which their villages could qualify for Bureau of Indian Affairs (BIA) services and other federal programs. Though they do not always agree, both the nongoverning Native corporations and the tribal governments "prove useful to Native Alaska's political endeavors within the national and state political system."[8]

These jurisdictional changes, the matrix of political entities, and the debates over them are the product of over 150 years of settler imperialism in Alaska. The opposition of state officials and lawmakers to Indian Country and tribal sovereignty in Alaska continue to reflect the rhetoric of racial distinctions and legal ambiguities they inherited from their predecessors. Following federal recognition of Alaska's 229 tribes in 1993, many politicians, lawmakers, and attorneys have been working to undermine the governing authority of the tribal governments in favor of the nongoverning ANCSA corporations. To do this, they repeatedly frame Alaska Native sovereignty as a recent invention in contravention of over a hundred years of legislation that, to them, established as fact that there were no tribes eligible for federal recognition in Alaska. As proof, they refer to the very constellation of legislation and statutes that constitute the settler imperial formation, thereby demonstrating how pervasive the narrative of racial and legal distinctions between Alaska Natives and Indigenous nations in the contiguous states remains. For example, Ted Stevens, Alaska's long-serving US senator, constantly sought to eliminate funding for Alaska Native tribes and to reduce their influence in the state.[9] Likewise, attorney Donald Craig Mitchell authored an entire monograph opposing the existence of tribal sovereignty in Alaska in which he repeatedly chastised Assistant Secretary Ada Deer's decision to empower Alaska Native nations by including them on the federal register of recognized tribes in 1993.[10]

What Deer knew, and what Stevens and Mitchell fail to recognize, is that Native sovereignty exists and persists regardless of recognition from the US federal government or any other entity. Their opposition to sovereignty and nationhood status reveals the ways ambiguity continues to function to the detriment of Alaska Native land rights and legal strategies and allows lawmakers and government officials to deny the persistence of Indigenous legal orders. Instead, they insist that the distinctions government officials made in the late nineteenth and early twentieth centuries and the unique settlement structure of ANCSA constitute the only legitimate and applicable framework for Native rights in Alaska. Rather than evaluating why federal Indian policy played out in Alaska the way it did, these attorneys and lawmakers take for granted that "Alaska Natives were not dealt with as tribes." Furthermore, because ANCSA corporation lands are not Indian Country, nor are the corporations sovereign governments, it is no surprise that state officials and lawmakers draw on the history of nonrecognition and legal uncertainty in their opposition to tribes and tribal sovereignty beyond ANCSA corporations. While a useful tool for Alaska Natives, the corporations are nevertheless interpreted by many non-Native people as consistent with the objectives of the 1884 Organic Act that equated Indigenous land rights with those of "other persons" to the exclusion of all other land regimes.[11]

What is lost on these politicians, attorneys, lawmakers, and government officials is that Alaska Native nations have always been sovereign. The ways they shaped their strategies in navigating the ambiguities of settler imperialism reveal their adherence to their own legal, political, social, and cultural orders and the land relations that sustained them. As they had done prior to Russian or US colonialism, Alaska Natives drew on their long histories of diplomacy to negotiate imperial and settler intrusions. Along the way, they incorporated elements of the US legal system and its institutions to render their sovereignties relevant and legible, ensuring their collective continuance as Indigenous Peoples and nations. As Frederick Moore's letter from the opening of this book demonstrates, Alaska Natives knew early on that the federal government was treating them distinctly from tribal nations in the contiguous states.[12] They also knew that the longer the federal government insisted on their ambiguous legal status, the longer they would continue to lose their land, though they were and remain wary of federal BIA oversight and management of their affairs. In this context, they developed strategies to engage US legal institutions such as citizenship while leveraging their ambiguous status against would-be corporate, settler, and federal projects on their homelands. They warned lawmakers that the legal ambiguities clouding their political status and that of their land rights within the US legal system also clouded titles that any non-Native entities sought to acquire until Native land rights were resolved. They held firm through the twentieth century, insisting that if the United States wanted access to their land, it would have to concede to Native ownership and engage in preemptive negotiations or face persistent and ongoing litigation for retroactive purchase. In doing so, they insisted on and achieved a plurality of legal systems that have allowed them to pursue a diverse array of strategies to protect their lands.

Underscoring the nineteenth-, twentieth-, and twenty-first-century struggles for Native land and sovereignty was the role government officials and lawmakers envisioned for Alaska in the schematic of US imperial objectives. From the 1867 initiation of possessory claims, Alaska was not conceived as the last frontier of the American West but rather understood as first empire. Thus, the Treaty of Cession with Russia marked a significant moment in imperial expansion by which the United States asserted possessory claims to strategic geographies without the explicit intention to incorporate them into the nation proper. In concert with Alaska's geographic distance from the contiguous states, the imperial orientation of Alaska significantly delayed the arrival of the "frontier rabble" and accompanying settler legal infrastructure.[13] This allowed government officials to delay defining the relationship of Alaska Natives to the federal government and to withhold the customary trappings of westward expansion. As we have seen, Congress's refusal to designate Alaska as Indian Country in tandem with the racialization of Alaska Natives as Asian established the means by which subsequent generations of lawmakers could avoid the requisite constitutionally prescribed negotiations for land with Alaska Natives as sovereigns. As a prerequisite of preemptive negotiation or redemptive purchase, Indian Country anticipated dispossession. Combined with the absence of treaties to facilitate the making and taking of land/property out of Indian Country, these imperial distinctions embedded ambiguity as the underlying framework of US–Indigenous relations in Alaska. This ambiguity, in turn, initiated a temporal pause in the dispossessive process whereby the uncertainty of Alaska's relationship to the nation proper allowed the federal government to avoid resolving the status of land or the land rights of Indigenous Alaskans. While seemingly innocuous in its lack of formal removals of Alaska Natives from their homelands, ambiguity nevertheless aided corporate mining and fishing interests who exercised extralegal seizure of and access to lands and waters considered external to the United States and inhabited by "dependent subjects" rather than political sovereigns.[14]

The seizure of additional noncontiguous territories following the Spanish-American War and settler anxieties around the supposed closing of the frontier forced an elaboration of the settler imperial framework and a relocation of ambiguity to the point of redemptive retroactive purchase in the dispossessive process. In the 1898 imperial moment, Alaska became a legal borderland against which lawmakers, government officials, and judges and lawmakers sought to manage the boundaries of the nation proper by creating a hierarchy of territorial categories with diverse corresponding constitutional statuses. Seeking a legal mechanism by which to exclude the inhabitants of Puerto Rico, the Philippines, and Guam from the constitutional provisions of citizenship, jurists crafted a frontier narrative to naturalize Alaska as always-already destined for full incorporation into the settler nation-state. In doing so, these officials codified the imperial process of constitutional differentiation in territorial possessions to facilitate the expansion of US empire in the Pacific. Despite this congealing of incorporated and unincorporated categories and the juridical pronouncement that Alaska was intended for inclusion in the nation proper, government officials and lawmakers continued to refuse any uniformity of law or political status of Alaska Natives with their counterparts in the contiguous states. Instead, they constructed legislation and construed court rulings to shift ambiguity and uncertainty from the status of land in Alaska vis-à-vis the nation proper to the recognition of Alaska Natives as potential prior owners of property vis-à-vis tribes in the contiguous states.

Following the designation of Alaska as an organized, incorporated territory, Alaska Natives mobilized around US citizenship as a method to assert ownership of their homelands in ways that would resonate with lawmakers and government officials. They appropriated and wielded the rhetoric of citizenship and property ownership in conjunction with their rights as Indigenous Alaskans to the constitutional protections to their homelands. This syncretizing of US citizenship, US law, and their own legal and political orders were and continue to be sovereign acts of diplomacy by which they challenged intrusions on their homelands as nations and as Alaska's first citizens. From the late nineteenth and early twentieth centuries, they refuted the ways the federal government defined what it considers an American Indian or Alaska Native tribe and worked to carve out their diplomatic relationships on their own terms. While the ambiguity that government officials and lawmakers sought to entrench in the Alaska landscape posed significant challenges to these objectives, it nevertheless proved useful as Alaska Natives mobilized US property regimes and notions of clear title against those seeking to deny the existence of tribes and tribally held lands in Alaska.

Settler imperialism is a constellation of statutory and case law made possible only by the stories government officials, lawmakers, judges, and corporate interests told themselves about who Alaska Natives were and what they intended Alaska to be. These stories relied on other fictions that racialized Alaska Natives as Asian and denied their status as sovereign nations, which the various agents of US empire anticipated would relieve them of the constitutionally prescribed methods of appropriating Native land and converting it into property. Despite narratives to the contrary, Alaska Native resistance to settler imperialism in Alaska reveals the tenuous, contingent, and disjointed nature of US empire and exposes its limitations. From the initiation of US possessory claims in 1867 to the current litigation over Native jurisdiction and trust lands, Alaska Natives have never conceded to US ambitions for their homelands either as sources of extractible wealth or as strategic staging grounds in support of hegemonic projects. Their persistent mobilization of their own diplomatic traditions as Indigenous nations have disabled and foreclosed the primary objectives of US imperialism, forcing the United States to concede to their status and ongoing presence as nations and ensuring Indigenous futures.

Acknowledgments

It is overwhelming to think about the many people I am grateful for in ensuring this book came to fruition. The thanks I can offer in exchange for the years of support seems profoundly inadequate, and as I reflect on the completion of this project, I am humbled by how fortunate I have been. This book reflects a trajectory of not only intellectual growth but personal growth, and I am grateful for the patience and grace my mentors and peers extended to me as I brought it through its many iterations.

I'd like to begin by thanking Jeani O'Brien, and it is truly a challenge to find words that can rise to this occasion. Before coming to the University of Minnesota, my pathway through academia had been circuitous and fraught. Originally waitlisted for the history PhD program when I applied in 2011, her encouragement to reapply the following year remains one of the most significant turning points in my life. In the many years since, her mentorship, guidance, and enthusiasm for my research provided me with the confidence to truly grow into a sense of myself as a researcher, educator, and colleague. The conversations I had with Jeani about the questions I had about Alaska, my suspicions about my archival findings, and the theoretical framework I was proposing have made this book what it is. Her sense that this was important propelled me forward (and her occasional offerings of a box of tissues and chocolate-covered almonds in times of immense stress certainly helped). Equally as important as the time and energy she devotes to her students is her investment not just in us as academics but also in who we are as people. In addition to celebrating our professional accomplishments and counseling us through academia's many frustrations, she revels in the triumphs and laments the disappointments in our personal lives as well, attending weddings, bridal showers, and birthdays. Her devotion to the field truly manifests in her seemingly boundless dedication to graduate students and junior scholars, serving both formally and informally as an adviser and advocate for so many of us throughout her career. I am grateful and humbled to be counted among them, and since graduating I strive to be the kind of mentor, friend, and colleague that she is.

Likewise, I struggle to find adequate words of thanks for Barbara Welke, who coadvised with Jeani. I sought Barbara as an adviser because I knew she would demand excellence and a meticulousness in my work that, combined with the intellectual rigor expected of me by both her and Jeani, would take my research to the next level. Barbara is also deeply invested in her students in a way that I strive to emulate every day. Her care in reading and commenting on every chapter, every article revision, along with job application materials, job talk rehearsals, and syllabi still astonishes me. My drafts would be covered in her handwritten comments such that I coined the term “Barbara’s Raindrops” to describe the way they sprinkled each page, pushing me to think more deeply and deliberately and to consider every sentence from every possible angle. I’ve retained those hard copy drafts and use them to this day in my classrooms to emphasize to my students the rigor of revision and to understand more concretely the intellectual process of thinking, writing, rethinking, and rewriting that is knowledge production.

Practically a third adviser, I owe special thanks to Juliana Hu Pegues, who immediately reached out with friendship, mentorship, and an eagerness to collaborate and deliberate on the intersections of our research on Indigenous Alaska and US empire. Our conversations on the puzzling configuration of Alaska within US settler colonial and imperial endeavors were critical to my confidence as a researcher and convinced me that I was truly on to something. Equally important, the opportunity to observe the evolution of the theoretical interventions of their own work inspired me to think more deeply about my own. I am also immensely grateful for Juliana’s support, guidance, and empathy while on the academic job market. Both of us hailing from nontraditional trajectories through academia, her perspective and understanding stewarded me through a number of difficult decisions, disappointing outcomes, and ultimately hard-earned successes.

In addition to my advisers, my dissertation committee members were indispensable in their careful consideration of my work, their encouragement, and the variety of disciplinary perspectives they provided. Their contributions enabled a richness and a complexity to this book that I would not have been capable of without them. I am thankful to David Aiona Chang, whose careful reading of multiple chapter drafts and generative questions over the years challenged me to think more expansively about the reach and relevance of my work. I recall often some of the most meaningful advice I've ever received as a researcher and a historian: In a moment of frustration while trying to reconcile some seemingly incongruent component of a chapter draft with my overall argument, he said, "Let the mess be the story itself." For the ten-plus years since, that phrase bubbles to the surface of my mind when I feel stuck in my thinking and writing, allowing me to relax just enough for the pieces to fall into place. I also relay that story to students in my research seminars every semester when they, too, encounter challenges or obstacles in their research. I'm thankful to Kat Hayes for her enthusiasm about my project and especially for the time she devoted to the private reading seminar early in my grad school experience. It was fundamental to situating Alaska within historical frameworks of race and Indigeneity. And finally, I'd like to thank M. Bianet Castellanos for her interest and encouragement in my project. The frameworks for comparative Indigeneities I gleaned from her own scholarship and her graduate seminar were crucial to understanding Alaska and the field more broadly. I feel incredibly fortunate to have had one of the most inspiring, encouraging, supportive, and gracious groups of mentors. This book would not be what it is without them.

Community is crucial in academia, and I consider this book a collective effort not only because of my committee members but also because of the cohort of graduate students I am so fortunate to have met at UMN. My time at the University of Minnesota brought me into the orbit of an amazing group of scholars with whom I have developed lifelong friendships for which I am infinitely grateful. During my time in graduate school, the American Indian and Indigenous Studies Graduate Student Workshop cultivated an environment of collaboration, cooperation, and collegiality that I have since discovered is difficult to replicate and hard to find. Not only did our weekly meetings provide a useful structure for completing our dissertations, preparing for conferences, and learning how to approach publishing and the job market, but it also greatly improved the quality of our work, thus demonstrating the ways community is central to scholarly success. I cannot thank this cohort enough. I'd like to especially thank Kasey Keeler for her immediate and enduring friendship, the writing, grading, and workshopping sessions, boxed wine and Cheetos evenings, and her straightforward advice and willingness to listen. She enthusiastically assisted myself and others in our circle, making graduate school a place where I could thrive. Likewise, Katie Phillips was also immensely formative in my development as a scholar, teacher, and colleague in similar ways. I am indebted to them both and grateful for the inspiration. Other members of the workshop cohort included Sasha Suarez, Bernadette Pérez, Jameson Sweet, Amber Annis, Rose Miron, and my 2014–2015 workshop cochair Jesús Estrada-Pérez. I'd also like to thank Evan Taparata, with whom I worked my way through coursework, prelims, and my dissertation defense nearly in lockstep. This synchronized progression and our concurrent struggles, challenges, triumphs, and disappointments at various stages in our matriculation made weathering academia much more tolerable.

I am also indebted to numerous individuals who contributed to the development of this book through conversations, conferences, and formal manuscript workshops. I'd like to thank Caskey Russell, whom I met at the 2015 Newberry Consortium in American Indian and Indigenous Studies graduate student conference. His family (Roy and Elizabeth Peratrovich, Frank Peratrovich) features prominently in this book, and his encouragement and enthusiasm from its nascent stages have been invaluable. I'm grateful for the many conversations and conference gatherings we shared that have shaped my understanding of Alaska Native land rights and civil rights activism. Along with his scholarship on Tlingit literary traditions, law, and Indigenous sovereignty, this book would not be what it is without his input. I'd like to thank Paige Raibmon and Keith Richotte, who graciously workshopped the manuscript for me in the spring of 2024. Their feedback and recommendations were the catalyst to all the pieces finally falling into place, allowing for a more sophisticated theorization of settler imperialism, a more cogently articulated argument, and more effective use of the extensive archival evidence to these ends. I'm also especially grateful to Lee Stephan, whom I met during his time as tribal council president for the Native Village of Eklutna. He is a wealth of specialized knowledge, and I learned much from him in our conversations. I reflect often on some of the more poignant phrases he used to describe his experiences and his hopes for the future. I'm thankful for the stories, salmon, and the four-wheeling adventure he and his family were so willing to share with me.

I brought this book to its final stages in my first three years of a tenure-track position at Oberlin College in northeast Ohio. Having moved around so much during my undergraduate years and as a product of the academic job market following graduate school, I haven't had much experience being in one place for more than a year or so except for my time at the University of Minnesota. Moving around so much doesn't exactly facilitate the formation of friendships beyond acquaintanceship, and I am quite grateful for the community of colleagues, friends, and mentors who welcomed me here and helped me navigate the turbulences of academia as I progress toward tenure. I'm grateful to Gina Pérez for mentorship and support, her stewarding of the Comparative American Studies Program, and her guidance on teaching, writing, and time management and for helping me say "no." Her collegiality is unparalleled, and the multiple gatherings she hosts should serve as an inspiration for what professional community can look like. I'd also like to thank Danielle Skeehan, Erika Hoffmann-Dilloway, Jessica Madison Pískatá, Amanda Zadorian, Leah Huntsinger, and Wendy Kozol. I'm grateful for our regular gatherings over food and drink, excursions into Cleveland, trivia nights, writing sessions, and the welcome distraction of memes and reels shared on the group text thread. I don't think I could find a better group of friends. Thank you for the laughter and the tears.

I also wouldn't be here without my family. There is a gritty determination that I inherited from both the Arnetts and the Bowsers, and while my academic and professional trajectory was circuitous, challenging, uncertain, and sometimes bleak, I refused to let go. I attribute my triumphs and successes to the long line of relatives who forged their own paths before me. I'm thankful for my mother, Wendy Anderson, for inspiring me with her creativity and her adventurous spirit. Watching her unflinchingly take up new hobbies, climb mountains, run, cycle, speed skate, play hockey, quilt, paint, and develop uncanny expertise in all of it gave me a sense that there wasn't anything I couldn't learn how to do. Likewise, my dad John Arnett's lifetime commitment to percussion showed me that our individual passions and the fulfillment they provide are as crucial to life as air or water and that we should never give up their pursuit so long as they bring us joy, challenge us, or soothe us. I'm grateful for my sister, Kirsten, for her sense of humor, her witty sarcasm, her honesty, and her no bs mentality. I'd also like to thank my nephew Milo for his purity of heart, his boundless imagination, and his commitment to always be a weirdo. His authenticity is a reminder that I, too, can embrace, indulge, and celebrate my true self. My stepdad,

Paul, and stepmother, Maggi, have also born witness to the evolution of this project. I'm grateful to Paul for the long conversations on Alaska politics and administration and for making sure I got regular, healthy doses of the mountains. I'm thankful to Maggi for her eagerness to celebrate each milestone of this journey and for the pragmatic nature of her encouragement at each juncture along the way—and there were many.

I'm incredibly grateful for my spouse, Adam, and my stepson, Ian. They have both enriched my life beyond words, and they have given me a fuller, deeper understanding of family. I'm incredibly thankful to Adam for supporting my professional endeavors and for reading every word of this book and offering insight, copy edits, and his expertise as an attorney in my unpacking of federal Indian law in Alaska. I couldn't ask for a better partner and best friend. I'm equally thankful to Ian for his contemplative curiosity, his compassion for others, and his courage to dream big. The two of them bring an aura of confident enthusiasm to my life that smooths over the anxiety that often accompanies long-term goals and the unknowns that may present themselves. Finally, I am forever indebted to the dogs who have been my constant companions for the duration of this journey. Phoebe, for making the move from Alaska to California, New York, Indiana, and Minnesota and the multitude of challenges that marked the passing of those years. Kenai, for her wisdom, intelligence, and playful demeanor, not to mention the miles upon miles running trails together. And Luna, for proving to me each day that no matter what challenges we face, we deserve love and are capable of joy. Thank you, girls, for taking such good care of me.

In addition to the strategic, academic, and emotional support, guidance, and advice of my colleagues, family, friends, and pets, this endeavor has also received financial support from a number of organizations and institutions. These included a Doctoral Dissertation Fellowship, a Graduate Research Partnership Program grant, and travel stipends from the University of Minnesota that supported archival research and writing at various stages. I also received a generous predoctoral research fellowship from the Andrew Mellon Council on Library and Information Resources that supported a year of archival research at over a dozen locations within the United States. The short-term research fellowship from the Newberry Consortium in American Indian and Indigenous Studies likewise supported travel to additional archives that otherwise may not have been possible. Smaller contributions from the Western Washington University James W. Scott Regional Research Fellowship, the Dwight D. Eisenhower Foundation Research Travel Grant, and the Harry S. Truman Library Institute Research Grant ensured access to collections that proved crucial to this project.

Notes

Introduction

1. Frederick L. Moore to Philander Chase Knox, April 12, 1902, Records of the US House of Representatives, 57th Cong., Hr57A-H26.1–26.3, Committee on Territories to Alaska and Hawaii, box 116, "Alaska" file, National Archives and Records Administration, Washington, DC (hereafter NARA).

2. Frederick L. Moore to Philander Chase Knox, April 12, 1902, NARA.

3. Philander Chase Knox to Robert Friedrich, May 9, 1902, Records of the US House of Representatives, 57th Cong., Hr57A-H26.1–26.3, Committee on Territories to Alaska and Hawaii, box 116, "Alaska" file, NARA.

4. Knox to Friedrich, May 9, 1902, NARA.

5. The Massachusetts Board of Trade to the United States House of Representatives, October 14, 1902, Records of the US House of Representatives, 57th Cong., Hr57A-H26.1–26.3, Committee on Territories to Alaska and Hawaii, box 116, "Alaska" file, NARA; St. Paul Minnesota Chamber of Commerce to E. C. Stevens, November 28, 1902 Records of the US House of Representatives, 57th Cong., Hr57A-H26.1–26.3, Committee on Territories to Alaska and Hawaii, box 116, "Alaska" file, NARA.

6. League of American Sportsman to M. C. Graham, April 2, 1902, "Resolutions Adopted by the League of American Sportsman at Its Annual Meeting, Feb. 12, 1902," Records of the US House of Representatives, 57th Cong., Hr57A-H26.1–26.3, Committee on Territories to Alaska and Hawaii, box 116, "Alaska" file, NARA.

7. Clearly Alaska is contiguous through what is today known as Canada. The borderlands region of Alaska, British Columbia, and the Yukon Territories constituted a hotly contested location characterized by what Andrea Geiger terms a "convergence of three empires." See Andrea Geiger, *Converging Empires: Citizens and Subjects in the North Pacific Borderlands, 1867–1945* (University of North Carolina Press, 2022).

8. Designation of land as Indian Country was arguably a precursor to dispossession, and BIA administration severely undermined the sovereignty of Native nations and Indigenous Peoples (Roy M. Huhndorf and Shari M. Huhndorf, "Alaska Native Politics Since the Alaska Native Claims Settlement Act," *South Atlantic Quarterly* 11, no. 2 [2011]: 385–401). Tlingit scholar Caskey Russell writes about the paradoxical nature of treaties and their simultaneous recognition and denial of sovereignty as a means to legalize the appropriation of lands and resources. As texts, treaties represented legal fictions that nevertheless delineated Indian experience over time ("The Paradox of Sovereignty: Contingencies of Meaning in American Indian Treaty Discourse," *American Indian Culture and*

Research Journal 32, no. 1 [2008]: 1–19). Juliana Hu Pegues describes implications for land and sovereignty following the racialization of Alaska Natives as Asian in *Space-Time Colonialism: Alaska's Indigenous and Asian Entanglements* (University of North Carolina Press, 2021).

9. David S. Case and David A. Voluck, *Alaska Natives and American Laws* (University of Alaska Press, 2012), 165.

10. Russian operations had been situated in Southeast Alaska, and for some time after US possession most military and government operations were similarly in Southeast Alaska, in Tlingit territory. US military officials were quite frequently compelled to respect and adhere to Tlingit law. See Rosita Worl, *Tlingit Law, American Injustice, and the Destruction of Tlingit Villages* (Sealaska Heritage Institute, 2019); Thomas F. Thornton, *Being and Place Among the Tlingit* (University of Washington Press, 2007).

11. Thornton, *Being and Place Among the Tlingit.*

12. Thornton, *Being and Place Among the Tlingit*; Worl, *Tlingit Law.*

13. Chickasaw scholar Jodi A. Byrd uses the term *settler imperialism* to denote the ways settler colonialism informs imperial objectives and ambitions. This book traces the ways this plays out on the ground and in law in Alaska, where tensions in these objectives and how to use Alaska to achieve them ultimately informed the structure that emerged therefrom. Jodi A. Byrd, *The Transit of Empire: Indigenous Critiques of Colonialism* (University of Minnesota Press, 2011).

14. Treaty making was by no means universal, as the existence of countless federally unrecognized tribes and tribes without reservations or other forms of reserved lands attests to, and it was unequivocally coercive and violent. What is important here is the full-scale reconfiguring of the methods and mechanics of dispossession.

15. Robert Nichols, *Theft Is Property! Dispossession and Critical Theory* (University of North Carolina Press, 2020).

16. Nichols, *Theft Is Property!*, 7, 31, 145.

17. Heidi Kiiwetinepinesiik Stark argues that treaties and the recognition of Indigenous sovereignty they represented reflect the paradox that the United States and Canada "require Indigenous sovereignty as their own legitimacy as nation-states is constituted through treaties" that "provide the perception of legality." Treaties also anticipate possession, with "cession becoming the given, the presumed." Heidi Kiiwetinepinesiik Stark, "Criminal Empire: The Making of the Savage in a Lawless Land," *Theory & Event* 19, no. 4 (2016): 12, https://muse.jhu.edu/article/633282.

18. Patrick Wolfe, "Settler Colonialism and the Elimination of the Native," *Journal of Genocide Research* 8, no. 4 (2006): 387–409; Lorenzo Veracini, *Settler Colonialism: A Theoretical Overview* (Palgrave Macmillan, 2010).

19. Through this process, Nichols contends that "theft quite literally produced property." Nichols, *Theft Is Property!*, 42.

20. Stephen Haycox, *Alaska: An American Colony* (University of Washington Press, 2002); Claus-M. Naske and Herman E. Slotnick, *Alaska: A History of the 49th State* (University of Oklahoma Press, 1987); Clause-M. Naske, *49 at Last! The Battle for Alaska Statehood* (Epicenter Press, 2009); Orlando W. Miller, *The Frontier in Alaska and the Matanuska Colony* (Yale University Press, 1975). For publications

on Alaska Native land claims, see Donald Craig Mitchell, *Sold American: The Story of Alaska Natives and Their Land, 1867–1959* (University of Alaska Press, 2003); Donald Craig Mitchell, *Take My Land, Take My Life* (University of Alaska Press, 2001); Peter Metcalfe, *A Dangerous Idea: The Alaska Native Brotherhood and the Struggle for Indigenous Rights* (University of Alaska Press, 2014).

21. This does not mean that ad hoc dispossession was not happening. As many scholars point out, Indigenous people have been dispossessed without formal removal in instances in which their lands become degraded or polluted such that they are useless and uninhabitable in ways that allow the continuance of their Indigenous stewards as distinct peoples. See Kyle Whyte, "Settler Colonialism, Ecology, and Environmental Justice," in *Indigenous Resurgence: Decolonialization and Movements for Environmental Justice,* ed. Jaskiran Dhillon (Berghahn Books, 2022).

22. Knox to Friedrich, May 9, 1902, NARA.

23. In literatures addressing US empire and territorial possessions, Alaska is often initially enumerated alongside Puerto Rico, Guam, the Philippines, and Hawai'i within the first few pages of such works; however, after this brief mention, it vanishes from the discussion and is typically not addressed again (see Christina Duffy Burnett and Burke Marshall, eds., *Foreign in a Domestic Sense: Puerto Rico, American Expansion, and the Constitution* [Duke University Press, 2001]; Alfred McCoy and Francisco Scarano, eds., *Colonial Crucible: Empire in the Making of the Modern American State* [University of Wisconsin Press, 2009]; Bartholomew Sparrow, *The Insular Cases and the Emergence of American Empire* [University of Kansas Press, 2006]; Gerald L. Neuman and Tomiko Brown-Nagin, *Reconsidering the Insular Cases: The Past and Future of the American Empire* [Harvard University Press, 2015]; Julian Go and Anne Foster, eds., *The American Colonial State in the Philippines: Global Perspectives* [Duke University Press, 2003]). Also important here are studies that examine contiguous territorial incorporation, including Sanford Levinson and Bartholomew Sparrow, *The Louisiana Purchase and American Expansion, 1803–1898* (Rowman & Littlefield, 2005), and Bethel Saler, *The Settlers' Empire: Colonialism and State Formation in America's Old Northwest* (University of Pennsylvania Press, 2015). Saler's study of the territories, specifically Wisconsin and what she refers to as its "prolonged political incubation period" prior to statehood, is mechanically useful, though narrates the United States as a "postcolonial republic" in which Euro-American citizens in the Northwest Territories experienced a "double colonial governance" alongside Indigenous people and polities (Saler, *Settler's Empire,* 88, 1, 77). As other scholars note, she also fails to recognize or thoroughly engage settler colonialism as a theoretical framework to adequately analyze the ways the processes her book traces were destructive to Wisconsin's Indigenous people. See Jeffrey Ostler, review of *The Settlers' Empire: Colonialism and State Formation in America's Old Northwest,* by Bethel Saler, *Journal of Colonialism and Colonial History* 17, no. 3 (2016): https://dx.doi.org/10.1353/cch.2016.0049.

24. For federal Indian law, Native sovereignty, treaties, and dispossession, see David E. Wilkins and Tsianina Lomawaima, *Uneven Ground: American Indian Sovereignty and Federal Indian Law* (University of Oklahoma Press, 2002); David E. Wilkins and Heidi Kiiwepinetinesiik Stark, *American Indian Politics*

and the American Political System (Rowman & Littlefield, 2017); Heidi Kiiwetinepinesiik Stark, "Marked by Fire: Anishinaabe Articulations of Nationhood in Treaty-Making with the United States and Canada," *American Indian Quarterly* 36, no. 2 (2021): 119–49; Jean M. O'Brien, *Dispossession by Degrees: Indian Land and Identity in Natick, Massachusetts, 1650–1790* (University of Nebraska Press, 2003); Alexandra Harmon, *The Power of Promises: Rethinking Indian Treaties in the Pacific Northwest* (University of Washington Press, 2008); Michael Witgen, *An Infinity of Nations: How the Native New World Shaped Early North America* (University of Pennsylvania Press, 2013); Michael Witgen, *Seeing Red: Indigenous Land, American Expansion, and the Political Economy of Plunder in North America* (University of North Carolina Press, 2022). For examples of settler property logics and Indigenous land relations, see Aileen Moreton-Robinson, *The White Possessive: Property, Power, and Indigenous Sovereignty* (University of Minnesota Press, 2015); Nichols, *Theft Is Property!*; Leanne Betasamosake Simpson, *As We Have Always Done: Indigenous Freedom Through Radical Resistance* (University of Minnesota Press, 2020).

25. Hu Pegues, *Space-Time Colonialism*, 5; Roy M. Huhndorf and Shari M. Huhndorf, "Alaska Native Politics Since the Alaska Native Claims Settlement Act," *South Atlantic Quarterly* 11, no. 2 (2011): 385–401.

26. Francis Walker to C. Delano, March 14, 1872, H.R. Exec. Doc. No. 197, 42nd Cong., 2nd Sess. (1872); Hu Pegues, *Space-Time Colonialism*, 5–6.

27. Thomas Michael Swensen, "The Relationship Between Indigenous Rights, Citizenship, and Land in Territorial Alaska: How the Past Opened the Door to the Future," *Journal of the Alaska Native Studies Council* 2 (2015): 49, 50.

28. Evon Peter, "Undermining Our Tribal Governments: The Stripping of Land, Resources, and Rights from Alaska Native Nations," in *The Alaska Native Reader: History, Culture, Politics*, ed. Maria Shaa Tláa Williams (Duke University Press, 2009), 179; Huhndorf and Huhndorf, "Alaska Native Politics."

29. Indigenous resistance to settler colonialism and the persistence of Indigenous sovereignty and land relations has always been dynamic and multifaceted, engaging settler laws and institutions in diverse ways from negotiating recognition to refusal and resurgence. See Frederick E. Hoxie, *This Indian Country: American Indian Activists and the Place They Made* (Penguin, 2012); Philip J. Deloria, "Four Thousand Invitations," *American Indian Quarterly* 37, no. 3 (2013): 25–43; Tsianina Lomawaima, "The Mutuality of Citizenship and Sovereignty: The Society of American Indians and the Battle to Inherit America," *American Indian Quarterly* 37, no. 3 (2013): 333–51; Kevin Bruyneel, *The Third Space of Sovereignty: The Postcolonial Politics of U.S.-Indigenous Relations* (University of Minnesota Press, 2007); Byrd, *Transit of Empire*; Miranda Johnson, *The Land Is Our History: Indigeneity, Law, and the Settler State* (Oxford University Press, 2016); Audra Simpson, *Mohawk Interruptus: Political Life Across the Borders of Settler States* (Duke University Press, 2014); Leanne Betasamosake Simpson, *As We Have Always Done: Indigenous Freedom Through Radical Resistance* (University of Minnesota Press, 2020); Glen Sean Coulthard, *Red Skin, White Masks: Rejecting the Colonial Politics of Recognition* (University of Minnesota Press, 2014); Joanne Barker, *Native Acts: Law, Recognition, and Cultural Authenticity* (Duke University Press, 2011).

30. This concept in federal Indian law emanates from Chief Justice John Marshall's opinion in *Cherokee Nation v. Georgia* in which he reasoned that tribal nations constitute "domestic dependent nations" occupying a position like a

"ward to its guardian" (Cherokee Nation v. Georgia 30 U.S. 1 [1831]). While problematic, it was the basis for other critical elements of federal Indian law, specifically the Trust Doctrine (see Heidi Kiiwetinepinesiik Stark, "Transforming the Trickster: Federal Indian Law Encounters Anishinaabe Diplomacy," in *Centering Anishinaabeg Studies: Understanding the World Through Stories,* ed. Jill Doerfler, Niigaanwewidam James Sinclair, and Heidi Kiiwetinepinesiik Stark [University of Minnesota Press, 2013]). Stark argues that US courts and policymakers "have frequently reconfigured their trust responsibility to tribes, conflating protection with dependency, and dependency with limited or 'quasi' sovereignty" (Stark, "Transforming the Trickster," 267). See also Wilkins and Lomawaima, *Uneven Ground*; David E. Wilkins, *American Indian Sovereignty and Federal Law* (University of Oklahoma Press, 2001); Wilkins and Stark, *American Indian Politics*; Stark, "Marked by Fire"; Robert A. Williams Jr., *Like a Loaded Weapon: The Rehnquist Court, Indian Rights, and the Legal History of Racism in America* (University of Minnesota Press, 2005).

31. For example, see Cristina Stanciu, "Americanization on Native Terms: The Society of American Indians, Citizenship Debates, and Tropes of 'Racial Difference,'" *Native American and Indigenous Studies* 6, no. 1 (2019): 111–48; Catherine D. Cahill, "'Our Democracy and the American Indian': Citizenship, Sovereignty, and the Native Vote in the 1920s," *Journal of Women's History* 32, no. 1 (2020): 41–51.

32. The phenomenon by which policies and practices of subjugation, surveillance, and colonial management were applied domestically is explored in the edited volume by Alfred W. McCoy and Francisco A. Scarano, eds., *Colonial Crucible: Empire in the Making of the Modern American State* (University of Wisconsin Press, 2009).

33. Byrd, *Transit of Empire,* xiii; Hu Pegues, *Space-Time Colonialism,* 21.

34. Christina D. Ponsa-Kraus (as Christina Duffy Burnett), "The Edges of Empire and the Limits of Sovereignty: American Guano Islands," *American Quarterly* 57, no. 3 (2005): 779–803.

35. *In re Sah Quah* 31 F. 327 (D. Alaska 1886), 140.

36. Michele Connolly and Bette Jacobs, "Counting Indigenous American Indians and Alaska Natives in the US Census," *Statistical Journal of the IAOS* 36, no. 1 (2020): 201–10, https://journals.sagepub.com/doi/10.3233/SJI-200615.

37. Williams, *Alaska Native Reader,* 4.

38. In her new book, Jen Rose Smith articulates what she has termed "temperate-normativity," whereby Western Euro-American societies perpetuated the myth "that only from temperate zones could proper forms of civilization grounded in agricultural practices and settled livelihoods flourish" and that, conversely, "climates of tropical and ice geographies supposedly produce inferior human subjects." Importantly, she also critiques the ways the designation, defining, and redefining of so-called climate zones flatten and obscure "Indigenous historical and ongoing claims to space" and their knowledges of and relationships to the ice geographies—"formulated through a millennium of lived experience; accumulation of expertise and science; aesthetic and artistic interpretations; cosmological, philosophical, and theoretical rubrics; and juridical structures of accountability"—so frequently imagined by Westerners as hostile and empty. *Ice Geographies: The Colonial Politics of Race and Indigeneity in the Arctic* (Duke University Press, 2025), 12–13, 16, 24.

1. Creating an Imperial Jurisdiction

1. I use the phrase *possessory claims* to indicate that such exchanges of territory were fictions of empire between colonizing nations. Neither the Russian Empire nor the United States had the means to assert possession or governing authority sufficient enough to support claims of a "sale" or "purchase" of territory. What is now called Alaska remained under Indigenous governance long after 1867.

2. Rosita Ḵaaháni Worl, *Tlingit Law, American Injustice, and the Destruction of Tlingit Villages* (Sealaska Heritage Institute, 2019), 1–3.

3. Caskey Russell, "Cultures in Collision: Cosmology, Jurisprudence, and Religion in Tlingit Territory," *American Indian Quarterly* 33, no. 2 (2009): 239–52.

4. Russell, "Cultures in Collision"; Thomas F. Thornton, *Being and Place Among the Tlingit* (University of Washington Press, 2007).

5. Worl, *Tlingit Law*; Russell, "Cultures in Collision."

6. Russell, "Cultures in Collision."

7. Worl, *Tlingit Law*; Thornton, *Being and Place Among the Tlingit.*

8. Oliver R. Seward, ed., *William H. Seward's Travels Around the World* (Appleton and Co., 1873), 34.

9. According to the ruling in *Johnson & Graham's Lessee v. McIntosh,* 21 U.S. 543 (1823), "discovering" nations obtained rights to Indigenous homelands that included the right to dispose of such claimed lands to other European nations.

10. Treaty Concerning the Cession of the Russian Possessions in North America by His Majesty the Emperor of All the Russias to the United States of America, U.S.-R.F., Mar. 30, 1867, 15 Stat. 539.

11. Juliana Hu Pegues, *Space-Time Colonialism: Alaska's Indigenous and Asian Entanglements* (University of North Carolina Press, 2021), 5.

12. Treaty Between the United States of America and the French Republic, U.S.-Fr., Apr. 30, 1803, 8 Stat. 200.

13. Treaty of Peace, Friendship, Limits, and Settlement with the Republic of Mexico, U.S.-Mex., Feb. 2, 1848, 9 Stat. 922.

14. Brian Delay, "Independent Indians and the U.S.-Mexican War," *American Historical Review* 112, no. 1 (2007): 35–68.

15. Treaty Concerning the Cession of the Russian Possessions in North America.

16. William H. Seward to Edward de Stoeckl, March 23, 1867, document 338, Papers Relating to Foreign Affairs, Accompanying the Annual Message of the President to the Second Session of the Fortieth Congress, Part I, Correspondence with the Russian Legation, Office of the Historian, https://history.state.gov/historicaldocuments/frus1867p1/d338.

17. See Miller v. United States, 159 F.2d 997 (9th Cir. 1947).

18. After 1867, treaties between the United States and other "discovering" nations neither extended citizenship to nor recognized the nation-to-nation negotiating status of Indigenous Peoples in any other noncontiguous territory. Thirty years later, when the United States signed the Treaty of Paris at the conclusion of the Spanish-American War in 1898, it employed similar language. The treaty, in similar fashion to the Treaty of Cession with Russia, stated with specific regard to the Indigenous inhabitants "of the territories hereby ceded to the United States" from Spain that their "civil rights and political status . . . shall be

determined by Congress." Treaty of Peace Between the United States and Spain, U.S.-Spain, Dec. 10, 1898, 30 Stat. 1788.

19. An Act to Extend the Laws of the United States Relating to Customs, Commerce, and Navigation over the Territory Ceded in the United States by Russia, 15 Stat. 240 (1868).

20. Russell, "Cultures in Collision." In this passage, Caskey Russell is quoting Rosita Worl, "Tlingit At.oow: Tangible and Intangible Property" (PhD diss., Harvard University, 1998).

21. H. W. Halleck to Jefferson C. Davis, September 6, 1867, Alaska-Military Orders and Instructions, box 1, folder 7, Jefferson Columbus Davis Papers, VAULT-Ayer-MS-3057, Newberry Library, Chicago.

22. For detailed accounts of the bombardments, see Zachary Jones, "'Search for and Destroy': U.S. Army Relations with Alaska's Tlingit Indians and the Kake War of 1869," *Ethnohistory* 60, no. 1 (2013): 1–26.

23. Jones, "'Search for and Destroy.'"

24. Robert Scott to Jefferson C. Davis, February 15, 1869, Alaska-Correspondence, box 1, folder 3, Jefferson Columbus Davis Papers, VAULT-Ayer-MS-3057, Newberry Library, Chicago.

25. Report of the Secretary of War, H.R. Exec. Doc. No. 1, Part 2, 41st Cong., 3rd Sess. (1870).

26. Olivia Chilcote, "Time out of Mind: The San Luis Rey Band of Mission Indians and the Historical Origins of a Struggle for Federal Recognition," *California History* 96, no. 4 (2019): 38–53. Olivia Chilcote elaborates on the challenges facing unrecognized tribes in California in *Unrecognized in California: Federal Acknowledgment and the San Luis Rey Band of Mission Indians* (University of Washington Press, 2024). Additionally, in territory acquired in the Treaty of Guadalupe Hidalgo, the question of whether the Pueblos in what became New Mexico were Indians as defined in US law was challenged in two court cases, *United States v. Joseph* (94 U.S. 614, 617 [1876]) and *United States v. Sandoval* (231 U.S. 28 [1913]). *Joseph* held that the Pueblos were not an Indian tribe, whereas *Sandoval* reversed the decision, revealing that the technique of relegating tribes on land sought after by settlers as outside the legal parameters of "Indian" was an emerging technique in individual incidents resulting from continental westward expansion, though this becomes a blanket technique for the hundreds of Native nations in Alaska, setting a precedent for all other future territorial acquisitions.

27. Letter from the Secretary of the Interior Relative to the Condition of the Inhabitants of Alaska Who Resided There Prior to the Date of Our Acquisition of That Territory, H.R. Exec. Doc. No. 197, 42nd Cong., 2nd Sess. (1872).

28. Letter from the Secretary of the Interior.

29. Letter from the Secretary of the Interior.

30. United States v. Seveloff, 27 F. Cas. 1012, 1 Alaska Fed. 64 (D. Or. 1872) (No. 16,252).

31. *Creole* was a term used by the Russian American Company when referring to those of Alaska Native and Russian ancestry, and it came to denote a specific cultural, ethnic, and social category in the nineteenth and twentieth centuries. Seveloff is often described as a "Sitka Creole" in secondary source literature. See Sidney Harring, *Crow Dog's Case: American Indian Sovereignty, Tribal Law, and United States Law in the Nineteenth Century* (Cambridge University Press, 1994).

For more on the history of the term *creole* in Alaska, see Susan Smith-Peter, "'A Class of People Admitted to the Better Ranks': The First Generation of Creoles in Russian America, 1810s–1820s," *Ethnohistory* 60, no. 3 (2013): 363–84.

32. Nella Lee, "Impossible Mission: A History of the Legal Control of Native Drinking in Alaska," *Wicazō Ṡa Review* 12, no. 2 (1997): 95–109.

33. Deborah Niedermeyer, "The True Interests of a White Population: The Alaska Indian Country Decisions of Judge Matthew P. Deady," *New York University Journal of International Law and Politics* 21 (1988–1989): 195.

34. United States v. Tom, 1 Or. 26, 27 (1853); Niedermeyer, "True Interests of a White Population."

35. William Seward to Edward Stanton, January 30, 1869, quoted in Jurisdiction of the War Department over the Territory of Alaska, H.R. Exec. Doc. No. 135, 44th Cong., 1st Sess. (1876).

36. *United States v. Seveloff.*

37. An Act Making Appropriations for Sundry Civil Expenses of the Government for the Fiscal Year Ending June 30, 1874, and for Other Purposes, Act of March 3, 1873, 17 Stat. 530.

38. An Act to Regulate Trade and Intercourse with the Indian Tribes, 4 Stat. 279 (1834); David Wilkins and Tsianina Lomawaima, *Uneven Ground: American Indian Sovereignty and Federal Indian Law* (University of Oklahoma Press, 2002), 51.

39. The other cases are *In re Carr* (5 F. Cas. 115 [D. Or. 1875]), involving military enforcement of Sections 20 and 21 of the Trade and Intercourse Acts, and *Waters v. Campbell* (29 F. Cas. 411 [C.C.D. Or. 1876] [No. 17,264]) and *Waters v. Campbell* (29 F. Cas. 412, 415 [C.C.D. Or. 1877]) (referred to as *Waters I* and *Waters II*), involving civil suits likewise arising from the nature of military enforcement of the Trade and Intercourse Acts. *United States v. Williams* (2 F. 61 [D. Or. 1880]) involved a murder between two white settlers, and *United States v. Stephens* (12 F. 52 [C.C.D. Or. 1882]) involved another case of bootlegging. Deady's last Indian Country case regarding Alaska was *Nelson v. United States* (30 F. 112 [C.C.D. Or. 1887]), which also involved bootlegging (Niedermeyer, "True Interests of a White Population"). For a discussion of *In re Carr* and *Waters v. Campbell* (1876) in which Judge Deady upholds his decision in *Seveloff,* see Sidney L. Harring, "The Incorporation of Alaska Natives Under American Law: The United States and Tlingit Sovereignty, 1867–1900," *Arizona Law Review* 31 (1989): 279–327; Sidney L. Harring, *Crow Dog's Case: American Indian Sovereignty, Tribal Law, and United States Law in the Nineteenth Century* (Cambridge University Press, 1994).

40. Deady granted the writ of error, but only in the sense that the District Court of Alaska had imposed a sentence twenty days longer than the law allowed. He thus remanded the case with instructions only to revise the prison term.

41. United States v. Kie, District Court, D. Alaska, May Term, (1885), 26 F. Cas. 776, 777. See Harring, *Crow Dog's Case*; Harring, "Incorporation of Alaska Natives Under American Law."

42. Kie v. United States, 1 Alaska Fed. 125, 27 F. 351, 354 (1886).

43. Sitka Case 35, United States District Court, Civil Cases 1884–1900, Series 1825G AS32239, Alaska State Archives, Juneau. See also Jeff Landfield, Paxson Woelber, and Lee Baxter, *Sah Quah* (Sealaska Heritage Institute, 2022).

44. Legal scholar Sidney L. Harring speculates that *In re Sah Quah* was a carefully selected test case prepared by white settlers with the aim of condemning

Tlingit culture and asserting white control over their affairs (*Crow Dog's Case,* 233–34). It is also important to note the distinctions between slavery among Indigenous Northwest Coast societies and colonial enslaved societies developing out of the African slave trade. See Leland Donald, *Aboriginal Slavery on the Northwest Coast of North America* (University of California Press, 1997).

45. Sitka Case 35.

46. Sitka Case 35.

47. Sitka Case 35.

48. Sitka Case 35.

49. Sitka Case 35.

50. With regard to Northwest Coast societies, see Donald, *Aboriginal Slavery on the Northwest Coast.*

51. Donald, *Aboriginal Slavery on the Northwest Coast,* 34.

52. Juliana Barr, "From Captives to Slaves: Commodifying Indian Women in the Borderlands," *Journal of American History* 92, no. 1 (2005): 19–46. Juliana Barr argues that scholarly focus on enslavement practices of Indigenous North Americans has pushed United States historians to examine the diverse history of slavery beyond African American chattel slavery in the US South. Specifically, she refers to James F. Brooks, *Captives and Cousins: Slavery, Kinship, and Community in the Southwest Borderlands* (University of North Carolina Press, 2022), and Alan Gallay, *The Indian Slave Trade: The Rist of the English Empire in the American South, 1670–1717* (Yale University Press, 2003).

53. Sitka Case 35.

54. Sitka Case 35.

55. "Slavery Among the Alaska Indians—the Decision of the U.S. District Court Overthrows Its Last Defense," *Alaskan,* May 8, 1886.

56. Some have recently posited that Sah Quah genuinely sought American help in defying the system that enslaved him, refuting suspicions that the case was collusive on behalf of white objectives. This would suggest that Sah Quah perceived a binary between Tlingit culture and US law, which perpetuates notions of Indigenous savagery and American modernity. Given his testimony, it seems unlikely that his intentions and understanding of what he was doing were that simple, and in fact both are likely true in part. Missionaries and the attorneys and judges saw an opportunity to rebuke Tlingit culture as savage and primitive, and Sah Quah perhaps saw a way to navigate both Tlingit and settler societies in a rapidly changing landscape. See Landfield et al., *Sah Quah.*

57. *In re Sah Quah,* 31 F. 327 (D. Alaska 1886), 139.

58. *In re Sah Quah,* 138, 139.

59. *In re Sah Quah,* 140.

60. Natasha Singh (Dinyee Hu'tanna), interviewed by William Schneider in *The Tanana Chiefs: Native Rights and Western Law* (University of Alaska Press, 2018), 117.

2. Conceiving a New Frontier

1. Chief Koogh-see, Meeting Held in the Public School House of Juneau, Alaska, by Request of Indian Chiefs on Account of the Presence of His Honor, Governor John G. Brady, June 20, 1899, Alaska State Library Document

Collection, ASL-MF-Ar5-Roll5-f651, Alaska's Digital Archives, Juneau, 6, https://vilda.alaska.edu/digital/collection/cdmg22/id/104/rec/1.

2. Chief Shoo-we-Kah, Meeting Held in the Public School House, 9.

3. Organic Act of 1884, ch. 53, 23 Stat. 24 (1884).

4. See Bartholomew H. Sparrow, *The Insular Cases and the Emergence of American Empire* (University Press of Kansas, 2006); Gerald L. Neuman and Tomiko Brown-Nagin, *Reconsidering the Insular Cases: The Past and Future of the American Empire* (Harvard University Press, 2015); Christina Duffy Burnett and Burke Marshall, eds., *Foreign in a Domestic Sense: Puerto Rico, American Expansion, and the Constitution* (Duke University Press, 2001).

5. David S. Case and David A. Voluck, *Alaska Natives and American Laws* (University of Alaska Press, 2012), 65.

6. Organic Act of 1884.

7. Organic Act of 1884.

8. William L. Hensley, "'What Rights to Land Have the Alaska Natives? The Primary Question,' – May, 1966 by William L. Hensley with May 2001 Introduction," Alaska Historical Society, accessed January 22, 2026, https://alaskahistoricalsociety.org/wp-content/uploads/Hensley-paper-of-1966.pdf.

9. Case and Voluck, *Alaska Natives and American Laws,* 24.

10. 48 Cong. Rec. 530–31 (1884).

11. 48 Cong. Rec. 531 (1884).

12. 48 Cong. Rec. 531 (1884).

13. 48 Cong. Rec. 566 (1884).

14. Rev. Stat. § 1891 (1874).

15. 48 Cong. Rec. 595–96 (1884).

16. Juliana Hu Pegues, *Space-Time Colonialism: Alaska's Indigenous and Asian Entanglements* (University of North Carolina Press, 2021), 21.

17. 48 Cong. Rec. 631 (1884).

18. 48 Cong. Rec. 635 (1884).

19. The US census declared the US frontier closed in 1890, with no land available for settlement, leading many to speculate a crisis of national identity and social cohesion fueled by increasing anxieties around urbanization, wage labor, and modernity. Historian Frederick Jackson Turner articulated the concept of the frontier in 1893 in his frontier thesis, solidifying the myth of American settlement of the west in the American consciousness (Frederick Jackson Turner, "The Frontier in American History," *Annual Report of the American Historical Association* [1893]: 197–227). Some works on this phenomenon or critiques of the concept of the frontier generally include William Cronon, *Nature's Metropolis: Chicago and the Great West* (W. W. Norton, 1992); Mark David Spence, *Dispossessing the Wilderness: Indian Removal and the Making of the National Parks* (Oxford University Press, 2000); Jeffrey Ostler, *The Plains Sioux and U.S. Colonialism from Lewis and Clark to Wounded Knee* (Cambridge University Press, 2004); Sanford Levinson and Bartholomew Sparrow, eds., *The Louisiana Purchase and American Expansion, 1803–1898* (Rowman and Littlefield, 2005).

20. Endleman et al. v. United States, 86 F. 456, 458, 459 (9th Cir. 1898).

21. Joel Andrews Cosme-Morales, "Palmyra Atoll: America's 51st State?" *Southern University Law Review* 49, no. 97 (2021): 120, 121, 122.

22. Simeon E. Baldwin, "The Constitutional Questions Incident to the

Acquisition and Government by the United States of Island Territory," *Harvard Law Review* 12, no. 393 (1899): 411.

23. Carman F. Randolph, "Constitutional Aspects of Annexation," *Harvard Law Review* 12, no. 291 (1898): 295.

24. Randolph, "Constitutional Aspects of Annexation," 305. This same author also speculated that Hawai'i would likely achieve self-government through absorption with another Pacific state rather than remain attached to the United States. See also Elmer B. Adams, "The Causes and Results of Our War with Spain from a Legal Standpoint," *Yale Law Journal* 8, no. 119 (1898): 199–233.

25. Abbott Lawrence Lowell, "The Status of Our New Possessions—a Third View," *Harvard Law Review* 13, no. 155 (1899): 171, 172; Randolph, "Constitutional Aspects of Annexation."

26. Treaty of Peace Between the United States and Spain, 30 Stat. 1754 (1898), 8; Downes v. Bidwell, 182 U.S. 244 (1901), 339, 340.

27. Treaty of Peace Between the United States and Spain, 9; Treaty Concerning the Cession of the Russian Possessions in North America by His Majesty the Emperor of All the Russias to the United States of America, 15 Stat. 539 (1867).

28. Robert Nichols, *Theft Is Property! Dispossession and Critical Theory* (University of Minnesota Press, 2019), 39.

29. Nora Marks Dauenhauer (Tlingit, Lukaax̱.ádi) and Richard Dauenhauer write about this historic meeting and the speeches given by the Tlingit representatives in the tradition of Tlingit oratory and as part of the long history of Native protests against land theft. Nora Marks Dauenhauer and Richard Dauenhauer, eds., *Haa Tuwunáagu Yís, for Healing Our Spirit: Tlingit Oratory* (University of Washington Press and Sealaska Heritage Foundation, 1990), 135–36.

30. Dauenhauer and Dauenhauer, *Haa Tuwunáagu Yís*, 135. A poignant example of land as at.óow is reflected in Amy Marvin's story "Glacier Bay History" recounted in *Haa Shuká, Our Ancestors: Tlingit Oral Narratives*, ed. Nora Marks Dauenhauer and Richard Dauenhauer (University of Washington Press and Sealaska Heritage Foundation, 1987). Caskey Russell likewise demonstrates the ways Tlingit clan identity and a clan's claim to property ownership are embedded in totemic law (Caskey Russell, "Cultures in Collision: Cosmology, Jurisprudence, and Religion in Tlingit Territory," *American Indian Quarterly* 33, no. 2 [2009]: 239–52).

31. Meeting Held in the Public School House, 2.

32. Thomas Thornton, *Being and Place Among the Tlingit* (University of Washington Press, 2007), 136.

33. Meeting Held in the Public School House, 4.

34. Thornton, *Being and Place Among the Tlingit*, 136.

35. Meeting Held in the Public School House, 4–6.

36. Meeting Held in the Public School House, 6–10.

37. Meeting Held in the Public School House, 11–13.

38. Meeting Held in the Public School House, 13.

39. Thornton, *Being and Place Among the Tlingit*, 137.

40. "Governor John G. Brady's Address to the Thlingit in the Public School House, December 14th, 1898," 1–3, ASL-MF-Ar5-Roll5-f651, Alaska's Digital Archives, Juneau, 6 https://library.alaska.gov/hist/fulltext/ASL-MF-Ar5-Roll5-F65.html. The Dauenhauers rightly argue that Brady "goes down in history as particularly unsympathetic regarding Tlingit land use and possession," having

"personally seized Tlingit land and directed the building of a road through the center of the Tlingit burial grounds in Sitka" (Dauenhauer and Dauenhauer, *Haa Tuwunáagu Yís,* 136).

41. Case and Voluck, *Alaska Natives and American Laws,* 66–67; Sutter v. Heckman, 1 D. Alaska 188 (1901).

42. Heckman v. Sutter, 119 F. 83, 88 (9th Cir. 1902). Legal scholars David S. Case and David A. Voluck argue that the Ninth Circuit did not fully adopt the Alaska District Court's "right-to-convey theory," though the court certainly refrained from acknowledging Aboriginal title. See Case and Voluck, *Alaska Natives and American Laws,* 67.

43. James Wickersham was a profoundly problematic individual whose actions as a judge, attorney, and congressional delegate reflected his thinking on racial hierarchies that perpetuated ongoing violences of settler colonialism and exclusionary processes of nation-state building. He was heavily involved in Alaska Native land claims litigation in the early twentieth century, and he had also spent time in Washington state, during which he participated as a leading member of the Committee of Fifteen who had violently driven Chinese laborers from the city of Tacoma. He also counseled the Alaska Native Brotherhood and Alaska Native Sisterhood out of personal interest, recommending that he and William Paul would serve as the attorneys for any lawsuits brought under the jurisdictional act.

44. In re Naturalization of Minook, 2 Alaska 200 (D. Alaska 1904).

45. *Minook,* 200, 201.

46. Rassmussen v. United States, 197 U.S. 516, 519, 525, 522 (1905).

47. *Rassmussen v. United States*; Bartholomew Sparrow, "Public Response to Controversial Supreme Court Decisions: The Insular Cases," *Journal of Supreme Court History* 30, no. 3 (2005): 197–210.

48. United States v. Berrigan, Case #270F AS 30921, Alaska State Archives, Juneau.

49. United States v. Berrigan, 2 Alaska 442 (D. Alaska 1905).

50. *United States v. Berrigan,* 447, 442, 451.

51. William Schneider, *The Tanana Chiefs: Native Rights and Western Law* (University of Alaska Press, 2018), 117.

52. Report of Lt. G.T. Emmons to Congress, S. Doc. No. 106, 58th Cong., 3d Sess. (1905), 3, 15.

53. Report of Lt. G.T. Emmons to Congress, 3. See also Michael Witgen, *An Infinity of Nations: How the Native New World Shaped Early North America* (University of Pennsylvania Press, 2013). Emmons and others were viewing Alaska Native land regimes through the "lens of discovery," which rendered them incapable of perceiving the persistence of Indigenous institutions.

54. Russell, "Cultures in Collision," 236.

55. Alaska Native Allotment Act, 34 Stat. 197 (1906).

56. Case and Voluck, *Alaska Natives and American Laws,* 135.

57. On citizenship and Indigenous rights in Alaska, see Thomas Michael Swensen, "The Relationship Between Indigenous Rights, Citizenship, and Land in Territorial Alaska: How the Past Opened the Door to the Future," *Growing Our Own: Indigenous Research, Scholars, and Education Journal of the Alaska Naïve Studies Council* 2 (2015): 44–58.

58. In 1914, the Ninth Circuit affirmed the ruling in *Berrigan* when the new district judge issued an injunction against white settlers who claimed to have purchased land that had been set aside as an Indian mission. Judge Fuller concluded that the lands in question were trust lands and that Alaska Natives were wards of the government and could not convey title (U.S. v. Cadzow, 1953F, AS 31064, RG 626, United States District Court Civil case files, Series 1825B US District Court Civil Cases 1900–1955 Fourth Division [Fairbanks], Case 1953F, Alaska State Archives, Juneau). The name of the Indigenous owner of the cabin is not listed in court records. These findings were short-lived, though, when the US Ninth Circuit considered a dispute over the use of tidelands in *Worthen Lumber Mills v. Alaska Juneau Gold Mining Company,* 229 F. 966 (9th Cir. 1916) just two years later. The court found in favor of the Alaska Juneau Gold Mining Company, validating their title to adjacent land that they had previously acquired from an Indigenous owner. See Case and Voluck, *Alaska Natives and American Laws,* 69.

59. An Act to Provide a Civil Government for Puerto Rico and for Other Purposes, 39 Stat. 951 (1917).

60. Muratti v. Foote, 25 P.R. Dec. 568, 581; In re Tapia, 9 P.R. Fed. 560; Cosme-Morales, "Palmyra Atoll."

61. Balzac v. Porto Rico, 258 U.S. 298, 309 (1922); Gerald Neuman and Tomiko Brown-Nagin, eds., *Reconsidering the Insular Cases: The Past and Future of the American Empire* (Harvard University Press, 2015), 48.

62. Kyle Whyte argues that Indigenous sovereignty is contingent on "the capacity of Indigenous peoples to rebuild and continue complex moral relationships that can promote economic, cultural, and social resilience." While Alaska Native activists realized that expelling settlers and corporations was an unlikely outcome of their efforts, they sought ways to ensure the persistence of their relationships to the land, to each other, and to the nonhuman nations of beings that had sustained them for generations. Kyle Whyte, "Critical Investigations of Resilience: A Brief Introduction to Indigenous Environmental Studies and Sciences," *Daedalus* 147, no. 2 (2018): 145.

3. Asserting Native Land Relations

1. Alaska Native Brotherhood minutes, 1920 Convention November 21–27, box 2, folder 1, Judson Brown Papers, William L. Paul Sr. Archives and Special Collections, Sealaska Heritage Institute, Juneau, 1.

2. The 1924 Indian Citizenship Act unilaterally conveyed US citizenship on all American Indians and Alaska Natives.

3. An Act to Provide for the Allotment of Lands in Severalty to Indians on the Various Reservations, 24 Stat. 388, 25 U.S.C. §§ 331–334, 339, 341, 342, 348, 349, 354, 381 (1887).

4. Alaska Native Brotherhood minutes, 2.

5. An Act Providing a Civil Government for Alaska, May 17, 1884, 23 Stat. 24, 48th Cong., 1st Sess., Ch. 53 (1884), 26.

6. Nora Marks Dauenhauer and Richard Dauenhauer, eds., *Haa Kusteeyí, Our Culture: Tlingit Life Stories* (University of Washington Press, 1994), 3; Peter Metcalf, *A Dangerous Idea: The Alaska Native Brotherhood and the Struggle for*

Indigenous Rights (University of Alaska Press, 2014), 8, 20–21; Juliana Hu Pegues, "Beyond Settler Feminism: Tillie Paul's Arrest and Indigenous Feminist Activism," presentation given at Cornell University, February 21, 2024.

7. Alaska Native Brotherhood minutes, 2, 3.

8. Alaska Native Brotherhood minutes, 3.

9. Alaska Native Brotherhood minutes, 1–27, 3.

10. Alaska Native Brotherhood minutes, 5–6. For the ways Metlakatlans preserved their social, cultural, and political orders through migration and missionary pressures on their societies, see Mique'l Icesis Dangeli, "Bringing to Light a Counternarrative of Our History: B. A. Haldane, Nineteenth-Century Tsimshian Photographer," in *Sharing Our Knowledge: The Tlingit and Their Coastal Neighbors*, ed. Sergei Kan (University of Nebraska Press, 2015). On Tsimshian migration, see Susan Neylan, "'Choose Your Flag': Perspectives on the Tsimshian Migration from Metlakatla, British Columbia, to New Metlakatla, Alaska, 1887," in *New Histories for Old: Changing Perspectives on Canada's Native Pasts*, ed. Ted Binnema and Susan Neylan (University of British Columbia Press, 2008). Andrea Geiger also chronicles this cross-border migration in *Converging Empires: Citizens and Subjects in the North Pacific Borderlands, 1867–1945* (University of North Carolina Press, 2022).

11. Steve Colt, "Salmon Fish Traps in Alaska: An Economic History Perspective," ISER Working Paper 2000.2, February 15, 2000, http://www.alaskool.org/projects/traditionalife/fishtrap/fishtrap.htm.

12. For histories of contests over Indigenous fishing rights in the contiguous states, see Larry Nesper, *The Walleye War: The Struggle for Ojibwe Spearfishing and Treaty Rights* (University of Nebraska Press, 2002); Chantal Norrgard, *Seasons of Change: Labor, Treaty Rights, and Ojibwe Nationhood* (University of North Carolina Press, 2014); Larry Nesper, "Twenty-Five Years of Ojibwe Treaty Rights in Wisconsin, Michigan, and Minnesota," *American Indian Culture and Research Journal* 36, no. 1 (2012): 47–78; Douglas C. Harris, "The Boldt Decision in Canada: Aboriginal Treaty Rights to Fish on the Pacific," and "Reserved for Whom? Defending and Defining Treaty Rights on the Columbia River, 1880–1920," in *The Power of Promises: Rethinking Indian Treaties in the Pacific Northwest*, ed. Alexandra Harmon (University of Washington Press, 2008); Charles Wilkinson, *Treaty Justice: The Northwest Tribes, the Boldt Decision, and the Recognition of Fishing Rights* (University of Washington Press, 2024); Douglas C. Harris, *Landing Native Fisheries: Indian Reserves and Fishing Rights in British Columbia, 1849–1925* (University of British Columbia Press, 2008); Heidi Kiiwetinepinesiik Stark and Kekek Stark, "Nenabozho Goes Fishing: A Sovereignty Story," *Daedalus* 147, no. 2 (2018): 17–26.

13. Alaska Native Brotherhood minutes, 4. *Humpies* refers to pink salmon, which was sometimes considered less desirable than red salmon, thus incentivizing some fishermen to discard them.

14. Caskey Russell elaborates on this relationship and the evolution and adaptation of Tlingit tradition and values as a critical mode of resistance to colonization in his analysis of Nora Marks Dauenhauer's poem "How to Make Good Baked Salmon from the River" in "Tools of Self Definition: Nora Marks Dauenhauer's 'How to Make Good Baked Salmon,'" *Studies in American Indian Literatures* 16, no. 3 (2004): 29–46.

15. Nora Marks Dauenhauer, "How to Make Good Baked Salmon from the River," quoted in Russell, "Tools of Self Definition," 34–35.

16. Alaska Delegate Dan Sutherland, 74 Cong. Rec. 608 (1930).

17. David S. Case and David A. Voluck, *Alaska Natives and American Laws* (University of Alaska Press, 2012), 201; 53 Interior Dec. 605 (1932).

18. *Hearing Before the Committee on Indian Affairs on S. 1196 a Bill Authorizing the Tlingit and Haida Indians of Alaska to Bring Suit in the United States Court of Claims*, 72nd Cong. 11 (1932).

19. In his discussion of dispossession, Robert Nichols cites Leanne Betasamosake Simpson in reference to Indigenous land relations prior to dispossession. She argues that the opposite of dispossession is not "possession" but rather a "deep, reciprocal, relational attachment." This is likely the aim of Tlingit and Haida in this instance; however, they frequently mobilize the language of possession to these ends to prompt action from lawmakers. Robert Nichols, *Theft Is Property! Dispossession and Critical Theory* (University of Minnesota Press, 2020), 151; Leanne Betasamosake Simpson, *As We Have Always Done: Indigenous Freedom Through Radical Resistance* (University of Minnesota Press, 2017), 43.

20. Memorandum from Commissioner of Indian Affairs Charles J. Rhoads, in *Hearing Before the Committee on Indian Affairs on S. 1196*, 12–15.

21. Wickersham likely sought to validate his Alaska District Court rulings in *Berrigan* and *Cadzow*, which had relied on designation of Alaska as an incorporated territory and the explicit mention of "uncivilized" tribes in contrast to other "inhabitants." *Hearing Before the Committee on Indian Affairs on S. 1196*, 3–4, 11.

22. *Hearing Before the Committee on Indian Affairs on S. 1196*, 5–7; United States v. Berrigan, 2 D. Alaska 442 (1905); U.S. v. Cadzow, 2 D. Alaska 125 (1914).

23. *Hearing Before the Committee on Indian Affairs on S. 1196*, 17.

24. The ANB was drawing on a long genealogy of citizenship debates among Indigenous peoples in the United States. See Tsianina Lomawaima, "The Mutuality of Citizenship and Sovereignty: The Society of American Indians and the Battle to Inherit America," *American Indian Quarterly* 37, no. 3 (2013): 331–51; Cristina Stanciu, "Americanization on Native Terms: The Society of American Indians, Citizenship Debates, and Tropes of 'Racial Difference,'" *Native American and Indigenous Studies* 6, no. 1 (2019): 111–48.

25. George T. Stormont to William H. Blair, March 13, 1934, box 4, file 49, Anthony Dimond Papers, Alaska and Polar Regions Collections and Archives, Elmer E. Rasmuson Library, University of Alaska Fairbanks.

26. Stormont to Blair.

27. Harold Ickes to William Rogers, March 8, 1935, box 4, file 49, Anthony Dimond Papers, Alaska and Polar Regions Collections and Archives, Elmer E. Rasmuson Library, University of Alaska Fairbanks.

28. Paul was undoubtedly motivated by his desire to serve as the attorney for Tlingit and Haida claimants, though his arguments are important in understanding the ways citizenship was useful in shaping land rights.

29. William L. Paul Sr. to Anthony Dimond, November 1, 1934, box 4, file 49, Anthony Dimond Papers, Alaska and Polar Regions Collections and Archives, Elmer E. Rasmuson Library, University of Alaska Fairbanks.

30. Indian Reorganization Act, 48 Stat. 984 (1934).

31. William L. Paul Sr., Felix Cohen, Paul Gordon to John Collier, January 22, 1936, series 3, box 1, folder 10, Anthony Dimond Papers, Alaska and Polar Regions

Collections and Archives, Elmer E. Rasmuson Library, University of Alaska Fairbanks.

32. The Federal Credit Union Act of 1934, 48 Stat. 1216, ch. 750 (1934), 1, 1219.

33. "Extending Wheeler-Howard Act to the Territory of Alaska," report accompanying S.B. 4420, February 24, 1936, S. Rep. No. 1748 (1936).

34. William L. Paul Sr. to Harold Ickes, September 21, 1937, William Paul Sr. Papers, Accession No. 1885–7, box 4, file 22, University of Washington Special Collections, Seattle.

35. Westbrook provided multiple accounts of the colony, its origins, and its purpose. Lawrence Westbrook, "The True Story of Matanuska," October 6, 1935, box 398, General Alaska Reports file, RG 126 Records of the Office of Territories, National Archives and Records Administration, College Park, MD; Lawrence Westbrook, "The Story of America's New Frontier," undated, box 399, Speeches file, RG 126 Records of the Office of Territories, National Archives and Records Administration, College Park, MD.

36. Clarence Hulley, "A Historical Survey of the Matanuska Valley Settlement in Alaska," *Pacific Northwest Quarterly* 40, no. 4 (1949): 327–40.

37. Anthony Dimond, "The Matanuska Valley Colonization Project in Alaska," May 14, 1935, in response to former Congressman Cyrenus Cole's denouncing of the colony in the Iowa press, 74 Cong. Rec. 7537–7538 (1935).

38. "Explanatory Memorandum," January 5, 1939, box 25, file 406 Committee on Alaska Meetings, Felix Cohen Papers, Yale Collection of Western Americana, Beinecke Rare Book and Manuscript Library, Yale University, New Haven, CT.

39. *The Problem of Alaskan Development* (US Department of the Interior, 1940).

40. *The Problem of Alaskan Development,* 9. For a history of the 1924 Immigration Act, see Mae Ngai, *Impossible Subjects: Illegal Aliens and the Making of Modern America* (Princeton University Press, 2014).

41. 51 Cong. Rec. 10092 (1890).

42. *The Problem of Alaskan Development,* 45.

43. *The Problem of Alaskan Development,* 48.

44. *The Problem of Alaskan Development,* 53.

45. A Bill to Provide for the Settlement and Development of Alaska, 76 H.R. 3577 (1940); A Bill Providing for the Utilization of Unfilled Immigration Quotas in Order to Colonize Alaska for Purposes of National Defense and as a Market for Surplus Production, 77 H.R. 2791 (1941).

46. *Hearings Before a Subcommittee of the Committee on Territories and Insular Affairs on S. 3577,* Committee on Territories and Insular Affairs, 76th Cong. 1–4 (1940).

47. *Hearings Before a Subcommittee of the Committee on Territories,* 1–4.

48. *Hearings Before a Subcommittee of the Committee on Territories,* 7.

49. *Hearings Before a Subcommittee of the Committee on Territories,* 234.

50. *Programs with Respect to Relief and Rescue of Refugees-Temporary Havens (Alaska and Virgin Islands),* box 54, Projects and Documents file: January 1944–September 1945, Records of the War Refugee Board, 1944–1945, Franklin Roosevelt Presidential Library and Museum Digital Collections, http://www.fdrlibrary.marist.edu/archives/collections/franklin/.

51. *Hearings Before the Committee on Immigration and Naturalization on H.R. 2791,* 77th Cong. 4 (1941).

52. *Hearings Before a Subcommittee of the Committee on Territories and Insular Possessions*, Senate, 76th Cong. 231 (1940).

4. Denying Sovereignty

1. An Act Authorizing the Tlingit and Haida Indians of Alaska to Bring Suit in the United States Court of Claims, ch. 275, 49 Stat. 388 (1935); An Act to Extend Certain Provisions of the Act Approved June 18, 1934, Commonly Known as the Wheeler-Howard Act, to the Territory of Alaska, ch. 254, 49 Stat. 1250 (1936).

2. Tlingit and Haida Indians of Alaska v. United States, 147 Ct. Cls. 315, 177 F. Supp 452 (1959).

3. Information on the moiety, house, clan, and village membership for Roy and Frank Peratrovich was shared with the author by Caskey Russell on July 1, 2025.

4. Roy and Elizabeth Peratrovich to Ernest Gruening, December 30, 1941, ms129, folder 1, Peratrovich Papers, Alaska State Library.

5. See Thomas Borstelmann, *The Cold War and the Color Line: American Race Relations in the Global Arena* (Harvard University Press, 2001); Mary L. Dudziak, *Cold War Civil Rights: Race and the Image of American Democracy* (Princeton University Press, 2011).

6. Holly Guise, *Alaska Native Resilience: Voices from World War II* (University of Washington Press, 2024). Holly Guise's rich oral histories reveal how Native service in the Alaska Territorial Guard functioned as a critical site of sovereignty and diplomacy as Alaska Natives allied with the United States in defense of their homelands. See also Terrence M. Cole, "Jim Crow in Alaska: The Passage of the Alaska Equal Rights Act of 1945," *Western Historical Quarterly* 23, no. 4 (1992): 429–49. For a comprehensive legal history of civil rights from *Plessy* to *Brown*, see Michael Klarman, *From Jim Crow to Civil Rights: The Supreme Court and the Struggle for Racial Equality* (Oxford University Press, 2004). On labor and the civil rights movement, see Nancy MacLean, *Freedom Is Not Enough: The Opening of the American Workplace* (Harvard University Press, 2008); Robert Samuel Smith, *Race, Labor, and Civil Rights: "Griggs Versus Duke Power" and the Struggle for Equal Employment Opportunity* (Louisiana State University Press, 2008); Zaragosa Vargas, *Labor Rights Are Civil Rights: Mexican American Workers in Twentieth-Century America* (Princeton University Press, 2005); Emilio Zamora, *Claiming Rights and Righting Wrongs in Texas: Mexican Workers and Job Politics During World War II* (Texas A&M University Press, 2009); Risa Goluboff, *The Lost Promise of Civil Rights* (Harvard University Press, 2007). Tomiko Brown-Nagin decenters the Supreme Court and the NAACP and considers the civil rights movement from the bottom up in *Courage to Dissent: Atlanta and the Long History of the Civil Rights Movement* (Oxford University Press, 2012); Laurel Bill, "The Alaska Territorial Guard," *Alaska* 80, no. 8 (2014): 50. Members of the Alaska Territorial Guard were not recognized as military veterans until 2004.

7. Ernest Gruening to Harold Ickes, December 11, 1944, box 331, Alaska Indian Reservations file, General Records of the Office of Territories and Its Predecessors, 1885–1971, RG 126, National Archives and Records Administration, College Park, MD (hereafter *NARA*).

8. Harold Ickes to Henry L. Stimson, November 1, 1943, RG 370, box 40,

Pribilof Islands Rehabilitation 1942–1945 file, National Archives and Records Administration, Seattle, WA. This endeavor was contingent on the forced labor of Unangax̂ peoples, a condition that persisted into the 1960s. Holly Guise's rich oral history exposes the inhumane treatment Unangax̂ experienced while interned in Southeast Alaska and the ways they forged alliances with Tlingit communities and developed strategies for survival. Guise, *Alaska Native Resilience.*

9. David Vine, "Islands of Imperialism: Military Bases and the Ethnography of U.S. Empire," in *Ethnographies of U.S. Empire,* ed. Carole McGranahan and John F. Collins (Duke University Press, 2018); Victoria De Grazia, *Irresistible Empire: America's Advance Through Twentieth-Century Europe* (Harvard University Press, 2006); Alfred McCoy, *Policing America's Empire: The United States, the Philippines, and the Rise of the Surveillance State* (University of Wisconsin Press, 2009).

10. Wilcox Air Base Act, ch. 511, 49 Stat. 610 (1935).

11. Alaska Airlines, "Alaska Airlines COO: 'A Mission of Mercy and Incredible Caring.' How Alaska Supported Afghan Refugee Charter Flights," September 17, 2021, https://news.alaskaair.com/care/alaska-coo-afghan-refugee-charter-flights/. Operation Magic Carpet was also the name of the operation to repatriate US personnel back in the years following WWII. On the Wings of Eagles is also used to for the 1949 operation that transported Yemeni settlers to Israel.

12. Tongass Timber Act, ch. 481, 61 Stat. 920 (1947).

13. Alaska Anti-Discrimination Act, H.B. 14, ch. 2, Laws of Alaska, 17th Regular Session, Territorial Legislature (1945).

14. For the ways territorial administration influences domestic policy, see Alfred W. McCoy and Francisco A. Scarano, eds., *Colonial Crucible: Empire in the Making of the Modern American State* (University of Wisconsin Press, 2009).

15. David S. Case and David A. Voluck, *Alaska Natives and American Laws* (University of Alaska Press, 2012), 100.

16. Department of the Interior, Fish and Wildlife Service, *Laws and Regulations for Protection of the Commercial Fisheries of Alaska, 1943,* Sec. 201.21b (Government Printing Office, 1943), 16.

17. Nathan Margold, "Fishing Rights of Alaskan Indians," February 13, 1942, in *Opinions of the Solicitor of the Department of the Interior Relating to Indian Affairs 1917–1974,* vol. 1 (US Department of the Interior, 1975), 1096.

18. Margold, "Fishing Rights of Alaskan Indians," 1105.

19. M. D. L. Fuller (Law Offices of Pillsbury, Madison, and Sutro) to A. K. Tichnor, April 18, 1939, and Jack Underwood to Edward Allen, November 25, 1939, box 14, file 12 "Native Land and Fishing Rights 1939–1946," Alaska Packers Association Papers, Center for Pacific Northwest Studies, Western Washington University, Bellingham, WA (hereafter *CPNS*).

20. M. D. L. Fuller (Law Offices of Pillsbury, Madison, and Sutro) to A. K. Tichnor, November 25, 1939, and Edward Allen to Victor H. Elfendahl, April 24, 1942, box 14, file 12, Records of the Alaska Packers Association, CPNS.

21. Law Offices of Allen, Hilen, Froude, and De Garmo to the Law Offices of Pillsbury, Madison, and Sutro, June 13, 1942, box 14, file 12, Records of the Alaska Packers Association, CPNS.

22. Ernest Gruening to Harold Ickes, August 12, 1944, box 332, general file 9-1-52 part 3, RG126 Records of the Office of Territories, NARA. It is important to note that, as discussed in chapters 2 and 3, Gruening is not entirely accurate in his

statements. Executive order reservations and land reserves of varying sizes had been created in Alaska for the exclusive benefit of Alaska Natives. See Case and Voluck, *Alaska Indians and American Laws.*

23. Ernest Gruening to Harold Ickes, December 11, 1944, box 331, Alaska Indian Reservations file, RG126 Records of the Office of Territories, NARA.

24. Gruening to Ickes, December 11, 1944.

25. Petition of William Paul on Behalf of Himself and the Tee-Hit-Ton Tribe, April 3, 1944, box 14, file 12, Records of the Alaska Packers Association, CPNS.

26. H. L. Faulkner to Alaska Packers Association, April 12, 1944, box 14, file 12, Records of the Alaska Packers Association, CPNS.

27. H. L. Faulkner to Alaska Packers Association, April 12, 1944.

28. Petition of William Paul on behalf of himself and the Tee-Hit-Ton Tribe, April 3, 1944, box 14, file 12, Records of the Alaska Packers Association, CPNS.

29. Tsianina Lomawaima, "The Mutuality of Citizenship and Sovereignty: The Society of American Indians and the Battle to Inherit America," *American Indian Quarterly* 37, no. 3 (2013): 333–51; Cristina Stanciu, "Americanization on Native Terms: The Society of American Indians, Citizenship Debates, and Tropes of 'Racial Difference,'" *Native American and Indigenous Studies* 6, no. 1 (2019): 111–48.

30. Gruening to Alaska Native Brotherhood Convention, November 4–8, 1944, box 14, file 12, Records of the Alaska Packers Association, CPNS.

31. Gruening to the Alaska Native Brotherhood Convention, 1943, box 14, file 12, Records of the Alaska Packers Association, CPNS.

32. H. L. Faulkner to A. K. Tichnor, July 31, 1944, box 14, file 12, Records of the Alaska Packers Association, CPNS.

33. Peter Metcalfe, *A Dangerous Idea: The Alaska Native Brotherhood and the Struggle for Indigenous Rights* (University of Alaska Press, 2014), 48.

34. *Daily Alaska Empire,* January 31, 1945; Cole, "Jim Crow in Alaska."

35. The IRA was controversial across Indian Country, with nearly 30 percent of tribes voting against it and many bristling at Interior Department authority over IRA tribal governments. See David E. Wilkins and Heidi Kiiwetinepinesiik Stark, *American Indian Politics and the American Political System* (Rowman & Littlefield, 2017).

36. Memorandum, Irwin Silverman to Julius Krug, November 8, 1946, box 332, General file, RG 126, Records of the Office of Territories, NARA.

37. George Folta to Roy Peratrovich, November 8, 1944, ms129, folder 2, Peratrovich Papers, Alaska State Library, Juneau.

38. A Bill to Authorize the Selection, Construction, and Installation of Frontier Defense Bases for the Army Air Corps, 74 H.R. 4130 (1935), 1.

39. Narratives of WWII Alaska that generally do not account for the contingency of US militarization on the dispossession of Alaska Natives include Stephen Haycox, *Alaska: An American Colony* (University of Washington Press, 2002); Claus M. Naske and Herman E. Slotnick, *Alaska: A History of the 49th State* (University of Oklahoma Press, 1994). While they note the disruption to Native life, the emphasis is more oriented around militarization as a precursor to statehood. For a history of Indigenous dispossession and displacement as a result of WWII and Cold War militarization, see Amber Annis, "The River Calls Me Home: Cold War Diplomacy, US Militarization, and Environmental Justice Within the Cheyenne River Sioux Tribe" (PhD diss., University of Minnesota, 2023). Experiences

of Indigenous people in WWII have been cataloged in numerous recent works, including Guise, *Alaska Native Resilience*; Lin Poyer, *War at the Margins: Indigenous Experiences in World War II* (University of Hawai'i Press, 2022); Kenneth William Townsend, *World War II and the American Indian* (University of New Mexico Press, 2002).

40. *Hearings Before the Committee on Military Affairs on H.R. 6621 and H.R. 4130*, 74th Cong. 121 (1935).

41. *Hearings Before the Committee on Military Affairs*, 5. For a history of Japanese interest in Alaska and the Pacific Northwest Coast, see Andrea Geiger, *Converging Empires: Citizens and Subjects in the North Pacific Borderlands, 1867–1945* (University of North Carolina Press, 2022).

42. *Hearings Before the Committee on Military Affairs*, 112–14.

43. *Hearings Before the Committee on Military Affairs*, 32–33.

44. Theodore Joseph Crackel, *A History of the Civil Reserve Air Fleet* (Air Force History & Museums Program, 1998), 40, 41, 42.

45. Scholars of Indigenous studies and settler colonial studies have long interpreted Zionist activities and intentions through the framework of settler colonialism. See Patrick Wolfe, "Settler Colonialism and the Elimination of the Native," *Journal of Genocide Research* 8, no. 4 (2006): 387–409; Wolfe, "Purchase by Other Means: The Palestinian Nakba and Zionism's Conquest of Economics," *Settler Colonial Studies* 2, no. 1 (2012): 133–71; Lorenzo Veracini, "The Other Shift: Settler Colonialism, Israel and the Occupation," *Journal of Palestine Studies* 42, no. 2 (2013): 26–42.

46. Steven Fleischman, "Israel, Neocolonialism, and U.S. Hegemony," *Nature, Society, and Thought* 17, no. 3 (2004): 309.

47. Crackel, *History of the Civil Reserve Air Fleet*, 57.

48. Crackel, *History of the Civil Reserve Air Fleet*, 59.

49. Crackel, *History of the Civil Reserve Air Fleet*, 87, 223–24.

50. Edwin Meredith Secretary of Agriculture to Secretary of the Interior, July 31, 1920, box 384, General file, RG 126, Records of the Office of Territories, NARA.

51. *Hearings Before the Committee on the Territories to Conduct a Study and Investigation of the Various Questions and Problems Relating to the Territory of Alaska*, 79th Cong. 8 (1945).

52. *Hearings Before the Committee on the Territories*, 116.

53. *Hearings Before the Committee on the Territories*, 11, 13, 54.

54. *Hearings Before the Committee on the Territories*, 34–35.

55. *Hearings Before the Committee on the Territories*, 50, 55, 116.

56. Oscar Chapman to Solicitor, June 14, 1946, box 332, General file 9-1-52 Part 3, Records of the Office of Territories, NARA.

57. See Harold Ickes, "Claims of the Natives of Hydaburg, Klawock, and Kake, Alaska," submitted to Congress as part of *Hearings Before the Committee on the Territories*, 141–47; Walter R. Goldschmidt and Theodore H. Haas, eds., *Haa Aaní, Our Land: Tlingit and Haida Land Rights and Use* (University of Washington Press, 1998).

58. H.R.J. Res. 205, 80th Cong. (1947). The Tongass Timber Act reflects the title applied to the majority of Southeast Alaska in 1907 when 16.7 million acres of the region was designated a national forest.

59. *Hearings Before the Committee on Agriculture on H.J. Res. 205 to Authorize the Secretary of Agriculture to Sell Timber Within the Tongass National Forest,* 80th Cong. 151–54 (1947).

60. *Hearings Before the Committee on Agriculture,* 155, 161. For Tlingit land regimes, diplomacy, and jurisprudence, see Thomas F. Thornton, *Being and Place Among the Tlingit* (University of Washington Press, 2007); Caskey Russell, "Cultures in Collision: Cosmology, Jurisprudence, and Religion in Tlingit Territory," *American Indian Quarterly* 33, no. 1 (2009): 1–24.

61. *Hearings Before the Committee on Agriculture,* 156.

62. James Curry to Ruth Bronson, May 10, 1947, Curry-Weissbrodt Papers, box 1B, file 17.2, Sealaska Heritage Institute, Juneau.

63. John P. Van Orsdel, Puget Sound Pulp & Timber Co. to Lyle Watts, U.S. Forest Service, June 30, 1947, in *Hearings Before the Committee on Agriculture,* 167.

64. *Hearings Before the Committee on Agriculture,* 43, 131–35.

65. *Hearings Before the Subcommittee of the Committee on Interior and Insular Affairs on S.2037 and S.J. Res. 162,* 80th Cong. (1948), 2.

66. *Hearings Before the Subcommittee of the Committee on Interior and Insular Affairs,* 295.

67. *Hearings Before the Subcommittee of the Committee on Interior and Insular Affairs,* 4.

68. *Hearings Before the Subcommittee of the Committee on Interior and Insular Affairs,* 295, 298, 310.

69. *Hearings Before the Subcommittee of the Committee on Interior and Insular Affairs,* 273, 277.

70. *Hearings Before the Subcommittee of the Committee on Interior and Insular Affairs,* 296.

71. *Hearings Before the Subcommittee of the Committee on Interior and Insular Affairs,* 321.

72. *Hearing Before the Committee on Interior and Insular Affairs on the Nomination of Oscar L. Chapman to Be Secretary of the Interior,* 81st Cong. (1950), 11–12.

73. *Hearing Before the Committee on Interior and Insular Affairs on the Nomination of Oscar L. Chapman,* 17.

74. Heintzleman quoted in Diane J. Purvis, *The Drive of Civilization: The Stikine Forest Versus Americanism* (pub. by author, 2016), 141.

5. Domesticating Empire

1. Gertrude Smith to Mike Stepovich, September 12, 1957, RG 101, box 4899, Alaska Native Service File 1957–58, Alaska State Archives, Juneau.

2. M. J. Walsh to Mildred Herman, August 21, 1958, RG 313, box 3, file 18, Alaska State Archives, Juneau.

3. Smith to Stepovich, September 12, 1957.

4. The late 1950s are characterized by concerns among US national security officials that the rise of China and the decolonization movements in Africa and Asia might lead to the decline of US global influence, fueling efforts to reify and expand US hegemony by establishing a global network of military bases in addition to methods of resource control and economic imperialism. See David Vine, "Military Bases and the Ethnography of U.S. Empire," in *Ethnographies of U.S.*

Empire, ed. Carole McGranahan and John F. Collins (Duke University Press, 2018); Catherine Lutz, ed., *The Bases of Empire: The Global Struggle Against U.S. Military Posts* (New York University Press, 2009); Victoria de Grazia, *Irresistible Empire: America's Advance Through Twentieth-Century Europe* (Belknap Press, 2005).

5. The 1959 Alaska Statehood Act authorized the State of Alaska to select approximately 105 million acres of federal lands to be transferred to the State of Alaska. The land selection process was seen as a necessary step to ensure that Alaska would be "economically self-supporting." "State Entitlements," US Bureau of Land Management, accessed October 10, 2024, https://www.blm.gov/programs/lands-and-realty/regional-information/alaska/land_transfer/state-entitlements.

6. *Hearings Before the Subcommittee of the Committee on Interior and Insular Affairs on S.2037 and S.J. Res. 162*, 80th Cong. (1948), 310.

7. US Congress, *Hearings Before Subcommittee on Territorial and Insular Possessions of the Committee on Public Lands House of Representatives, 80th Congress, 1st Session on H.R. 206 and H.R. 1808* (Government Printing Office, 1947), 428–29, 126, 134.

8. US Congress, *Hearings Before Subcommittee on Territorial and Insular Possessions*, 134.

9. US Congress, *Hearings Before Subcommittee on Territorial and Insular Possessions*, 428.

10. Heidi Kiiwetinepinesiik Stark traces a similar entrapment in which the stories that lawmakers and courts in settler societies use to legitimate their claims often leave them "caught in their own riddle" as they "slip between the real and the imagined . . . as settler narratives of the state disorientate and misguide the listener as they traverse the legal landscape." Alaska Native refusal to accept these stories exposes their tenuous nature, as the exchange between Faulkner and Lemke illustrates. See Heidi Kiiwetinepinesiik Stark, "Transforming the Trickster: Federal Indian Law Encounters Anishinaabe Diplomacy," in *Centering Anishinaabeg Studies: Understanding the World Through Stories*, ed. Jill Doerfler, Niiganwewidam James Sinclair, and Heidi Kiiwetinepinesiik Stark (Michigan State University Press, 2013), 265.

11. US Congress, *Hearings Before Subcommittee on Territorial and Insular Possessions*, 136.

12. A Bill to Provide for the Admission of Alaska to the Union, H.R. 5666, 80th Cong., 2nd Sess. (1948).

13. House of Representatives Committee on Public Lands Rep. No. 1731, to accompany H.R. 5666, April 14, 1948, 14, 15.

14. Petitions of the Alaska Native Sisterhood, Petersburg, Angoon, Sitka, Klawock, (1948), box 1B, file 14.9, Curry-Weissbrodt Papers, Sealaska Heritage Institute, Juneau.

15. Amy Yax Yeidí Hallingstad to Julius Krug, December 20, 1948, and Amy Yax Yeidí Hallingstad to E. L. Bartlett, December 30, 1948, Curry-Weissbrodt Papers, box 1A, file 11.16, Sealaska Heritage Center, Juneau.

16. US Congress, *Hearings Before the Committee on Interior and Insular Affairs on H.R. 331 an Act to Provide for the Admission of Alaska to the Union* (Government Printing Office, 1950), 76–77, 78, 149.

17. US Congress, *Hearings Before the Committee on Interior and Insular Affairs on H.R. 331*, 287, 286, 288.

18. US Congress, *Hearings Before the Committee on Interior and Insular Affairs on H.R. 331*, 348.

19. James Curry to Arthur V. Watkins, November 27, 1950, Curry-Weissbrodt Papers, box 1A, file 14.2, Sealaska Heritage Institute, Juneau.

20. For examples, see James Curry to Lester C. Hunt, December 8, 1950; James Curry to Arthur V. Watkins, November 27, 1950; and Harry Douglas, ANB Grand President at Hoonah to James Curry, November 30, 1950, box 1A, file 14.2, Curry-Weissbrodt Papers, Sealaska Heritage Institute, Juneau.

21. A Bill to Settle Native Land Claims in the Territory of Alaska and to Assist the Natives of Alaska in Stabilizing Their Economy, H.R. 4388, 82nd Cong. (1951). This was not the first time extinguishment legislation was introduced. In 1948, A Bill to Settle and Extinguish Land Claims to the Public Domain in the Territory of Alaska, H.R. 7002, 80th Cong. (1948), was submitted to Congress; however, after swift and forceful condemnation by James Curry, Felix Cohen, the NCAI, and other organizations, it was abandoned. See box 1, file 11.7, Sealaska Heritage Institute, Juneau.

22. *Hearings Before the Subcommittee on Indian Affairs of the Committee on Interior and Insular Affairs on H.R. 4388, a Bill to Settle Native Land Claims in the Territory of Alaska and to Assist the Natives of Alaska in Stabilizing Their Economy*, 82nd Cong. 24–25 (1951).

23. *Hearings Before the Subcommittee on Indian Affairs of the Committee on Interior and Insular Affairs on H.R. 4388*, 10–12.

24. *Hearings Before the Subcommittee on Indian Affairs of the Committee on Interior and Insular Affairs on H.R. 4388*, 12–14, 17, 25–27.

25. *Hearings Before the Subcommittee on Indian Affairs of the Committee on Interior and Insular Affairs on H.R. 4388*, 12–14.

26. *Tee-Hit-Ton Indians v. United States*, 348 U.S. 272, 277 (1955); David E. Wilkins and Tsianina Lomawaima, *Uneven Ground: American Indian Sovereignty and Federal Indian Law* (University of Oklahoma Press, 2002), 24, 134. On *Tee-Hit-Ton*, see Robert A. Williams, *Like a Loaded Weapon: The Rehnquist Court, Indian Rights, and the Legal History of Racism in America* (University of Minnesota Press, 2005); Walter R. Echo-Hawk, *In the Courts of the Conqueror: The 10 Worst Indian Law Cases Ever Decided* (Fulcrum, 2010); David E. Wilkins, *American Indian Sovereignty and the U.S. Supreme Court: The Masking of Justice* (University of Texas Press, 1997); Peter Metcalfe, *A Dangerous Idea: The Alaska Native Brotherhood and the Struggle for Indigenous Rights* (University of Alaska Press, 2014).

27. Wilkins and Lomawaima, *Uneven Ground*, 24; *Tee-Hit-Ton v. United States.*

28. Tongass Timber Act, ch. 515, 61 Stat. 920 (1947); Case and Voluck, *Alaska Natives and American Laws*, 71.

29. *Tee-Hit-Ton Indians v. United States*, 348 U.S. 272, 278 (1955).

30. Case and Voluck, *Alaska Natives and American Laws*, 71.

31. See *Hearings Before the Committee on Interior and Insular Affairs United States Senate on S. 50 and S. 224*, 83rd Cong. 1 (1953); "Providing for the Admission of Alaska Into the Union," Senate Committee on Interior and Insular Affairs Committee Report 1028 to accompany S.50 83rd Cong., 2nd Sess. (1954); *Hearings Before the Committee on Interior and Insular Affairs United States Senate on S.49, S.399 and S.402*, 84th Cong. 1 (1955).

32. Claus M. Naske, *49 at Last! The Battle for Alaska Statehood* (Epicenter Press,

2009); Stephen Haycox, *Alaska: An American Colony* (University of Washington Press, 2002).

33. Eisenhower's Press and Radio Conference July 14, 1954, February 25, 1953, box 630, file OF147 D Alaska (1), White House Central Files, Dwight D. Eisenhower Library, Abilene, KS.

34. See Efrén Rivera Ramos, "Deconstructing Colonialism: The 'Unincorporated Territory' as a Category of Domination," in *Foreign in a Domestic Sense: Puerto Rico, American Expansion, and the Constitution*, ed. Christina Duffy Burnett and Burke Marshall (Duke University Press, 2001); Christina D. Ponsa-Kraus, "The Edges of Empire and the Limits of Sovereignty: American Guano Islands," *American Quarterly* 57, no. 3 (2005): 779–803.

35. Secretary of Defense to Chairman Engle, February 15, 1955, Bryce Harlow Records, box 29, Statehood Alaska and Hawaii (2) file, Dwight D. Eisenhower Library, Abilene, KS.

36. Dwight D. Eisenhower to Senator Henry Jackson, March 31, 1955, Records as President, box 630, Official file, OF-147-D-1 Alaskan Statehood (2), Dwight D. Eisenhower Library, Abilene, KS.

37. Governor B. Frank Heintzleman argued in a letter to House Speaker Joseph Martin that partition might be an acceptable compromise for immediate statehood. April 3, 1954, box 4, file 53, Operation Statehood Records, Alaska and Polar Regions Archives, University of Alaska, Fairbanks.

38. Enabling the People of Hawaii and Alaska Each to Form a Constitution and State Government and to Be Admitted to the Union on an Equal Footing with the Original States, H.R. Rep. No. 88, Committee on Interior and Insular Affairs Report to accompany H.R. 2535, 84th Cong., 1st sess. (1955).

39. E. L. Bartlett to Hugh Butler, December 2, 1950, box 2 subseries 83, file 5 Bartlett Correspondence, RG 313, Alaska State Archives, Juneau; Naske, *49 at Last!*, 197.

40. Senator Eastland, 85 Cong. Rec. 12017–18 (1958).

41. In thinking about the relationship of plunder, settler economies, and extractable raw materials from Native land, see Michael Witgen, *Seeing Red: Indigenous Land, American Expansion, and the Political Economy of Plunder in North America* (University of North Carolina Press, 2022).

42. Senator James Eastland, 85 Cong. Rec. 12017–18 (1958).

43. Some prominent examples include Noenoe Silva, *Aloha Betrayed: Native Hawaiian Resistance to American Colonialism* (Duke University Press, 2004); J. Kēhaulani Kauanui, *Hawaiian Blood: Colonialism and the Politics of Sovereignty and Indigeneity* (Duke University Press, 2008); J. Kēhaulani Kauanui, *Paradoxes of Hawaiian Sovereignty: Land, Sex, and the Colonial Politics of State Nationalism* (Duke University Press, 2018); Lisa Kahaleole Hall, "Strategies of Erasure: U.S. Colonialism and Native Hawaiian Feminism," *American Quarterly* 60, no. 2 (2008): 273–80; Lisa Kahaleole Hall, "'Hawaiian at Heart' and Other Fictions," *Contemporary Pacific* 17, no. 2 (2005): 404–13.

44. J. Kēhaulani Kauanui, "Native Hawaiian Decolonization and the Politics of Gender," *American Quarterly* 60, no. 2 (2008): 281–87.

45. Kauanui, *Hawaiian Blood*, 3–4.

46. Hawaii Statehood Admission Act, Pub. L. No. 86-3, 73 Stat. 4 (1959).

47. Ponsa-Kraus, "Edges of Empire and the Limits of Sovereignty."

6. Disrupting Dispossession

1. *Hearings Before the Subcommittee on Indian Affairs of the Committee on Interior and Insular Affairs on H.R. 13142, H.R. 10193, and H.R. 14212* (Government Printing Office, 1970), 585.

2. Fourth and Gambell is now a major intersection in downtown Anchorage.

3. *Hearings Before the Subcommittee on Indian Affairs*, 585.

4. Now Joint Base Elmendorf-Richardson.

5. *Hearings Before the Subcommittee on Indian Affairs*, 585.

6. *Dena'ina Time Travel*, Anchorage Museum resources, accessed January 2, 2024, https://denaina.anchoragemuseum.org/pdfs/timelines/TT6%20Territory%20of%20Alaska.pdf.

7. I. S. Weissbrodt of Cobb and Weissbrodt to William L. Paul Sr., May 11, 1959, box 22, file 13, Accession No. 1885–007, William Lewis Paul Sr. Papers, University of Washington Libraries Special Collections, Seattle.

8. David S. Case and David A. Voluck, *Alaska Natives and American Laws* (University of Alaska Press, 2012), 72.

9. Chris McNeil, "The Tlingit & Haida Indians of Alaska v. United States," lecture, posted November 5, 2019, by Sealaska Heritage Institute, YouTube, https://youtu.be/z6A_rpUymls?si=H4nO6t1NRQEWt-mR. See also Chris McNeil, *The Significance of Tlingit and Haida Indians of Alaska v. United States* (Sealaska Heritage Institute, 2023), 6.

10. Thomas R. Berger's 1985 publication *Village Journey: The Report of the Alaska Native Review Commission* (Hill and Wang, 1985) is often referred to as an important review of ANCSA in its first fifteen years. Berger notes a number of impending issues, such as the alienability of shares after a twenty-year period and the disproportionate funding of regional versus village corporations, among other structural issues with ANCSA, that endangered Native land retention. See also Evon Peter, "Undermining Our Tribal Governments: The Stripping of Land, Resources, and Rights from Alaska Native Nations," in *The Alaska Native Reader: History, Culture, Politics*, ed. Maria Shaa Tláa Williams (Duke University Press, 2009); Benjamin Hugh Velaise, "The Incorporation of Life and Land: The Alaska Native Claims Settlement Act," in *Allotment Stories: Indigenous Land Relations Under Settler Siege*, ed. Daniel Heath Justice and Jean M. O'Brien (University of Minnesota Press, 2021), 213.

11. Susan Stark Christianson, ed., *Central Council Historical Profile* (Tlingit and Haida Indian Tribes of Alaska, 1995), 7. Peter Metcalfe performed the research and writing of the original publication in 1985. "About Eklutna Inc.," Eklutna Inc., accessed July 2, 2025, https://www.eklutnainc.com/about/; Sealaska, accessed July 2, 2025, https://sealaska.com/.

12. Tlingit and Haida Indians of Alaska v. United States, 177 F. Supp. 452 (Ct. Cl. 1959).

13. The CCTHITA also included the creation of the Metlakatla Indian Reservation and Glacier Bay National Monument as substantial takings in addition to the Tongass.

14. Christianson, *Central Council Historical Profile*, 6.

15. McNeil, *Significance of Tlingit and Haida Indians of Alaska v. United States*, 13. McNeil (Tlingit, Nisga'a) points out the absurdity of this argument in which the

federal government is contending that Tlingit and Haida "were an Indian tribe sufficient enough to be the subject of a jurisdictional act to take their lands away, but insufficient to be compensated." He describes this as one way in which the government used its plenary power to manage and cloud what it would recognize as an Alaska Native tribe, which frustrated but informed subsequent strategies among land rights activists.

16. Manu Karuka, *Empire's Tracks: Indigenous Nations, Chinese Workers, and the Transcontinental Railroad* (University of California Press, 2019); James Kari and James A. Fall, *Shem Pete's Alaska: The Territory of the Upper Cook Inlet Dena'ina* (University of Alaska Press, 2003).

17. Alaska Railroad Corporation, *Alaska Railroad Corporation Historic Timeline* (Alaska Railroad Corporation Corporate and External Affairs Department, 2023), https://www.alaskarailroad.com/sites/default/files/Communications/Alaska_Railroad_Historic_Timeline_or.pdf.

18. *Dena'ina Time Travel.*

19. Case and Voluck, *Alaska Natives and American Laws,* 97; An Act for the Establishment of Industrial Schools for Alaska Native Children, Pub. L. No. 468, 43 Stat. 978 (1925).

20. *Hearings Before the Subcommittee on Indian Affairs of the Committee on Interior and Insular Affairs,* 91st Cong. 587–88 (1969).

21. *Dena'ina Time Travel.*

22. Kristy Hollinger, *The Early Electrification of Anchorage* (Center for Environmental Management of Military Lands, Colorado State University, 2002), 21.

23. *Hearings Before the Subcommittee on Indian Affairs,* 587–88.

24. *Natives of Palmer, Alaska v. United States,* Petition Filed with the Indian Claims Commission, August 13, 1951, RG 279: Records of the Indian Claims Commission, Entry 11-A: Closed Case Files, Docket 370, box 3216, National Archives and Records Administration, Washington, DC (hereafter *NARA*).

25. Indian Claims Commission Act, Pub. L. No. 79-726, 60 Stat. 1049 (1946). The ICC was an agency established by Congress in 1946 to hear the claims of "any Indian tribe, band, or other identifiable groups of American Indians residing within the territorial limits of the United States or Alaska." Case and Voluck, *Alaska Natives and American Laws,* 72; Motion for Summary Judgement, May 25, 1964, *Natives of Palmer, Alaska v. United States,* Records of the Indian Claims Commission, Docket 370, NARA.

26. Ramsey Clark Motion for Summary Judgement, May 25, 1964, RG 279: Records of the Indian Claims Commission, Entry 11-A: Closed Case Files, Docket 370, box 3216, NARA.

27. Michele Connolly and Bette Jacobs, "Counting Indigenous American Indians and Alaska Natives in the US Census," *Statistical Journal of the IAOS* 36, no. 1 (2020): 201–10, https://content.iospress.com/articles/statistical-journal-of-the-iaos/sji200615; Beverly M. Pratt, Lindsay Hixson, and Nicholas A. Jones, "Measuring Race and Ethnicity Across the Decades: 1790–2010," US Census Bureau, September 24, 2015, https://www.census.gov/data-tools/demo/race/MREAD_1790_2010.html.

28. Ramsey Clark Motion for Summary Judgement, May 25, 1964. This is likely a reference to the recommendation of Commissioner of Indian Affairs Francis A. Walker to exclude Alaska Natives from BIA jurisdiction on account

of his perception of their racial distinctions. The 1940 and 1960 censuses further demonstrate the ways Walker's Asian racialization of Alaska Natives and subsequent decision to exclude them from BIA jurisdiction congealed in institutions that created, defined, and regulated race-based systems of rights in the US legal system. For Alaska Natives, the categories engendered by Walker's racial musings would undermine their legibility in the US legal system from 1872 to the present day.

29. Ramsey Clark Motion for Summary Judgement, May 25, 1964; *Natives of Palmer, Alaska v. United States,* Petition Filed with the Indian Claims Commission, August 13, 1951.

30. Ramsey Clark Motion for Summary Judgement, May 25, 1964; *Natives of Palmer, Alaska v. United States,* Petition Filed with the Indian Claims Commission, August 13, 1951.

31. Alaska is by no means the only context in which the federal government challenged Indigenous land claims by creating ambiguity around specific instances of legal taking. It is, however, significant when this approach is employed as a blanket policy across the state as a function of the long history of distinct racial and legal categories for Alaska Natives.

32. A full list of the Alaska claims in the ICC includes St. Paul Island, Dkt. 352; Aleut Tribe et al., Dkt. 369; Athabaska Indians, Stevens Village, Dkt. 199; Chitina, Natives of, Dkt. 187; Gambell, Native Village of, et al., Dkt. 284; Nisgah Tribe, Dkt. 287; Palmer, Alaska, Natives of, Dkt. 370; Shungnak, Native Village of, and Kowagmut Tribe, Dkt. 286; Tatitlek Village, Natives of, Dkt. 200; Tee-hit-ton, Dkt. 171; Tlingit and Haida et al., Dkts. 278–278A; Tlingit and Haida and Angoon Tribe, Dkt. 278-B; Unalakleet, Native Village of, et al., Dkt. 285; Aleut Community of St. George Island, Dkt. 369-A. See *United States Indian Claims Commission Final Report: August 13, 1946–September 30, 1978.*

33. Petition Before the Indian Claims Commission, Native Village of Gambell, August 10, 1951, RG 279: Records of the Indian Claims Commission, Entry 11-UD, Closed Case Files, Docket 284–287, box 2607, NARA.

34. Petition Before the Indian Claims Commission, Native Village of Gambell, August 10, 1951.

35. Petition of the Natives of Tatitlek, Alaska, August 6, 1951, RG 279: Records of the Indian Claims Commission, Entry 11-UD, Closed Docketed Case Files, Docket 199–201, box 1895, NARA.

36. Perry W. Morton, Motion to Dismiss, May 8, 1957, RG 279: Records of the Indian Claims Commission, Entry 11-UD, Closed Docketed Case Files, Docket 199–201, box 1895, NARA.

37. Ramsey Clark, Motion to Dismiss, August 26, 1963, RG 279: Records of the Indian Claims Commission, Entry 11-UD, Closed Case Files, Docket 284–287, box 2607, NARA.

38. An Act Authorizing the Tlingit and Haida Indians of Alaska to Bring Suit in the United States Court of Claims, and Conferring Jurisdiction upon Said Court to Hear, Examine, Adjudicate, and Enter Judgment upon Any and All Claims Which Said Indians May Have, or Claim to Have, Against the United States, and for Other Purposes, 49 Stat. 388 (1935).

39. *Hearings Before the Subcommittee on Indian Affairs of the Committee on Interior and Insular Affairs to Amend the Act of June 19, 1935,* 89th Cong. 21 (1965).

40. *Hearings Before the Subcommittee on Indian Affairs*, 27, 36.

41. An Act to Amend the Act of June 19, 1935 (49 Stat. 388), as Amended, Relating to the Tlingit and Haida Indians of Alaska, 79 Stat. 543 (1965).

42. McNeil, *Significance of Tlingit and Haida Indians of Alaska v. United States*, 14–15.

43. McNeil, *Significance of Tlingit and Haida Indians of Alaska v. United States*, 18.

44. State of Alaska v. Udall, 420 F.2d 938 (9th Cir. 1969); Case and Voluck, *Alaska Natives and American Laws*, 74.

45. *Hearings Before the Committee on Interior and Insular Affairs on S. 2906 a Bill to Authorize the Secretary of the Interior to Grant Certain Lands to Alaska Natives, Settle Alaska Native Land Claims*, 90th Cong. 63–65 (1968).

46. *Hearings Before the Committee on Interior and Insular Affairs on S. 2906*, 16–17.

47. *Hearings Before the Committee on Interior and Insular Affairs on S. 2906*, 33.

48. *Hearings Before the Committee on Interior and Insular Affairs on S. 2906*, 50–51.

49. *Hearings Before the Subcommittee on Indian Affairs of the Committee on Interior and Insular Affairs on H.R. 13142, H.R. 10193*, 91st Cong. 51–52 (1969).

50. The Alaska Native Claims Settlement Act of 1971, Pub. L. No. 92-03, 85 Stat. 688 (1971).

51. Act of December 18, 1971 Pub. Law 92–203.

52. Case and Voluck, *Alaska Natives and American Laws*, 292; H.R. Rep. No. 92–746 (1972) (Conf. Rep.).

53. The Alaska National Interest Lands Conservation Act, Pub. L. No. 96-487, 94 Stat. 2371 (1980).

54. Case and Voluck, *Alaska Natives and American Laws*, 36.

55. For example, see Alaska v. Native Village of Venetie Tribal Government et al. 522 U.S. 520 (1998); Katie John v. United States, 247 F.3d 1032 (9th Cir. 2001); Yellen v. Confederate Tribes of the Chehalis Indian Reservation, 594 U.S. 338 (2021).

Conclusion

1. An Act to Confer Jurisdiction on the States of California, Minnesota, Nebraska, Oregon, and Wisconsin, with Respect to Criminal Offenses and Civil Causes of Action Committed or Arising on Indian Reservations Within Such States, and for Other Purposes, ch. 505, 67 Stat. 588 (1953).

2. James Brooks, "New Department of Interior Opinion Promises to Recognize Expanded Tribal Jurisdiction in Alaska," *Alaska Beacon*, March 15, 2024, https://alaskabeacon.com/2024/03/15/new-department-of-interior-opinion-promises-to-expand-tribal-jurisdiction-in-alaska/; "A Tiny Juneau Lot Is the Latest Battleground in a Dispute over Tribal Sovereignty," KTOO, January 20, 2023, https://www.ktoo.org/2023/01/20/a-tiny-juneau-lot-is-the-latest-battleground-in-a-dispute-over-tribal-sovereignty/; "FAQs on Alaska Native Allotments (Eklutna Litigation)," State of Alaska Department of Law, accessed July 3, 2025, https://law.alaska.gov/department/tribal-relations-FAQ-ANA.html.

3. James Brooks, "Federal Agency, Reversing Prior Rulings, Greenlights Eklutna Tribal Gaming Hall," Alaska Public Media, July 31, 2024, https://

alaskapublic.org/2024/07/31/federal-agency-reversing-prior-rulings-greenlights-eklutna-tribal-gaming-hall/.

4. Brooks, "Federal Agency, Reversing Prior Ruling." At the time of this writing (July 2025), Eklutna Village had opened its temporary Chin'an Gaming Hall in January and has plans to construct a permanent facility. The tribe recently won a court case filed by homeowners in the surrounding area claiming that the tribe is not federally recognized. The US district court ruled in the tribe's favor.

5. Brooks, "New Department of Interior Opinion."

6. State of Alaska Department of Law, "FAQs on Lands into Trust Litigation," February 22, 2024, https://www.documentcloud.org/documents/24465200-faqs-on-lands-into-trust-litigation-feb-22-2024.

7. Coronavirus Aid, Relief, and Economic Stimulus Act, Pub. L. No. 116-136, 134 Stat. 281 (2020).

8. Yellen v. Confederated Tribes of the Chehalis Reservation, 594 U.S. 338 (2021). Also Thomas Michael Swensen, "Of Subjection and Sovereignty: Alaska Native Corporations and Tribal Government in the Twenty-First Century," *Wicazō Ṡa Review* 30, no. 1 (2015): 100–17.

9. Swensen, "Of Subjection and Sovereignty."

10. Donald Craig Mitchell, *Tribal Sovereignty in Alaska: How It Happened, What It Means* (Carolina Academic Press, 2022).

11. An Act Providing a Civil Government for Alaska, ch. 53, 23 Stat. 24 (1884).

12. Frederick L. Moore to Philander Chase Knox, April 12, 1902, Records of the US House of Representatives, 57th Cong., Hr57A-H26.1–26.3, Committee on Territories to Alaska and Hawaii, box 116, "Alaska" file, National Archives and Records Administration, Washington, DC.

13. Patrick Wolfe, "Settler Colonialism and the Elimination of the Native," *Journal of Genocide Research* 8, no. 4 (2006): 392.

14. *In re Sah Quah,* 31 F. 327 (D. Alaska 1886), 140.

Index